HOW TO MAKE MONEY

Scoring Soundtracks
and Jingles

by Jeffrey P. Fisher

6400 Hollis Street
Emeryville, CA 94608

Library of Congress Catalog Card Number: 97-71392

Book design, layout, and cover art: Linda Gough

Production staff: Mike Lawson: publisher; Lisa Duran: editor; Randy Antin: editorial assistant;
Sally Engelfried: editorial assistance; Teresa Poss: administrative assistant; Ellen Richman: production director;
Sherry Bloom: production assistant

6400 Hollis Street
Emeryville, CA 94608
(510) 653-3307

Also from MixBooks:
The Art of Mixing: A Visual Guide to Recording, Engineering, and Production
500 Songwriting Ideas (For Brave and Passionate People)
Music Publishing: The Real Road to Music Business Success, Rev. and Exp. 4th Ed.
How to Run a Recording Session
The Songwriters Guide to Collaboration, Rev. and Exp. 2nd Ed.
Critical Listening and Auditory Perception
Keyfax Omnibus Edition
The AudioPro Home Recording Course
Modular Digital Multitracks: The Power User's Guide
Concert Sound
Sound for Picture
Music Producers
Live Sound Reinforcement

Also from EMBooks:
Making the Ultimate Demo
Tech Terms: A Practical Dictionary for Audio and Music Production
Making Music With Your Computer

Also from CBM Music and Entertainment Group:
Recording Industry Sourcebook
Mix Reference Disc
Mix Master Directory
Digital Piano Buyer's Guide

MixBooks is a division of Cardinal Business Media Inc.

Printed in Auburn Hills, Michigan

ISBN 0-918371-18-X

DEDICATION

This book is for my wife, Lisa, to thank her for her
kindness, understanding, encouragement, tolerance, and
love. It's not easy being married to me, I know, but I do
love you for trying!

Contents

About This Book

"Fisher's focus is on marketing rather than music, which is sensible. Most musicians have an instinct for their craft, but don't have a clue when it comes to selling their talent. This book could improve your bottom line."

—MUSICIAN MAGAZINE

"Hugely popular career guide. The best business advice on writing and selling commercial jingles and scoring for video, film, and multimedia. This how-to book will help you understand the markets, set up a business, make your demo, market your services, find clients, and get them to buy."

—MIX BOOKSHELF

"In its third edition, Fisher's book gives practical knowledge to composers about how to break into the music business. The manual gives step-by-step information on ways to start a successful commercial music business."

—SCREEN

"This is valuable information from someone who does this for a living and can save anyone many times the cover price in mistakes you will learn to avoid in advance. This is still a good reference book for anyone wanting to know how to make a stab at making money in the soundtrack business. You can't go wrong."

—THE MUSIC AND SOUND RETAILER

"I am glad to see that someone finally put together a complete package showing how to make money with music at home. Thank you for dedicating the time and effort it must have taken to put it all together."

—D. J. SAMMONS, CLINTON, NC

"Within four months of buying your book, setting up my project studio, and working your strategies one step at a time, I've had my first success: a great piece of music for a Fortune 500 company. Plus, I get a check for doing what I love to do. Your book and encouragement really has made a difference."

—MARY BROOKS, ROWAYTON, CT

"Your book is simply fantastic and has already helped me. I'm recommending it to all my musician friends as a totally user-friendly reference."

—WILL GREGA, POP FRONT PRESS, NEW YORK, NY

"I have learned so much from your insights and experience. I am so excited about the positive and profitable direction I see my music career taking. THANK YOU, THANK YOU, THANK YOU!!!"

—ANTHONEY SEAVERS, CHICAGO, IL

"The depth and frankness of the information you supply in the book surprised me. Your wanting to help others get started in this business is a rare personal trait. If everyone else ran their business as you run yours, my life as a musician would be a lot less hectic."

—BARRY SHELL, CLAYTON, GA

"This book is filled with tons of valuable information! How to get the work, where to look for jobs, what to charge your clients, and more. Trust me, if you want to succeed in the commercial music business, please get this book."

—KEVAN PATTEN, PATTEN SOUND, SAN GABRIEL, CA

"I have found your book both comprehensive and inspirational as a guide to getting started in the music business."

—CLIFFORD LYON, BIG EAR MUSIC, SOMERVILLE, MA

"Jeffrey P. Fisher is a music marketing guru."

—BOB BAKER, SPOTLIGHT PUBLICATIONS

"Thank you for giving me a boost. I respect that you keep your promise and welcome phone calls and letters. Your book and reports are not only very informative, but motivating and inspiring as well."

—DAN ZEMANEK, SAVOY, IL

"I received your book about 1½ weeks ago and I am very happy with it. The marketing techniques you describe are right on the money. Your book is an excellent refresher course. Can't wait to start making $$$ with the music!"

—DEVIN KIRSCHNER, DWK MUSIC, UNIONVILLE, NY

Acknowledgments

----

*The only sensible ends of literature are, first,
the pleasurable toil of writing; second, the
gratification of one's family and friends;
and, lastly, the solid cash.*
—Nathaniel Hawthorne

Many people contributed to this book—none of
them knowingly: Roddy Frame, Mel Brooks,
George Martin, Mark Isham, Bernard Herrmann,
Leon Russell, Gustav Mahler, Ray Harryhausen, Jeffrey Lant, David Lynch, Herman Holtz, Patrick
O'Hearn, Marsha Sinetar, Robert Gunning, Bruce
Bendinger, Brian Holmsten, Jan Hammer, Willie
Nelson, Len Kuzmicki, Sears, Craig Anderton, Dennis Muren, Jim Shorts, Ken Tobias, Andy Summers,
Miro Ledajaks, Rob Kole, Jane Talisman, Bill
Forsyth, Patricia Pribyl, Sting, Ed Brunke, Steve
Armstrong, Marshall Cook, Alfred Hitchcock, John
Gardner, David Carradine, Peter McWilliams, David
Torn, Ensoniq, Mom and Pops, me brother Charlie
and me other brother Charlie, Peggy, Sandy, a man
called Tuna, all those nieces and nephews, the President and CEO of Skoober Enterprises, my delightful son Adam, and mostly that little voice inside my
head that simply said: *Do It!*

I'd also like to take a few inches to offer my
gratitude to those people without whom this book
would not have been. Many thanks go to Mike Lawson for believing in the project; Linda Gough for
her splendid book design; the many readers of the
previous editions who shared experiences, proffered suggestions, and inspired me to improve the
book; and mostly to Lisa Duran and her capable
editorial assistants who transformed my workmanlike text into lucid, accessible, and robust prose.

Introduction

YOU CAN DO IT

Movies, radio, TV, cable, video, slide, multimedia, the Internet, and other audiovisual presentations desperately need your original music scores and jingles. The traditional music-users, such as advertisers, TV, and theatrical motion pictures, are not the only companies needing original music. Business TV, cable, the Web, and other outlets are also demanding quality compositions, so opportunities for you in the commercial music industry abound. Once you understand this market and develop a plan to reach it—and this guide shows you precisely how—you'll enjoy a successful career making money from your music.

Don't think for one minute this is some get-rich-quick scheme. This book is for people who truly want success for their music and their life. Success doesn't come overnight. It requires hard work, dedication, constant purpose, and a carefully considered strategy that you work at every day. Follow this process and you will, slowly and steadily, build your soundtrack scoring and jingle business to the level of success you desire. It's you, your talent, and your commitment that will make this happen.

One person, working alone from a well-equipped home project studio, can make a decent living composing scores and jingles for corporations, radio, TV, cable, and commercials. I'm proof of it. This book shows you how to do it. These techniques work for me, and they'll work for you. I know you can do it. So, let's get started!

WHY I WROTE THIS BOOK

*The only thing one can do with good advice is to
pass it on. It is never of any use to oneself.*
—OSCAR WILDE

Having record contracts and playing in bars are not the only way for you to earn your living from music. Unfortunately, most so-called guides to making money in the music business rarely mention any alternative careers. And if they do, it's only in a scant two or three paragraphs—hardly enough information to get you started, let alone succeed. This book fills that void by showing you exactly how to make money scoring soundtrack music and commercial jingles.

Sadly, many other books about the music business contain more information about what to do than how to do it. I'm out to change that. This book presents step-by-step details in an honest, no-nonsense approach. You may not always admire my candor, but I guarantee this opinionated book is practical and instantly usable with loads of proven advice. No theory, no statistics; in short: no BS. You see, I want you to succeed. And you will, if you follow the advice offered in this book.

But like all books, this one doesn't contain everything you may need or want to know. Think of it as the foundation—solid, thorough, but not complete. I'll do everything I can to help by giving you my suggestions as we progress, but it's up to *you* to build your dream. And, since no single resource can tell you everything, I'll recommend many other resources throughout the text. You should consult them all if you really want to prosper from your own commercial music business. Yes, I have read—and continue to profit from—every resource I recommend! You will, too.

Reading a book is like rewriting it for yourself . . .
You bring to it all your experience of the world and
you read it in your own terms.

—ANGELA CARTER

- -

This is an intense book. I make no apology for that fact. It provides you with all the information you need to manage your music business. I've worked very hard to show you exactly what you must do and precisely how you must do it to be successful, and I've provided you with *complete* follow-up information for all the other resources that can round out your education. Maybe you thought this book was too expensive, or you may have been skeptical of its value. After you start reading it, though, you'll discover its true value. This genuine, useful, easy to apply, and proven advice is designed so that this book lives up to the promise of its title. The reason is simple: *I wrote this book for you, to help you succeed.*

Most of all, I hope you keep coming back to it when you need some help or just a little encouragement. And when you are successful, I hope you'll remember me, too. I'd love to hear from you. Follow my advice and avoid the mistakes I've made along the way. Use this book, work hard, and you will have a successful and profitable commercial music business.

WHAT YOU GET IN THIS BOOK

Education is not filling a bucket,
but lighting a fire.

—WILLIAM BUTLER YEATS

- -

The first chapter in *How to Make Money Scoring Soundtracks and Jingles,* "What You Need to Begin," explains precisely what you need to know and do to start making money scoring soundtracks and jingles. You learn the crucial steps to success, including the most important secret to making it in today's commercial music business.

"Your Project Studio" is where you learn how to organize your talents and equipment so you are ready to produce the kind of music people want to buy.

"Creating the Killer Demo Tape" gives you the essentials of preparing and presenting your music demo tape. Here is where you learn the one surefire way to get your demo tape requested and listened to so you sell more of your commercial music services.

"Your Typical Gigs" explains how the business works and the steps you need to take to work with clients. Also, you learn the eight steps you must take to improve your composition skills.

If you don't understand the marketing and promotional aspects of this business, you are doomed to fail. That's why this book devotes page after page to helping you master these skills. "Finding Prospects Who Buy Original Music" tells you how and where to contact the people who will buy your scores and jingles.

"Reaching Prospects and Turning Them Into Paying Music Clients" delivers the step-by-step marketing plan that brings you to the attention of music buyers in a carefully structured program. Follow these precise details and you're on your way. Note: This is a dense chapter. You should read it twice.

"The Secrets to Moneymaking Sales Letters, Brochures, and Other Promotional Material" teaches you to craft profit-producing copy that gets people to purchase your commercial music services. Plus, you learn how to use information about your clients to your advantage.

In "Overlooked Promotional Opportunities," you discover more ways to get additional clients using specific promotional methods including free media, newsletters, word of mouth, and much more.

The next chapter concentrates on how you can "Profit From the Internet."

"Taking Care of Business" shows you all the vital information you must know to run your business right and build profits. You also get tips on how to use your computer effectively. Don't ignore this essential information. Study it carefully and apply it to your situation. Trust me, it's for your own good!

"The Money Stuff" concentrates on matters financial. You discover how to get, report, keep, and leverage your money into more cash. Use these tips to swell your bank account.

The rights issue is all too often misunderstood. "Copyrights and Other Rights" cuts through the fog and tells you exactly what you must do to protect your work and get the money you deserve.

Next, follow the simple formula in "How to Set Your Fee and Get It" and learn to handle quotes with ease, close sales faster, and make sure you profit.

Pay close attention to this next point. The key to making a decent living is found in "Diversify and Thrive." Diversity is the secret to making big money in the music business. Most of you will be more successful if you exploit all your musical talent. You should record, perform, produce, write songs, teach, and compose scores and jingles. And because this point is so important, there's an entire chapter devoted to several alternative moneymaking ways to turn your talent into cash.

At the end of the book is the "Samples" section, which is filled with many useful documents you can start using right away. All the letters, ads, flyers, news releases, and such are to help you sell your original music. Just add your specific information, print the samples on your letterhead, and start to profit right away. What could be easier?

It furthers one to have someplace to go.
—I CHING

I primarily compose and produce soundtrack music and jingles. After years of struggling and learning how to make my commercial music business a success, I decided to share this information and knowledge with others—like you! You shouldn't have to learn the hard way, as I did.

As you read through this book and realize all that you must do to succeed, you may want some additional attention. Perhaps you just need a point clarified, want more detailed explanations, or could use a push in the proper direction. You may choose to work directly with me—in addition to writing this book, I am also a business consultant. Consider my role in your life as an advisor, coach, and friend as you read through this manual. Let me help you improve your business, increase your sales, and be a success. You can be assured that I will:

• Tell you what has worked and show you how to duplicate these results

• Point out important points you may be missing and help you find practical solutions to the problems you and your business may face

• Be the sympathetic ear, confidant, and sounding board for both your problems and your inevitable triumphs

Please note: I do provide personal assistance in the areas of music, recording, and business. If you'd like me to help you promote your music products and services, write your sales copy, start and develop your business, or help with other music and business activities, just write me at **Fisher Creative Group, 323 Inner Circle Drive, Bolingbrook, IL 60490**; e-mail me at **fishercg@mcs.com**; or call me at **(630) 378-4109**. I'm usually available to start immediately helping you achieve your goals.

There are very few authors who would give you their telephone number so readily. Unlike them, I'm eager to help you in any way that I can. Your buying this book is not the end of our relationship. On the contrary, this is just the beginning. You and I will cover a lot of ground in this book. Make sure you take advantage of all the opportunities that can and will make your music endeavors—and your life!—rewarding, satisfying, and complete.

Additionally, I regularly share new information

about the commercial music industry—and how to get your own slice of it—in my *Musician's Business Building Bookshelf* newsletter. You can get a *free* one-year subscription to my newsletter by simply giving me your name, address, and telephone number. Why not do it right now? I'll happily send you the next issue.

With those thoughts, let's begin your journey toward making big money scoring soundtrack music and jingles . . . together.

----

*Quotations from the great minds of history
provide inspiration, comfort, knowledge, insight,
and enjoyment. That's why you'll find several
of my favorites sprinkled throughout the text.
Many of them teach us important ideas, and
some are just plain fun.*

CHAPTER 1

What You Need to Begin

The only good is knowledge

and the only evil is ignorance.

—Socrates

There has been a fundamental shift in the commercial music industry in recent years. This revolution of sorts can be summarized in three ways:

- The proliferation of inexpensive, high-quality music production and recording equipment
- A growing audiovisual market, such as business TV, computer games, the Internet, and multimedia presentations desperately needing original music and sound
- An increase in musicians seeking more meaningful work and nontraditional outlets for their musical creations. Many just aren't interested in playing in a band or going after record deals.

Isn't it time all your music and recording equipment stopped costing you money and started *making* you money? Whether you're in a band or just a serious hobbyist, you can make money composing scores and jingles. This guide shows you how to succeed. I'm not talking about Hollywood here, folks. There are other places to sell original music, and this market keeps getting bigger. It's just outside your door.

Corporations make videos, slide, and multimedia presentations for sales, training, and other communications. Local broadcast and cable TV shows need music for themes and underscoring. There are student and other low budget films and videos that need music. Don't forget new media such as video and computer games and the Internet. Local commercials on radio and TV always need jingles and catchy music

scores. They can *all* benefit from your music. And you can make good money selling your music services to them. This is a strong market that can put cash in your pocket while you do something you love—make music!

There is some competition out there and not just from where you might expect. The big music houses in Chicago, New York, and Los Angeles are not your only competition. Your main competition is royalty-free, buyout, and needle-drop production library music. You know what I'm talking about. Those bland, unimaginative, generic music cuts that proliferate cheap videos and boring corporate slide shows. But hey, when you can get 60 minutes of music for $60, it's no wonder producers reach for the latest music factory CD.

You can change all that. I'll show you how to position yourself against library tracks so you come out as the better deal. And you'll discover some unique methods to beat other music houses in your area. This will take some hard work and creativity, but you'll love the challenge because the reward is so great: *You get paid for your music.* You won't have to share royalties, you won't have to go on long tours to promote your record, and you won't have to bend to the record company's whims. It will be your music and you'll be in charge the whole time. And the best part is you keep *all* the profits.

Don't be afraid to take a big step if one is indicated.
You can't cross a chasm in two small jumps.

—David Lloyd George

Beginning your commercial music business doesn't require unreasonable action or vast amounts of money. You won't need to give up your job or take other foolish steps. The purpose of this book is to show you what you need to know and do. This resource will start you on your way toward your dream. It takes hard work, perseverance, and skill. And it takes confidence, faith, and a sincere desire to succeed.

Reading this manual is passive. Nothing will happen until you apply these ideas to your life. Take them, shape them, make them your own. Use them, learn, and success will come. Others can guide, can push, but only you can teach yourself the ultimate knowledge. It comes from within and it comes from without. Learn. Grow. Succeed. Whatever your background, means, skills, and talents, you can make it in the commercial music industry. It always puzzles me the way some people say they want success, yet they never do what is really necessary to be successful. I hope you are not like that. It is your sole responsibility to take charge of your life right now.

I'm assuming you chose this book because you're interested in writing commercial music. And I'm sure you'd like to earn your living from music. The first step to success is recognizing that you need a formal structure. You can't pursue this business piecemeal or ad hoc. You must immerse yourself fully into the commercial world and follow a specific system. Only starting your own commercial music business affords the advantages and benefits you need to reach the level of success you desire. Commit today to learning about general business practices, understanding the commercial music world, and applying your skills to running your own small business. This is an important factor to success, and unless you accept that fact, you are doomed to fail.

So why not start your own company and keep it all for yourself? There are many advantages to running your own commercial music business. The challenge is stimulating and the prize worthwhile. Frankly, I just don't understand why more people don't run a simple, humble, small business on the side. The benefits are tremendous. Plus, by turning your hobby or music skill into a tangible business, you can write off (deduct from your taxes) your current lifestyle. You will be leading the life you want, need, and deserve. Isn't that what this is all about?

Getting started in this lucrative business is a twelve-step process. Here's a map for you to follow:

- Prepare yourself to be in business by developing a plan. Make sure you write down your goals, both personal and professional.
- Save money to build a solid financial cushion both for your personal life and for the start of your business.
- Research your business, your area, your market, and your competition. Use this information to find people and companies who buy original music. You must first identify your target market and discover what they need so you can adapt your music services accordingly.
- Talk to others and learn from their experience. Don't reinvent the wheel. There is plenty of information and there are experienced people available to answer your questions and give you insight.
- Learn to market, promote, and sell your commercial music services. You must consider how you will make people aware of both their needs and your ability to meet them. Use many promotional strategies to get to the level of success you desire.
- Practice both your music and business skills. Be confident, courageous, and have faith in your abilities and your plan.
- Organize your project studio, equipment, and resources.
- Prepare your demo reel.
- Produce and record your commercial music projects.
- Manage your business carefully and effectively. Take control of your career as a business owner and focus on results.
- Start right *now* and do it.
- Persist.

I'm assuming, of course, you already possess the necessary composition and technical skills to write and record music. This is not a book about how to compose. This book is about how to sell music scores and jingles. One word of caution: If you think your music is art, then making and selling commercial music is not for you. Your music is your product and all the traditional business rules apply. If you can't stomach that your music can be packaged and sold like gym shoes, this business is not for you. Also, if you think you'll mind that your music will play a supporting role under dialogue and narration—that means your incredible guitar solo won't get noticed—then you better not get into this business. Scoring soundtracks and jingles for corporations, TV, and commercials is a *business!*

Yes, you need musical ability and originality. But you must have business savvy, too. You'll be selling your services and running your music business just like any other business. It will astonish you how little time you actually spend composing. Don't let this scare you off, just be practical. If you don't have any clients, you can't sell your music. So, which really needs to come first? The music? Or the market?

UNDERSTAND THESE SOBERING THOUGHTS

In a recent magazine survey, *Home Office Computing* asked readers what business areas they needed help with. The results were not surprising:
- 53% need help with selling and marketing.
- 48% need help in financial areas.
- 35% need to know more about their competition.
- 35% need to improve their people skills.
- 30% need more general information about their specific industry.

In another survey, *HOC* asked readers to indicate their toughest job. Once again the results were typical:
- 64% need to get more business.
- 56% need to know how to grow and expand.
- 51% need to know how to promote their products and services.

It should come as no surprise to you that the major emphasis of this book is marketing and selling. Mastering these skills is crucial to your success. You must study, practice, work hard, and apply the concepts and ideas you find in these pages. In short, your formula for making money scoring soundtracks and jingles is this:
- Own your own business. This way you get all the success as you learn to manage all the consequences. Though you can learn while working for others, you'll never make the big money unless you work for yourself. Now, that doesn't mean you should quit your job—quite the reverse—keep your steady paycheck and work part-time on your own commercial music business ventures. You get the best of both worlds: security and endless possibilities.
- Be flexible and make sure you adapt easily to changing circumstances. This is a major benefit of being a one-person shop. You can seize an opportunity quickly and take full advantage of it. You may discover a product, service, or market that others have missed.
- Stay close to your clients. Make sure you are always accessible. Don't put up barriers between you and your market. Most of all, make sure you deliver what your clients want and need. Ask them how you can serve them better. Stay in touch and learn what you must do to keep your clients buying your music services.
- Get help by using specialists to fill in the gaps in your knowledge. Don't think of these services as expenses, but rather as investments in your future success. Add the right people to your team and you will be better off in the long run.
- Make sure you carefully control your resources of both time and money.

Why would you want to start and run your own music business? *Business Week* reported the top seven reasons people go into business for themselves:
- To use my skills
- To gain control over my life
- To build for the family
- To find a challenge
- To live how and where I like
- To gain respect and recognition
- To earn lots of money

Does this sound like you? Maybe you are a born entrepreneur who enjoys a different view of life. We entrepreneurs tend to be:
- Self-reliant. We look to ourselves to find and make what we want. We know the only way to succeed is to use our personal resources of time and talent.
- In control. We direct our life and create our own destiny. Nobody is going to take care of us, so we manage our affairs in our own way.
- Balanced. We recognize the diverse facets of our life and strive for harmony. We are not workaholics and know how to properly juggle work, leisure, and other personal obligations.
- Humane. We care about family, friends, and Mother Earth. We are decent and ethical. Most important, we are smart and savvy. We use our knowledge to find a better quality of life in everything we do.

THE KEY IS PROMOTION

It amazes me how people believe that just because they're in business, clients will automatically come to their door. Nothing could be further from the truth. You want to make music, right? You want to make a living from your music, right? Or, at the very least, some extra cash? Well, you must promote, promote, promote to make your dream come true.

No, you don't need to turn into some corporate suit, but you will have to put forth a professional image. And you won't have to spend many dollars either. I'll show you exactly what to do—and how to do it—later. But right now you must realize that your music and related services are a commodity. And you will sell them. For profit. Big money. You must target your marketing and spend time making it successful. This strategy takes time, effort, imagination, and creativity, *not* cash. You'll see exactly what you need to do to get the most bang for your buck. Don't underestimate the need for constant promotion. It is the vital—dare I say crucial?—element to your business success.

MASTERING RUTHLESS SELF-PROMOTION

*You can't build a reputation
on what you're going to do.*
—Henry Ford

I'm a promotion fanatic. If you're like me, you'd rather spend your *time* getting new business, not your money. You'll discover the real strategies that let you leverage your success and status to keep bringing in more business. Here are the basic steps:
• Prepare your mind for self-promotion.
• Master the technical aspects.
• Create an image.
• Clarify what you are trying to say.
• Gather marketing information about the commercial music industry.
• Understand and use many promotional tactics.
• Develop your marketing plan
• Use networking to establish and maintain your efforts.
• Gather and respond to information.
• Produce the promotional material you need.
• Learn basic sales techniques.
• Commit to success: Plan what you will do and how to do it.
• Determine how to measure your success.
• Review these steps regularly.

◗ PREPARE YOUR MIND FOR SELF-PROMOTION
Your personality will play a significant role in your success. Ruthless self-promotion requires a specific state of mind for which you must prepare. This business is both demanding and rewarding. You must make sure your mind is ready for the challenge. You need a solid determination and an interminable will to succeed. You must cultivate these two crucial characteristics. You must really want to be successful and truly desire to do whatever it takes get there. You need an objective, and that objective is to promote and sell your original music. You may even have decided on tactics you will use to accomplish your objective. Before all that, however, you must first recognize that you deserve the promotion when and only when you put forth the effort required. You must put your mind to the task and work hard all the time to promote your commercial music services . . . ruthlessly!

◗ MASTER THE TECHNICAL ASPECTS
Are your skills, image, presence, and other qualities showcasing your best work? If not, you need to concentrate on improving your technical skills. Besides your music composition skills, you need:
• Writing skills
• Oral presentation skills
• Business skills

You must be able to communicate effectively through both writing and speaking. Writing promotional material, handling interviews, and delivering sales presentations are crucial to sustain your promotions. You will be meeting with the media and clients by telephone and in person. You must learn to explain your business in ways they'll understand. You will sell yourself, your ideas, and your music. If you can't communicate effectively, you are destined to fail. You must understand the intricacies of these skills, practice using them, and ultimately master them. Feel like you need some help? Take some adult education courses in writing or speech. What about business skills? I advise you to run your musical career as a small business. There are many advantages to this, but it's up to you to discover what works for your particular situation and then exploit every possibility. You can't afford to take these important points for granted. Yes, your music matters, but your people and business skills are also vital to your success. Making it in today's commercial music world is a demanding job. You will need every single ounce of your talent, knowledge, stamina, and skills to thrive.

◗ CREATE AN IMAGE
You need to define an image for yourself. Think of all the celebrities and how their persona is really just a manufactured image. For example, Dennis Rodman of the Chicago Bulls is a notorious "bad boy." It's an image he first earned but now cultivates very carefully. Being on the same team as Michael Jordan leaves little room for another "good guy," so the Worm uses bad to his advantage. What other images come to mind? How about Bill Gates as a nerdy whiz-kid, Walter Cronkite as an elder statesman, Katie Couric as a sympathetic friend, Tom Peters as an eccentric genius? My own image is a bit of the rogue loner—not in the sense of a rapscallion but as someone outside the music industry norm. I don't accept traditional music roles or play games, and in my experience, that's rare in the commercial music world. This image positions my company with a unique reputation. I'm not a shark or a cutthroat. I'm an accessible, sincere music business professional. Take time to craft and portray an image for both you and your business.

◆ CLARIFY WHAT YOU ARE TRYING TO SAY

Do less, be more.

—MARSHA SINETAR

You need a message. This goes hand in hand with your image. For most people, the message is the products and services they sell. You must be more specific. For me, my business resources are designed to help the maximum number of people help themselves. This book's message is autonomy. I help people parlay their skills into a successful and profitable business. What are *you* trying to say?

◆ GATHER MARKETING INFORMATION ABOUT THE INDUSTRY

In the beginning, survival is more important than success. Survival is staying on the field, playing the game, learning the rules, and beginning to grow.

—PAUL HAWKENS

You can't proceed on your assumptions and perceptions about the industry alone. You need to get your music into the hands of those who need it, want it, and have the means to pay for it. Therefore, you must research carefully to find the information that provides useful insight into the commercial music world. Only when you discover how the industry works in your region can you formulate a proper plan of action. The first step is to find music buyers. Next, you must learn about their music requirements in detail. You need to know who buys music, for what kinds of projects (jingles, video soundtracks, computer games, etc.), what specific styles of music they buy, and how often. Now you must adapt what you discover to your business. Take what you learn and position your music products and services to fit the particular needs of your target market.

◆ UNDERSTAND AND USE MANY PROMOTIONAL TACTICS

You will use my *Business Success MAPS*. The *MAPS* center on these four areas:
- *Marketing:* everything you do to operate your business including people, location, promotional doodads, open houses, signs, etc.
- *Advertising*: the ads you place, coupons, mailers, direct mail, co-op, online, etc.
- *Publicity*: news releases, public relations, articles, books, booklets
- *Sales*: direct sales techniques on phone and in person, demos, people, etc.

To succeed, your image and your message must be conveyed at every step. Your promotions must expose the problems people have and then show how you solve these problems. At this point, think of publicity as something you start and put in motion but can't control. Conversely, you have complete control over your marketing, advertising, and sales opportunities. This is not a sequence of events; it's a loop. All the parts work in tandem. That's why you must take the time to craft a plan and execute it carefully.

◆ DEVELOP YOUR MARKETING PLAN

I don't know. I'm making it up as I go along.

—INDIANA JONES IN *RAIDERS OF THE LOST ARK*

All this talk is useless unless you have a plan. You can't run a successful commercial music business by the seat of your pants. You need to take the time to decide:
- Who is your market?
- What promotional tools will you use to reach these people?
- When and how will you promote?
- How do you want to be known?
- How much time and money will you devote to your efforts?

The marketing plan example below answers all these questions and more. Keep your plan as simple and straightforward as this. You don't need details at this point, just a road map for success. Later you can fill in the blanks as you explore the many ideas presented throughout the text. The format for this marketing plan is based on suggestions in Levinson's *Guerrilla Marketing*, cited later in the text.

Jeffrey P. Fisher Music marketing will build an increasing base of satisfied, repeat customers. This will be done by stressing our originality, quality, convenience, value, and affordability.

Our target audience is music-buying advertising agencies; film/video production and post production houses; radio, cable, and television stations; and music publishers, primarily those centered in the Midwest.

Marketing tools we will use include quarterly direct marketing letters and postcards, quarterly free client newsletters, monthly advertising in industry magazines, brochures, flyers, books and booklets, articles, audiotape and videotape demonstrations, free samples of rights-free/buyout music, reprints of ads/publicity/articles, seminars and lectures, testimonials, trade shows, sales presentations, and free consultations.

Our niche is targeted at smaller advertisers and film/video producers who can't afford the big bucks charged by our competition but still want all the benefits of original music that works, sounds great, and is affordable.

Our identity will be creative, knowledgeable, state-of-the-art, friendly, helpful, and hardworking as evidenced by our "YOU-centered" attitude. We will be easy and convenient to do business with, and we will provide free samples, free demos, free consultations, and money-back guarantees. Jeffrey P. Fisher Music will devote 5-10% of gross sales toward marketing.

Once you formulate your plan, follow it, review it periodically, and make necessary changes. Create a marketing scrapbook by gathering your plan, material, articles, brochures, letters, and more into a three-ring binder. Or better still, keep it all on your computer. Either way, you'll be able to review your efforts easily and use your old materials as the basis for new marketing materials.

◗ USE NETWORKING TO ESTABLISH AND MAINTAIN YOUR EFFORTS

As a direct follow-up to the previous steps, you need to create and maintain a promotional network. As you work to elevate the status of your business, you will encounter many people who have the power to help you. My suggestion is for you to help them first. Give them something of value, something they can use. At that point you are in a prime position to get something in return—some form of promotion. Go out of your way to help people because you help yourself by helping others. It is the professional and noble thing to do, and ultimately it contributes to the success of your business.

◗ GATHER AND RESPOND TO INFORMATION

Always be on the lookout for promotional opportunities. Even the most mundane activity can yield results. Make promotion a crucial part of your daily marketing routine. A recent *Music and Computers* article about making money in multimedia stated that there was no book available to help people break into this part of the music business. Multimedia is just another part of the commercial music world, and my book can give you the tools to succeed there. I immediately wrote a letter to the editor describing my book and how it would help readers of the multimedia article. They then promoted my book in the next issue. Stay alert to possibilities like these.

◗ PRODUCE THE PROMOTIONAL MATERIAL YOU NEED

Imagination is more important than knowledge.
—ALBERT EINSTEIN

Your demo tape and other collateral sales material needs to be designed to promote you and your work. No business can succeed without these necessary items. You need to develop this material yourself or find other professionals to help you put it together so you can sell your music products and services. If most musicians would put the time and attention they put into their music into promoting and selling their talents, there would be many more successful artists in the world. You can't exist with just a demo cassette and a stack of sticky notes. The basic ruthless self-promotion arsenal consists of brochures, sales letters, flyers, postcards, ads, company profiles, a composer biography, pictures, and more.

◗ LEARN BASIC SALES TECHNIQUES

Let me clarify an important promotional factor. Your business prospects are not interested in you. They are only interested in themselves. To succeed, you *must* make sure your promotional material—indeed, every sales opportunity—focuses completely on your prospect's wants and desires. It's a subtle but critical position. You can't use "I'm great, hire me" tactics in today's music world. You must shift your position to "You have a problem (or need) that I understand. By working with me we can solve that problem (or fulfill that need) together. Here's how . . ."

Do you see the difference? Do you feel the difference? Begin thinking about your clients. What do they want? How do your music products and services benefit them? You must concentrate on what your client wants, *not* what you offer. You don't sell music, you sell solutions. Your commercial music business relies on personal talent to solve problems for AV presentations by creating moods, enhancing images, and helping to deliver a message effectively. If you follow this advice, you will save tons of money you would otherwise waste on promotional gambits and materials that don't work and won't sell your music.

◗ COMMIT TO SUCCESS: PLAN WHAT YOU WILL DO AND HOW TO DO IT

I believe you can have *any*thing in the world but not *every*thing. To be the musical success you want to be, you need to sacrifice something, give something up. You can't have a full social calendar, a full-time job, a family, and a band and devote your full energy to each. Something's gotta give, and you must decide what it is going to be.

That may seem cold-hearted. Surely this is America, and the American dream is to "have it all!" Unfortunately, many well-intentioned people have failed miserably or even gone to an early grave while chanting that anthem. You must first decide *what* it is you want and then concentrate on getting it. There is no middle ground. I believe author Holbrook Jackson described it best when he said sacrifice is a form of bargaining. Suffice to say that *you* must determine where it is you wish to head and must commit, indeed pledge, that you will do what is necessary, and make the appropriate sacrifices to reach your goal. That is how it must be. You can blame nobody for your failure. All that prevents you from getting there is you. So, commit to the success of your self-promotion efforts. Pledge to make the appropriate sacrifices to reach your goals. And make sure you set aside some time each week to work on your promotions.

Next, scrutinize your competition, consider your promotional gambits, study the many options available to you, and determine a plan of action. You've set your goal and committed your resources of time and talent to attaining your success. Now you need a specific plan of action. This doesn't need to be some fancy doctoral thesis. Start with this simple format: Here's where I am. Here's where I wish to go. And here's how I plan to get there. You need a one-year plan, a five-year plan, and a life plan. Just remember that your life is a work in progress. Use the plan as a road map but be flexible.

◗ DETERMINE HOW TO MEASURE YOUR SUCCESS

When you set your goals and decide how you plan to achieve them, make sure you also include a measuring device. Is scoring the next David Lynch film your dream? What if you get a documentary for PBS—does that mean you've succeeded? These are hard questions, almost philosophical in nature. Set yourself some general goals with specific outcomes you desire. For example, you might want to make money from your music. Hold it. That's too vague. How about this instead: I will earn my living entirely from music-related ventures within two years. That's easy to measure. If you are still holding down a part-time job to pay the bills 25 months from now, you know you didn't reach the goal you set for yourself. Take a few minutes to think about how you would measure your success. Write it down. Keep it with your plans. And then take some action!

◗ REVIEW THESE STEPS REGULARLY

Experience is the name we give to our mistakes.
—OSCAR WILDE

Don't make the mistake of thinking about this once and then filing it away. You need to regularly review these steps and determine what is working so you can keep on doing it. You also need to determine what is failing so you can fix it *fast*. Take time out from pur-

suing your goals to reflect on what you did, are doing, and should do. It can sometimes be a sobering experience, but often it's a good feeling that will give you a sense of focus and accomplishment. Review your past, learn from it, and apply what you learn to either changing or staying on course.

Working hard on your self-promotion will keep your name alive, build credibility, and ultimately, put money in your pocket. Make sure everything you do adds value to your business. Present a strong, helpful image, solve problems, give others (people, clients, prospects, and the media) more than they give or expect to receive, and make sure they come away with a good feeling about you, your business, and your music.

Remember this: Ego has nothing to do with this. Ruthless self-promotion is about making your business stronger by leveraging the success you've achieved into more success. First, you must have an initial success—then go crazy telling the world about it. Recognize that your success comes through careful diligence, growing your business day-in and day-out, slowly and methodically. Keep your eye on the prize and the goals you've set for yourself, and make the most of every opportunity presented to you.

WHY SO MANY FAIL

Most business people fail because they don't recognize what business they are in, and what is more important, they don't understand what they are really selling. And now that you know this, remember: *You are not in the music business!* Yep, that's right. You don't sell music. You add value to business, broadcast, cable, and commercial audiovisual presentations. You help producers communicate their message and do a better job. Do you understand this?

Here's an example. The U.S. railroad industry is not the economic force it once was. Why do you think that is? Most experts agree that the railroads made one major miscalculation. They thought that they were in the railroad business. But they weren't. They were actually in the transportation business. See the difference? The trucking industry knew what they were selling. Not trucks, but the moving of goods around the country. You must understand this important distinction and sell your music the same way. You don't sell music. You sell what your music does, and music scores enhance audio and visual presentations, making them better, more memorable, more exciting, and more effective. Got it?

All of the material in this book applies to writing commercial music, whether it be jingles or scores. While I specialize in scoring instrumental tracks, the occasional jingle can also be very lucrative. Some jingles use instrumental underscoring, while others use lyrics. The age of the catchy lyric ebbs and flows—right now, very few jingles feature music and lyrics, but next year that may change.

It is important for you to understand that commercial music is either licensed or sold outright. Usually you grant specific licenses for specific uses of your music. This is the equivalent of renting your music for a period of time for a particular use. For example, you'd grant a client the right to use your music as a local advertising jingle for one year. After that the license expires, but the client can renew the license by paying an additional fee. In the case of a buyout, you sell your music outright for one fee. The client can do what they wish with the music as they now own all rights to it.

For this book, a jingle refers to music used exclusively for TV or radio advertising, whether it has vocals or not. A soundtrack is music used to underscore productions that are not specifically advertising (such as a business presentation). Jingles without words are really soundtracks, but I group them together because the jingle business is slightly different.

The main differences between the jingle business and scoring is that with jingles, you'll write lyrics (either by yourself or with help from ad agency copywriters) and hire more outside musicians, typically singers. If the jingle is a union gig, the unions, AFM and AFTRA, supply all the necessary paperwork. The client or ad agency handles all this. Sometimes you can hire an outside talent payment service to oversee all these union technicalities. You must also understand that most jingle projects will be buyouts where you relinquish all rights. Typically, you are paid a larger fee in advance but realize no future income from the jingle.

After reading *How to Make Money Scoring Soundtracks and Jingles* and following its strategies, you may decide to pursue the jingle business. All the tips and tricks in this book will help you, but if you need more training, here are the best resources about the traditional jingle music business:

- *Through the Jingle Jungle*, Steve Karmen. Billboard Publications; 1515 Broadway, New York, NY 10036. It's out of print, so try your library.
- *Jingles: How to Write, Produce, and Sell Commercial Music*, Al Stone. Writer's Digest Books; 1507 Dana Ave., Cincinnati, OH 45207. This is also out of print.

While the strategies presented here are also applicable to scoring motion pictures, be aware that this is the toughest market to crack. Writing local jingles and scoring small nonbroadcast productions and such *can* bring you fame and fortune. While you won't see your name on the big screen, the work is challenging and loads of fun, too. Cut your teeth on business TV and other local spots, *then* use your success to attract film producers and directors. Who knows, your commercial music business may lead to something bigger.

And for those of you in bands, scoring is a terrific way to supplement your performance income. It's also a natural extension of your talent. Look at Danny Elfman, Stewart Copeland, Mark Mothersbaugh, and others as examples of successful band members who made the transition to scoring. Many of these musicians still tour and record with their bands but score soundtracks and jingles as a big part of their career as well.

CHAPTER 2

Your Project Studio

A symphony must be like the world.

It must contain everything.

—Gustav Mahler

Since this is a business book, there won't be too much about equipment and the technical aspects of recording. This book is about making money, not *spending* money. I'll give you information about the basics, but there are many other books mentioned in the text that provide more detail in this area.

THE EQUIPMENT YOU NEED FOR SUCCESS

Not so many years ago, the idea of producing finished masters at home was a dream. All that has changed with the startling emergence of home project studios. These electronic cottages exist because of MIDI, which created a modular, expandable, and affordable approach to recording. With MIDI, you can now put together a system for composing, playing, and recording your music. All it takes is a handful of keyboards, sequencers, and drum machines; kick in some signal processing; run everything through a quality mixer; and you can record your masterpiece on DAT. This is the essence of modern project studio recording and composing.

Chances are your existing home equipment arsenal will get you through most of your assignments. When it doesn't, you can rent equipment or go out to a pro studio to record (you'll charge your clients these expenses, so don't think you'll be out any extra money, either). If you have a MIDI keyboard or two, drum machine, sequencer (hardware or software), multi-effects processor or two, mixer,

quality mixdown deck (¼-inch or DAT), and a decent cassette deck, you're well on your way. For mostly instrumental music, your MIDI tracks should cover the majority of your work. However, if you play another instrument (guitar, sax, etc.) or use singers, you might want to add a cassette or digital multitrack that can sync to your sequencer to handle the acoustic instruments and voices.

Often using a live solo instrument like sax or flute brings an added dimension to a mostly electronic score. I call this technique an electro-acoustic hybrid. It's my particular specialty. This method combines synthetic textures with real instruments like guitars, bass, and percussion for more versatility, flexibility, and a better sound. This is how I score most projects. When clients need rock, jazz, new age, exotic, or "out there," the synthesizer orchestra is the way to go. If you don't play keyboards, you'll need to find a partner (or use outside players). If you already have a band, you might consider working together on your commercial music projects. Of course, you'll make a little less money when you divide the proceeds, but you'll be more versatile and therefore more marketable. Just don't use your band name for your commercial music composition services.

To make the most money and keep your prices competitive, try to do everything yourself—write, play, record, produce, and mix. The more you farm out, the less you make on a given job. I can handle almost anything that comes along with my skills and equipment. This keeps the overhead and prices low, and clients get a good value.

YOUR SUCCESSFUL STUDIO

To give you an idea of a simple, effective, workable, and profitable project studio, here's my setup. (Keep in mind that if you bought all this at once, you'd pay lots of money up front.) It was built up over several years by adding equipment when the money justified it. I suggest you start small and make the best with what you have. Some items I consider indispensable, like a good compressor; others are optional. Spend wisely and look for bargains. It pays to shop around and look for close-outs. Last year's merchandise still does what it always did. It might not be the latest and greatest, but if it gets the job done—if it allows you to sell more music—it's worth the price.

The best time to find equipment at close-out prices is right after NAMM (the National Association of Music Merchants' conventions held in January and June of each year). Manufacturers introduce their new equipment at these shows. Subsequently, dealers get incentives to close-out the old line to make room for all the new stuff, often at ridiculously low discount prices. Plus, some manufacturers have an upgrade path. A few years ago, Ensoniq discounted their VFX-sd about 50% off the original price to make way for the SD-1, so you could buy the VFX-sd for a low price and then simply upgrade it to the newest model. This is an ideal way to begin, waiting to upgrade when the dough starts coming in.

▶ HERE'S MY EQUIPMENT LIST
- Ensoniq SD-1/32 synth workstation with built-in sequencer
- Yamaha DX-11 FM synth
- Yamaha RX-17 drum machine
- Casio CZ-101
- Tascam 688 MIDISTUDIO with 8-track cassette and 20-input mixer
- Alesis outboard gear—compressors, gates, reverb, etc.
- Digitech outboard gear—guitar processor, harmony processor, reverb, etc.
- Several guitars (acoustic and electric)
- Lots of miscellaneous ethnic percussion (cabasa, bells, guiro, tabla, rain stick, tambourine, kalimba, etc.)

You'll notice that I don't use a sampler. Personally, I prefer synthesizers, but that may soon change. This arrangement is more of a composition studio that contains just what I need to compose and record rough tracks. This is adequate for budget produc-

tions. For sophisticated projects, I usually rent equipment or commercial studio time. This is what works for me, but you may choose other paths. You don't need tons of fancy gear to make money in the commercial music business. The system detailed in this book will work with a moderate setup, but many of you may have a more extensive MIDI and recording setup; there is nothing wrong with that. You should choose the tools that you need to get the job done. I rent, borrow, or visit a commercial studio when a project is beyond my in-house means. Besides, the way some other authors push equipment, you'd think they had stock in the companies!

ON A BUDGET?

We're all children of George Martin and The Beatles. Those records are still the Bible to me. We go back to them as if we're going back to a manual. They were a great example of really utilizing your limitations instead of having unending possibilities. Limitations can be amazing and really breed personality and uniqueness.

—JOHN LEVENTHAL

For those who are just jumping in, start out small. A MIDI synth workstation is the ideal cornerstone to a basic project studio. The Ensoniq MR or AS series or the Alesis QS series all-in-one boxes give you tons of power and flexibility. Similar equipment is available from other manufacturers. For Enqoniq users there is a nifty little benefit called the *Transoniq Hacker*. This completely independent monthly magazine is devoted entirely to Ensoniq gear. Every month they show you how to get more out of your equipment.

- *Transoniq Hacker*. 1402 SW Upland Drive, Portland, OR 97221; (503) 227-6848; www.transoniq.com/~trnsoniq/
- Ensoniq. 155 Great Valley Parkway, Malvern, PA 19355; (800) 553-5151; www.ensoniq.com
- Alesis. 3630 Holdrege Ave., Los Angeles, CA 90016; (800) 525-3747; www.alesis.com

With a workstation under one arm, add a good mixdown deck (even high-quality cassette), and you're on your way. Then as you sell more and more music, invest part of every sale into increasing your equipment arsenal. Notice I said invest, not buy. Don't be frivolous. Choose only those items that will help you make better music or, what is more important, help you *sell* more music. You're in business now. Every dollar counts! And money invested to improve your business is money well spent.

If you're really on a tight budget and all you have is an older synth or tone module, you can update inexpensively. The easiest way to make an old synth sound new is to add effects. A single multi-effects processor brings new life to old gear. Just a cheap chorus pedal used for guitars can do wonders for a DX-7. Don't look for the expensive solution, get creative. By putting my CZ-101 through my Digitech GSP-5 guitar processor, the result is amazing. Most modern synths of the workstation variety use effects as an integral part of their sound anyway. It's easy and inexpensive to bring this feature to your older gear.

TO MIDI OR TO MULTITRACK?

The 8-track deck is important because I also do jingles, on-hold messages, various kinds of audio production, songwriter or band demos, and audio-for-video sweetening. Typically, I use my SD-1 to cover all my parts and then use my other synths for doubling and other effects. Guitars and percussion go on the multitrack with the SD-1 synced to tape using FSK (my multitrack has built-in MIDI sync and mix automation).

If you want more versatility, I suggest getting a 4- or 8-track cassette-based multitrack or digital system, such as the Alesis ADAT or Tascam DA-88 if your funds allow it. These little machines can help you in many ways (doubling up parts, adding narration or sound effects, and more). Again, take a long look at your skills and your budget. Buy what you need to get the job done right. And nothing else.

You might also consider a software-based studio centering around a MIDI/Digital audio multitrack system. Throw in some sound producing modules, a mixer, and such and you quickly have a desktop commercial music production studio. I've recently started using Digital Orchestrator Plus and love its elegant interface. I'll probably rebuild my project studio around it in the near future.

- Tascam. 7733 Telegraph Rd., Montebello, CA 90640; (213) 726-0303
- Voyetra. 5 Odell Plaza, Yonkers, NY 10701; (914) 966-0600; www.voyetra.com

GET SOME SPACE

You also need a place for your project studio. This doesn't need to be some fancy recording environment with expensive acoustical treatments. You just need an area to set up your equipment, compose, record, and mix. When the project is too big, go to a local studio to lay your tracks. By having most parts sequenced beforehand, you get in and out quickly and cheaply. You can easily save money and headaches in the studio by planning ahead; buying off-peak studio time for less; taking backups of sequences, samples, and disks; and preparing lead sheets for outside players.

A spare bedroom is my combined studio and control room. Most of my instruments, except percussion and voice, go directly to the mixing board, so I don't need a separate studio. When recording narration or singers, I set them up in a walk-in closet down the hall. This absolutely quiet and acoustically dry closet—it's full of clothes, y'know—is ideal for voice recording.

More and more people are working from their homes. There are tax, environmental, and lifestyle benefits. You get more flexibility, and you can work when you're at your best. (Personally, I'm sluggish in the morning, turbo-charged from one to six, and zonked by eight.) There is more time for work or play, less stress, and comfortable surroundings. It's sometimes crowded, but I wouldn't give up my ten-second commute for anything.

Running a business from home is terrific. It helps the cash flow, especially in the early going, and the overhead (the cost of staying in business) is very low, which is hard to beat. When I started out, I had some equipment, enough money for business cards, blank tapes, and a roll of stamps. If I had not worked from my home, my business never would have survived the first six months.

I recommend you work from home during the initial phases of your commercial music business. The advantages mentioned above can really make a difference. Of course, you'll need to check zoning and with your landlord (if applicable) before you work at home, but we'll discuss that later. If you don't want to locate your project studio in your home, you have three other choices:
- Rent office space.
- Work with another recording studio.
- Get an office in a studio complex.

▶ RENT OFFICE SPACE
This is, by far, your most expensive option. Paying rent and other utilities can zap you of precious resources during your critical first few months. If you don't have enough savings to support your business (and your personal life) for six months, stay home. Unless you are getting into the recording studio business and have clients coming and going at all hours, I don't see the need for an outside office. You'll handle most of your daily business at a keyboard (ivory or QWERTY). If you meet your clients at their place, you really have no need at all for an office. But if only an office will do, try the following.

▶ WORK WITH ANOTHER RECORDING STUDIO
You might offer your services to a recording facility whereby you become a kind of staff composer. They

give you an office in exchange for your doing all recordings at their facility. They get the benefit of a professional composer (you), and you get exposed to a client base you might not otherwise meet.

◗ OFFICE IN STUDIO COMPLEX

This is similar to the above arrangement, differing only in the number of area composers. In Chicago, there are several communities of composers centered around a well-equipped multiple studio complex. This arrangement can also help you get many other clients to which you might not otherwise have access. The downside is your direct competition surrounds you.

ORGANIZING YOUR WORK SPACE

*My father taught me to work;
he did not teach me to love it.*

—ABRAHAM LINCOLN

Since you'll be wearing many different hats, it's vital that you organize both your working routine and your project studio/office space. You need a place for handling your business functions: marketing, publicity, sales, accounting, etc. Also, you need a composing and recording area. For efficiency, I created four main areas for work: the computer, the SD-1, the mixing board, and the conference table. Follow this example or adapt it to your work area.

◗ COMPUTER

I use my computer a little for music and a lot for business (marketing, finances, mailing lists, newsletters, etc.). The sequencer in my SD-1 has always been fine for my music composition needs. However, the computer is becoming more and more integral to my music studio—my latest projects entail music and sound for computer-based presentations.

A small desk holds computer, monitor, mouse, and laser printer. Pertinent disks and manuals are within arm's reach, as is the telephone. By keeping most files on your computer, you'll need very little traditional paper file cabinets. Try to keep your business as paper-free as possible. About the only paper you'll need to keep are signed contracts, testimonials, receipts, and check stubs that match invoices. Everything else should be on your computer.

If you do store your entire business on computer as I do, *make sure you backup your data regularly.* One hard disk crash and you lose your entire business. More on using your computer later.

◗ SD-1

This is where I do all my composing. I rarely *play* my other synths, I just control them through the SD-1.

Using template sequences, I can configure my setup with the press of a button. Disks, manuals, and other pertinent material are on shelves nearby.

◗ MIXING POSITION

This area lets me reach my outboard effects and puts me right in the sweet spot of my stereo speakers. Lest you think I have a huge room, I don't. When sitting at the 688, I can reach everything in the room, including the computer and SD-1.

◗ CONFERENCE TABLE

This is the area I use for meetings, sorting mail, writing first drafts in longhand (stupid, ain't it?), and spinning my little webs.

WHAT ABOUT CLIENT VISITS?

Clients rarely visit my project studio. I make it a point to meet them on their turf. After all, the end product is the point. It's all they should concern themselves about. Just because I use my bathroom as an echo chamber doesn't make my music bad. Long-standing clients actually find this kind of fun. They know how creative and resourceful I am. And when it saves them some money, well, they think it's even better. I do, however, invite clients to outside sessions at commercial facilities and often meet them for lunch at convenient restaurants.

THE PROBLEM WITH EQUIPMENT

Face reality, buckaroo: You can't own everything. Nor should you want to. Hardware gets outdated so quickly that it's impossible to keep up. Even *trying* to keep up is both physically and mentally draining. Stick to the basics, only get the equipment you need to make your job easier and of the highest quality. Don't worry about the other stuff. Remember you can always rent equipment or go to your local recording studio when you need to cover special circumstances.

Here's an example: I contemplated getting a ¼-inch half-track mastering machine several years ago. I'm glad I didn't. On a recent project I was asked to mix to ¼-inch reel-to-reel. However, there are three distinctly different ¼-inch tape formats. Which was the right one?

I assumed this meant ¼-inch half-track. Instead, we needed ¼-inch quarter-track. The two formats are entirely incompatible. All it took was a quick phone call to the video editor to make sure we were compatible, but the experience was a reminder that you must be very careful when a producer specifies an audio format. Don't assume anything.

You must make sure you and the sound editor are absolutely simpatico when it comes time to mix music. Don't leave this to chance. Make sure everything is right before you mix the final master tape. Just how many different formats are there? Here's a handy little list:

▶ CASSETTE
- Normal, chrome, and metal tape formulations with various Dolby or DBX noise reduction systems

▶ REEL-TO-REEL
- ¼-inch quarter-track at 3.75, 7.5, and 15 inches per second (ips)
- ¼-inch half-track at 7.5 and 15 ips
- ¼-inch 4-track at 7.5 and 15 ips
- ½-inch half-track at 15 and 30 ips
- ½-inch 8-track and 16-track at 15 ips
- 1-inch 8-, 16-, and 24-track
- 2-inch 24-track

All the reel-to-reel formats have different noise reduction systems, such as Dolby A, B, C, and SR or DBX Type I or II. When you add in the different tape formulations, this becomes a real (or shall I say reel) nightmare.

For instance, most ¼-inch quarter-track machines are consumer decks that run at 3.75 or 7.5 ips. However, some professional decks run at 15 ips. If you record the music at 15 ips and your client uses a consumer machine, the speeds won't match. Also, some reel-to-reel decks use 10.5-inch NAB hubs for their reels while other machines only accept 7-inch reels. Wouldn't it be a shame if you got the format and tape speed right but you put it on the wrong kind of reel?

What's my advice? Well, unfortunately there are no standards—I once thought ½-inch half-track was standard, but not anymore. On three different projects I used ¼-inch quarter-track, cassette, and VHS hi-fi. If I owned the half-track deck, it would have simply gathered dust. Only cassette is the completely safe format—everybody has one.

▶ DIGITAL FORMATS
- Digital audio tape (DAT) at 44.1k or 48k sample rates
- Digital compact cassette (DCC)
- Digital multitracks by Alesis, Fostex, and Tascam
- Digital formats for PC's and the Internet, such as .wav, .aiff, and Real Audio

If you need a mastering machine, get a DAT deck and then find a duplicating house or recording studio that can transfer your DAT master to the (almost infinite) variety of formats. Owning all these different formats is costly and downright foolish. Let somebody else pay for the equipment maintenance and depreciation. Sure, it may cost some money to rent or buy transfer time at the local recording complex, but you'll simply charge these costs back to your clients and *save* money in the long run.

FINDING HELPFUL EQUIPMENT SUPPLIERS

One last word on building your project studio: Find a single-source music store that can handle everything you need. Also, find two or three suppliers of audio gear and one or two studios that can help you when an eventuality pops up. Do it now and start to build relationships with these vendors *before* you desperately need their help. I am indebted to several such places; one of them deserves particular mention.

Ken Tobias at Tobias Music is my one-stop source for everything having to do with guitars. I bought my first, second, and last guitar from him. I've never bought anything even remotely guitar-related from any other store (except when I won a guitar in a contest, but that doesn't count, does it?). He's a good person, of the sort one meets so rarely. No hype, only good advice and a practical view of life that I adore. I want to take a moment here to compliment and thank him for his encouragement and understanding. If you're ever in the Chicago area, stop by and tell him hello. Make sure you mention that you read about him here. That doesn't mean he'll give you a discount, though!
- Tobias Music. 5013 Fairview Ave., Downers Grove, IL, 60515; (630) 960-2455

FINDING AND USING OTHER MUSICIANS

Occasionally, you may need help with a score or jingle. Where do you get such help? If you are in a band, use the other members to cover parts. Otherwise try these resources:
- Music stores. Place notices or get numbers of solo and group musicians. Many stores have an ad hoc referral service. Use it.
- Telephone book under musicians or entertainment
- Musician's Union
- Bridal shops (many bands leave their cards there)
- Magazines and newsletters that list musicians and other talent in your area. Just turn to the music section in the *Standard Periodical Directory* (cited later) and you will find pages and pages of music press. Call or write for sample issues to see which ones have the information you need.

Make sure you find some musicians *before* you need them. Making friends with a few versatile, creative people can go a long way toward making your music better, not to mention meeting deadlines. Once you get a pool of musicians to draw from, you should be ready for just about any situation that comes up. Treat them well and stay in contact regularly. I send all my associates my newsletter. Remember, you'll be subcontracting their services. This doesn't require anything special. Hire them, get them to play, pay them, get them to sign a release. To sweeten the deal, throw in a free copy of the finished tape, especially if they are a featured performer.

You already know that some sound-producing equipment and a way to record them are the basic building blocks of your home studio. When you start to add equipment and expand your recording skills, you might be surprised to learn what the most essential items that you need for your home or project studio are. You see, to make the best recordings possible, these items are crucial. They will last longer and go further toward making your music sound better than any other pieces of equipment in your arsenal. And when your music sounds great, your clients will be happy, and that means more money for you. Here is what you need:
• Compressor
• Reverb (or multi-effects signal processor)
• Microphone
• Line stabilizer
• Monitor systems

▶ COMPRESSOR

This is the most crucial and most overlooked special effects device. I once heard that the number of gray hairs on an engineer's head is inversely proportional to the number of compressors and gates in the rack. Truer words were never spoken. You won't ever regret your purchase of a compressor. You simply can't get a modern rhythm section sounding right without a compressor. Compress the bass drum and bass tracks and get the bottom end really tight. It's the only way. Another important task for a compressor is ducking (explained later). Aside from using

compression on individual instruments and tracks, you can also use your compressor to reduce the dynamic range of an entire track. For example, if the final music is for videotape, use a 3:1 compression ratio on the whole mix.

It's my life's work to make sure everyone knows about the benefits of a good quality compressor (and ducker). It is, by far, the most neglected—but most useful—special effects device you can own. Here's a recommendation. Get the Alesis 3630 compressor/gate with side chain. This stereo (or dual mono) device is a good buy. You can compress, gate, and duck for well under 300 bucks. Better yet, get two!

▶ REVERB

To create convincing music mixes, you need to create spatial effects. Nothing works better at making sounds come alive and creating the right atmosphere than reverberation. If you are lucky to have a huge studio with controllable acoustics, you are set for life. But the rest of us who use synthesizers and close-miked instruments or instruments plugged right into the mixer need some artificial space.

Enter a digital reverb or multi-effects processor of some sort. If you have built-in effects with your synths, you won't need a separate reverb, but if you have older synths or are going to record acoustic instruments, a good reverb is necessary. Better yet, get a multi-effects processor like an Alesis Quadraverb or Digitech TSR 24. These powerful boxes make your tracks shine. If you have the space, the room on your mixer, and the money, buy many different processors. Use devices from different manufacturers because each has its own unique sound. I have four dedicated effects processors. Let's face it, effects are the key to sounding professional.

Here's a real world example. I had a couple of tracks recorded several years ago using my trusty X-15 cassette multitrack. Like many demos, it had a quality that I could not successfully recreate. Unfortunately, though my old tapes have some strong *performances*, they are rather mediocre *recordings* because I was learning the tricks of sound engineering when I made them. My music was obscured by my less-than-perfect attempts at recording and mixing.

So, I grabbed a couple of compressors, a digital reverb, and a guitar processor. The 4-track mixes were subjected to heavy processing to overcome the shortcomings of the recordings. I squashed the old drum tracks to a driving thump; smoothed the vocals with compression and spiced them up with a bright, splashy reverb; and turned the guitar track into a thing of beauty thanks to some mild compression, distortion, chorusing, and gating. I left the bass line alone and added some synth lines live while mixing, playing little bits where needed.

Do I believe in the power of signal processing? Yes!! Both old and new tracks came alive with the help of some liberal signal processing. These mixes sound as good as my newer work—plus I saved some terrific performances. Reverb, effects, and compressors are the key to a tight, clean, professional sound with plenty of impact and variety. Don't ever forget this point!

◗ MICROPHONE

Again, this is an optional item if your tracks will be mostly MIDI or electronic. For solo instruments, singers, narrators, and sampling, you need a quality, all-purpose microphone. An inexpensive microphone like the Shure SM57 or SM58 handles just about any circumstance that comes along. The only problem with the all-purpose microphone is that it's just like a sofa bed—it's neither a good sofa nor a good bed—but it gets the job done adequately and inexpensively.

Dynamic mics (those that don't need power) have a warm quality and character all their own. I like them on vocals (especially narration) and some solo instruments. Try the Shure SM57 or SM58 for vocals and electric guitar amps. I'm also fond of the Sennheiser 421 for female vocals, kick drums, and acoustic guitar.

Condenser mics (they need power from a battery or through your mixer) are more in your face. They tend to be dead-on accurate with no character. If accuracy is your bag (or you do a lot of sampling), check into one of these. The Shure SM81 is a good all-purpose condenser that should serve you well for many years.

Another type of condenser mic is a boundary mic or PZM (pressure zone microphone). This unique design capitalizes on the fact that all sounds are inherently in phase when reaching a flat boundary. By placing a microphone element slightly above a hard, smooth plate, sounds in the pressure zone are picked up. What is great about this is the sound doesn't suffer from the unfortunate side effects of a bad sounding room. We all know the hollow sound some mics can produce. PZMs don't suffer this fate. So if you have a bad room, get a PZM and solve some of those problems.

◗ LINE STABILIZER

If you have a computer or if you have synths (which are really small computers), you need one of these. I'm not talking about a cheap surge suppresser either. You need a line stabilizer, noise filter, surge protector, voltage regulator device (and backup power supply, if you prefer). Yes, it just sits there and does nothing, but

when you need it, it works hard for you.

My unit solves my line noise problem, keeps my computer from crashing, protects against surges and brownouts, makes a single-point grounding source that solves my ground loop problem, lets me shut everything down with one switch, and more. Everything gets power from it. When I shut down for the night, I turn it off and unplug it from the wall. My entire project studio is disconnected from the world. This is added protection when I'm not working because I simply don't trust the electric company. So get one of these fast—it's a safety feature that no studio should be without. If you've made a substantial investment in your gear, don't let it get ruined by a power surge or failure. Protect yourself or suffer the consequences!

Special note: Do you have excessive buzz or hum in your studio? If so, you probably have a ground loop. Without getting too technical, a ground loop simply means you have multiple paths to ground between your gear. Here's how to fix it. Make sure all your gear goes to one central source—your mixer or a patchbay is the ideal choice—either directly or indirectly.

Next, take a piece of speaker wire and attach one end to your central source (mixer chassis) and the other to the center post in an electrical wall outlet. Now, lift the ground of every piece of gear in your studio *except* the mixer. Use the little three prong to two prong adapters from your local hardware store. If you get a line stabilizer, plug your mixer into it with ground intact. Now you have only one path to ground, and all your hum should disappear.

Even if you don't have a problem with hum now, double-check your connections. You may still be able to improve your signal to noise ratio a few dB by following the above suggestions. In the age of digital recording, a few dB less noise is worth the extra effort.

◗ MONITOR SYSTEMS

That you need a good, accurate monitor system for your project studio goes without saying. However, you really need four (or more) separate monitor systems. Don't worry, it probably won't cost you another dime. Check all mixes on as many systems as you can—your car, a boom box, a typical home system, and a Walkman. You probably have most of these already; if not, find someone who does. Until you really know what you are doing, it pays to check your mixes on a variety of systems. It might surprise you how different a track can sound.

Though I have a decent monitor system, I take extra time to mix on systems that closely approximate where the final mix will be heard. Since most of my scores end up on videos, much of my best music winds up coming out of a three-inch speaker, so I check my mixes on a cheap TV. It's a challenge to make *that* sound good. Here's another tip: Listen to your favorite music on a crummy system and then mix to the same system, trying to get your music to sound as good as your beloved CD.

Know your audience and mix accordingly. Check the sound on any and everything you can get your hands on. Monitor through your full range system, of course, but check your mix on headphones, too. Instead of placing the cans on your ears, however, lay them face up on your mixer. You may need to crank the volume to hear, but the sound is the worst case scenario (very similar to a telephone earpiece). If your mix works on this setup, it'll be fine almost anywhere. Also, always check the mono compatibility for your music. Believe it or not, much of what you do will end up in mono, so make sure your music is OK.

"When I get home with my master tape, it never sounds as good as it did in the edit suite." I hear this all the time, and it happens all too often. Why? Because too many editors monitor on speaker systems that don't accurately reflect the sound your audience will hear. Here's a summary of the things you can do to make sure your soundtrack mix plays at its best on different audio systems:

- Don't rely on one speaker setup. The full range speakers can be misleading. You need to listen on other speakers before you'll know whether your mix is right.
- Listen on a regular old TV speaker, NS-10's (many suites and studios have these), and then the big system. Try to find the best sonic compromise between all these different possibilities. Remember that most of your audience will be listening to your music on crummy speakers. If you mix only for the high-priced audiophile, you'll be ignoring the majority of your audience.
- Check all music mixes on a full range system, cassette Walkman, TV speaker, car stereo, and boom box. Try to make a mix sound great using the worst possible scenario—a telephone. If it's intelligible over the phone, chances are it will be fantastic on fuller range systems.

Sure, it takes a little more time to make sure your soundtrack works on many different systems, but it's worth it. After all, it is *your* name on the credits!

CREATIVE MIXING TECHNIQUES

One problem you will face when preparing a soundtrack or jingle is how to mix the different elements together so they don't compete against one another.

The most difficult part is getting the music and voice track to work together.

The usual procedure when working with music and a voice track (be it singing, narration, or dialogue) is to reduce the volume of the music under the voice track. There's a problem with this method: When the voice track is silent, the music is usually too low in level, and if you increase its volume, it can quickly obscure the voice track. You're forced to either ride the gain by constantly raising and lowering the music track or just set it and forget it—hardly the most creative solution.

How do you prevent the music from stepping all over the voice track so you can understand all the words? Here's the secret: You must create a space for the voice track, a kind of hole in the soundtrack, reserved for speech with the music surrounding *but not enveloping* it. Here are five tricks of the trade you can use to create a strong, effective soundtrack. Three are electronic tricks you can do in the studio or editing suite; the other two are for particular types of music.

◗ CERTAIN INSTRUMENT FREQUENCIES INTERFERE WITH VOICE

Without going into the technical aspects, there are musical instruments that fight with the intelligibility of speech. For the male voice, the lower midrange instruments like acoustic guitar, tenor sax, and the middle of the piano are the culprits. For the female voice, the upper range instruments like alto sax, flute, solo violin, and screaming guitar solos tend to cover up and mask intelligibility. Any music track that predominantly features one of these instruments will conflict with the associated male or female voice.

Compose your music without these interfering frequencies so there is space for the voice track. For example, if you are using a female voice, avoid music with a hot guitar solo. It might help you to think of the voice track as another solo instrument and select appropriate music that lets you feature it prominently in the track.

◗ COMPOSE MUSIC THAT IS SOMEWHAT SPARSE

High-powered, high-density tracks work well for visual sequences, but they fight for space (and audience attention) when used under a voice track. In general, the less-is-more school of music is best. Choose music that is full range—with a tight low end and crisp highs—but has a somewhat reduced midrange.

◗ USE STEREO BALANCING TO CREATE A HOLE

If you're working in stereo—and I mean stereo all the way through to exhibition (most projects play in mono, not stereo)—make sure there is a hole in the center stereo field for the voice track. This mixing technique requires leaving solo and midrange instruments out of the stereo center and balancing them to either the left or right speakers. This way there is space in the middle for the voice track.

▶ USE FREQUENCY CONTROLS TO CREATE SPACE IN MONO

Though not as effective as the stereo trick above, you can create a hole by removing the troublesome midrange frequencies with an equalizer. The frequency band that most affects speech intelligibility (male and female) is between 3 and 4kHz. Reduce the music track by 2-4dB at those frequencies and correspondingly boost the same frequencies by 2-4dB on the voice track. This takes some experimentation to work exactly right, but a little knob diddling and careful listening will show you the way.

▶ USE A DUCKER TO MIX VOICE AND MUSIC TOGETHER

By far the best way to make sure the music and voice tracks don't interfere is to use a ducker. A what? A ducker is a function of most compressors. You use the compressor to automatically reduce the level of the music track below that of the narrator. You can do this manually, of course, but not with the same degree of accuracy. A ducker lets you control the background music level with the voice track.

When the voice track begins, the ducker reduces the music track level or ducks it out of the way. When the voice track is silent, the music plays at full volume. This device automatically controls the level of the music with the voice track. You get the perfect blend of voice and music, so you can concentrate on other important elements of your final production. If you want a cost-effective ducker, take a look at the Alesis 3630 mentioned earlier. It can really help you clean up your audio tracks and solve other sonic problems. I would never put together a soundtrack, especially a jingle, without this indispensable and versatile tool. You shouldn't either.

Use these five tricks of the trade to improve how you mix voice and music together. Never again worry whether voice tracks mixed with your music are intelligible or not.

REALISTIC SOURCE MUSIC

Occasionally you might need to add source (nondramatic) music to a production. This is music that is part of the scene, not dramatic underscore. Here are a few ways to make it more realistic:

• For music coming from a radio or boom box, use the equalization controls on your mixing board to cut all the highs and lows from the music. By reducing about 8-10dB at 10kHz and 100Hz, you get a boxy, cheap radio sound.

• If the music is coming from Walkman headphones, cut all the lows and midrange and boost the highs slightly. The result is that tinny sound everyone recognizes.

• When music is coming from a car that moves away in a scene, just cut the highs, and you're left with the thump. For the really adventurous, put the music on a tape deck with a variable speed control. As the car moves away from the scene, slow the music tape down slightly. This drops the music in pitch and sounds similar to the Doppler effect that occurs as a sound source moves away from our ears.

• For the sound of a scratchy old record, remove all the lows and all the highs and leave the honking midrange. If the recording you're using is already on an LP, skip this next step. Put an old LP on the turntable. Place the needle in the run-out groove at the end and mix in the sound of the crackling, thumping needle to your music. This only works if you don't have an automatic turntable that picks up the needle when it hits the run-out groove. Of course, you might have a hard time finding *any* turntable!

• To make a clean studio recording sound like a live performance, try adding some echo or reverb to the music.

• Another effective strategy is to cross-fade source music with dramatic music. You must work this out in advance. Sometimes you can create an interesting transition when the two music pieces overlap.

MORE SOUND ENGINEERING TIPS

The major tricks that make a great rock record are compression (the sound of rock), over-the-top EQ (the color of rock), and the many contrived echoes and reverbs, the phasing, the flanging, and the automatic double-tracking (the flavors of rock). And let's not forget that invaluable tool . . . the multitrack tape recorder! Rock sound is, and has been, extremely manipulated since it began.

—RICK CLARK

Here are my hottest recording tips, gleaned from experience, for you to use to make your commercial music sizzle. Pick out your favorites and give them a try the next time you fire up your musical gear.

• If your drum machine only has stereo outs, treat them as two individual mono outputs. Using the pan controls available through your drum machine, pan the kick drum hard left and pan the snare hard right. Bring these two feeds to your mixer, but keep them panned to the center. Now you can leave the kick dry and use different EQ and effects on the snare. For the other drums in the kit, strike a balance between the kick and snare treatment by panning these drums (using the drum machine pan controls) between the two outs. For instance, you could put the hi-hat about halfway between the dry kick and a heavily treated snare.

- Play your drum machine parts in real-time; don't sequence them. Or go back and add subtle variations at important points. When you do sequence, make your patterns four or more bars long, not two. This gives you more time to do interesting things before the sequence repeats again. Remember, a drummer has two hands and two feet. The feet are usually occupied hitting the kick and opening or closing the hi-hat, so the hands are free to hit only *two* other drums. Keep this in mind as you record your drum machine sequences. Of course, if you want an unrealistic sound, hit as many drums as you want. But for most modern band sounds, stick with no more than two hands and two feet!

- Layer your guitar parts using different brands. Each axe (and amp, for that matter) has its own unique quality. Or try this trick: Record a rhythm part using a standard tuning, then track a second part using a capo a few frets up. Adjust the song key accordingly, of course. This works great on acoustic guitar parts. Often I'll pan the two tracks hard left and right and open up space in the middle for vocals and other instruments.

- Use this tip to thicken the bass on all your recordings. Double-track all bass parts one octave lower. Use a deep Moog-type synth bass patch (all body, little attack, and short release) for extra impact. Also note that most bass parts tend to be monophonic. Bass players play one note at a time and very few chords.

- There are two ways to accomplish automatic double-tracking of any part. First, set a delay line to a short delay, between 5 and 30ms. Hard-pan the dry and delayed part for maximum effect. Alternatively, you can use a pitch shifter set between 2-4 cents. Eddie Van Halen tracks his guitar parts this way. His dry guitar sound goes hard left while the pitch shifted part is panned hard right. He controls the overall sound by the amount of pitch shifting.

- Stop sending full bandwidth mixes to your reverb. If your mixes are sounding muddy, it's because you're sending too much bass to your reverb. Use EQ to take the mud out of the track before it goes to reverb. In other words, put an EQ module between your effects send and reverb unit. Next, get rid of all frequencies below 3kHz. This is especially effective on vocals. You give a nice, bright splash on the plosives and hard consonant sounds. You can use this no-more-mud trick for slapback echo and longer delay lines, too.

- Lately I've been using the Digitech DHP-55 Harmony Processor as my signal processor of choice. Besides excellent—shall I say unbelievable?—instrument harmony processing, the DHP-55 has a couple of neat mix imager programs. Put your stereo mix through one of these programs and everything comes alive. The bass deepens while maintaining its punch, and the highs get clearer and more pristine without sounding brittle. All my mixes benefit from this box. In fact, the moment I started using it, people started calling to ask me how to get that sound on tape. Well, my secret's out. If you have or can get your hands on a Digitech DHP-55 or 5000, you must try these mix imaging programs.

  - Digitech. 8760 South Sandy Parkway, Sandy, UT 84070; (801) 566-8919; www.digitech.com

- Use equipment, especially synths and outboard gear, that others don't usually use. Old gear can give you a very distinct sound. I use a cheap Yamaha R100 effects processor for vocals and guitars. I love its delayed reverb programs.

- Speaking of delayed reverb, put a delay line before your reverb and set it to a 100% short delay with no feedback. Send a vocal line to the delay and then on to the reverb. You'll hear the dry vocal first in the mix. The delay line then creates a gap before the reverb begins. This makes the room seem bigger, without needing a long (read: muddy) reverb time. Adjust the delay time to fit your music. On choppy vocals it's cool. Dry sound . . . silence . . . reverb splash.

- Put a speaker and mic in your garage, basement, or tiled bathroom. Place them at opposite ends so you pick up the most room sound. Send instrument tracks to the speaker via your mixer's send and return system and add *real reverb* to your mix. I use my large tiled bathroom as an echo chamber. I put a small speaker in the room and use a PZM to pick up the sound and return it to the mix. This is the essence of my snare drum sound: bright, tight, crisp, and clean. It works well on snares, vocals, and some instruments. Experiment and get creative.

- Play those faders. As you begin mixing your music, keep moving the faders up and down slightly. You bring a little extra motion to your mix through this subtle manipulation of levels. Often I'll diddle with EQ and effects sends and returns, too. Nothing major—I'll just make a few minor tweaks live as the mix progresses.

- Play your synth bass parts all the way through; don't sequence them. If you must sequence them, go back and add fills, slaps, and other variations to humanize these parts.

- If you really want your synth to sound like a guitar, run your lead patches through a guitar combo amp and mike it up. Alternatively, or in addition, use some guitar effects processor. Jan Hammer used a Rockman for his solo guitar lines played on his Moog synth.
- More synth guitar emulation tips. Guitar power chords are usually just the root, fifth, and octave—no thirds—that's why they work in both major and minor keys! Guitarists tend to play monophonic leads and bend notes a half-step up generally. However, David Gilmour bends his guitar notes 2½ steps up on "Comfortably Numb"! A guitar player cannot bend a note *down*. To do that, the string must already be bent up, struck, and then released. Start with the pitch wheel up, press the key, and release the wheel so it springs back to pitch.
- Use a chorus effect on your vocal parts. The effect should be subtle, just a tiny hint. Or try this trick: Double-track your lead vocal part. Send the second vocal track to reverb and leave the main lead vocal part dry and up front in your mix. Don't let the second track be heard, just use it for the reverb send (pre-fader). This way the reverb around the lead vocal is actually a different take. It's the kind of subtlety that can make a song breathe.
- Don't forget about dynamics. I get lots of tapes and the one common thread is dynamics . . . or a lack of any. Get soft. Get loud. Swell. Fade. Mix it up. Subtract some instruments from the mix. Add in everything including the kitchen sink. If you don't know what I mean, listen to orchestral music, specifically the adagio in Mahler's Tenth Symphony. You'll learn what dynamics really are!

Start using these techniques to improve all your music recordings. Don't be afraid to tread new ground. Just because something sounds weird, doesn't mean it's not good.

TAKING CARE OF THE ROUTINE

*My sole inspiration is a telephone
call from a director.*
—COLE PORTER

The commercial music business requires you to be creative on demand, and dealing with that stress is often difficult. My tip is to keep the composing process hassle-free and keep the main steps of recording mutually exclusive. There are essentially two steps in all creative endeavors: Get the idea down quick and dirty and then go back and edit your idea relentlessly and turn it into a solid piece. Don't expect to get everything right the first time. The real work is in

the transformation from sketch to full blown song or score. Take care of the routine. Don't let technology interfere with your creative process. Your mind will find the true creativity within, and your music will be much better, believe me!

There are four steps to organizing your composition routine so that you are free to compose, not worry about the details. The point is to get your music down fast, while the ideas are flowing, and worry about tweaking it into a finished composition later, after the creative surge has passed.
- Organize your MIDI system.
- Streamline your composition tools.
- Program template sequences.
- Edit and mix later.

▶ ORGANIZE YOUR MIDI SYSTEM

Get all your individual components talking together on the right channels, the right programs, etc. If your setup is small, this is easy, but as your system grows, it gets tougher to keep it all straight. Take the time to organize patches, MIDI channels, effects programs, everything, and *write everything down*. You should be able to configure your system with just a few button presses. This way you're up and running quickly and optimally. You can take time later to change things—when you mix—but right now you need to compose *fast*.

▶ STREAMLINE YOUR COMPOSITION METHOD AND TOOLS

For composing, I use my SD-1 exclusively. Its onboard sequencer, built-in drums, effects, and master keyboard capabilities make it my ideal composition tool. I can turn it on and start writing music in seconds, which of course, speeds up the recording and composition process greatly. Now you can see why I'm a proponent of workstations! The ideal is to record tracks as fast as you can play them. You can augment your sketches later, but first get the parts down; workstations make writing and recording music much easier and more efficient.

▶ PROGRAM TEMPLATE SEQUENCES

I control my other synths through my master SD-1. Using template sequences to configure the setup with the press of a button means every composition session starts with a preset sequence on tracks one through six. For example:
- Drum kit (doubled on RX-17 MIDI channel 3)
- Bass (doubled on one CZ-101 MIDI channel 1)
- Piano (doubled electric piano on the DX-11 MIDI channel 4)
- Strings (doubled on other module MIDI channel 2)
- Solo sound (sax, trumpet, etc.)
- Effects (miscellaneous sound MIDI channel 5)

Immediately after my rough sketch is finished, I can bring in the other instruments and try combinations. I use several different templates, each geared to a particular style of music. For example, my orchestral template is:

• Strings
• Brass
• Woodwinds
• Double bass—cello
• Orchestral percussion

◗ EDIT AND MIX LATER

The three steps in the creative composition process—composing, recording, and mixing—should not overlap. Following my method means never start editing, tweaking, or mixing your composition until you finish the previous step. Edit after the composition is in reasonable sketch form. Avoid looking for special sounds until the song structure is complete. Don't send information to other synths until the editing stage. And don't start using effects until all the editing is complete!

After the track is down, it's time to start editing. Sure, you may rerecord a part, replace a part or a sound, or go in a different direction altogether—that's fine. But do it after you've first tried writing what you thought was good. Don't record a drum part and then tweak and quantize it to death before moving on to the bass. Use a preset drum pattern or two, drop in a bass line, move on to chords, etc. Build up the sketch, then stop. Take a short break and then come back to your composition and start editing. Once you finish editing, then it's time to mix, balance, and do all those fancy things we do to breathe life into our music. Try this method. It works.

YOUR OTHER STUDIO RESOURCES

When a man's education is finished, he is finished.
—E. A. FILENE
- -

Unsure about what equipment to buy? Or do you just need some recording advice? I heartily recommend the following resources:

• *Sound Studio Production Techniques*, Dennis N. Nardantonio. TAB Books; Blue Ridge Summit, PA 17294. Covers acoustics, equipment setup and operation, recording, MIDI, mixing, and more. This resource is richly detailed and not for the squeamish.
• *The Musician's Guide to Home Recording*, Peter McIan and Larry Wichman. Linden Press/Fireside, Simon and Schuster; Rockefeller Center, 1230 Avenue of the Americas, New York, NY 10020. A good primer for the novice, packed with basic recording information. This fine book was recently revised into its second edition. All the tips you learn make it worth

adding to your reference library.
• *The Studio Business Book*, Jim Mandell. MixBooks; 6400 Hollis St., Emeryville, CA 94608. I adore this book about making it in the recording studio business. This has exactly what you need to offer profitable studio services. An updated version of this classic text was recently published.
• *The Complete Business Plan for the Small Studio*, Al Stone. C.A.S. Advertising and Productions; 377 Hall Court, Noblesville, IN 46060. Another good studio business resource.
• *The Beatles Recording Sessions*, Mark Lewisohn. Harmony Books-Crown; 225 Park Ave South, New York, NY 10003. This one is just for fun. Read intricate details about these landmark recordings, told by the people who were there. The *Anthology* CDs make a perfect companion to this text, too.

Along with these books, I recommend the following monthly magazines as useful resources. All are available at most newsstands, bookstores, or by subscription.

• *EQ—The Project Recording and Sound Magazine.* 2 Park Ave., Suite 1820, New York, NY 10016
• *Keyboard.* 411 Borel Ave. #100, San Mateo, CA 94402
• *Mix* and *Electronic Musician* magazines. 6400 Hollis St., Suite 12, Emeryville, CA 94608
• *Recording.* 7318 Topanga Canyon Blvd., Suite 200, Canoga Park, CA 91303

EQUIPMENT'S LAST STAND

One machine can do the work of fifty ordinary men. No machine can do the work of one extraordinary man.
—ELBERT HUBBARD
- -

Setting up your studio is a complicated issue, and I've only provided the essentials. You don't necessarily need the newest equipment to have a career scoring soundtracks and jingles. Your composition skills will always outweigh your equipment list. As long as you can get a clean, quality recording on tape, you'll be successful, because the real skill is in the writing, not your equipment. Music equipment is only as good as the person using it and does not supplant ignorance of music theory.

Don't fret about having the latest and greatest toys. Build a system that works for your particular strengths. You can always rent equipment when necessary or pack up your gear and head out to a commercial studio to record.

Jan Hammer wrote all the music for *Miami Vice* from his home studio with only one sophisticated workstation: the Fairlight. He also used an old Memorymoog, a DX7, live guitar, and percussion. Hammer's setup was minimal, and today a workstation like the Ensoniq ASR or MR is almost as powerful as the old Fairlight. Together, the MR/ASR are probably even *more* powerful!

Bethune: The Making of a Hero composer Alan Reeves said in a *Mix* interview: "Any good composer who has a sampler or two—maybe some sample playback machines, some analog synths, even some FM synths—can do practically anything." Reeves didn't see this as a limitation in any way. He said that even an epic film such as *Bethune* can be scored at home on modest equipment. "You don't need a million-dollar control room to turn out great sounding work."

I admire people who push the limits of their imagination, creativity, and resources; that's my whole philosophy. Too many people rely on technology because it is easier than making do with a few simple tools. Mind you, this is quite a confession from someone who is an admitted (and recovering) tech-head. I used to adore gadgets, and keyboards, and mixers, and signal processors, and this, and that, ad infinitum . . . ad nauseam. Notice I said "used to." I now find the constant pursuit of technological superiority to be grossly depressing.

Not that we should throw out everything and migrate back to our ancestor's caves. On the contrary, technology is a good thing—but a little goes a long way, and when it starts to interfere with honest creativity, it's too much. So it always makes me quite happy to discover someone who has put together a superb piece of work on a shoestring.

Many of you may be familiar with the *El Mariachi* story, in which a whiz-kid produces a feature film for $7500, Hollywood picks it up for worldwide distribution, whiz-kid gets five million to direct the sequel— you know, your everyday, run-of-the-mill success story. Well, there is a musical sidelight to all this, too. Eric Guthrie, a pre-med student at the University of Texas, scored this film with no budget and a minuscule equipment list surprisingly similar to my own. No time code. No fancy gadgets. Just some basic gear, persistence, and a metric ton of creativity. Guthrie's gear:
• Mac computer
• Ensoniq EPS-16 sampler and SQ-R sound module
• Korg Wavestation synth
• Alesis Quadraverb signal processor
• Tascam 488 8-track recorder and mixer
• DAT master deck

Guthrie composed the score without seeing any scenes. He and director Robert Rodriquez discussed the film and the mood needed, and then Guthrie wrote. Without any reference, he was forced to record several versions of the individual music cues with different timings and instrumentation. When he finally saw finished cuts of the film, he made additional changes to the music before finally mixing to DAT.

"Robert wanted to fit the music to the picture," explained Guthrie in a recent magazine interview. "So I did several versions of every music cue with different lengths, tempos, and mixes." Great job, Eric! But I shouldn't be too surprised. I've been doing the exact same thing for several years now.

I know of a composer who has a Korg M1, a computer, and a notation program. He writes all the parts to his songs, prints the score, and takes it to a big studio for recording by live musicians. He's very successful and quite happy with his bare-bones home studio. I'm satisfied with the particular choices I made, too. How about you?

Now that you have what you need to compose and record your music, it's time to demonstrate your composition skills . . . and start making some money from your investment.

CHAPTER 3

Creating the Killer Demo Tape

The good composer is slowly discovered,

the bad composer is slowly found out.

—*Sir Ernest Newman*

The first step to your successful demo is to stop focusing on production and start focusing on promotion. If you are more concerned with getting a good drum sound on tape than getting your tape into a buyer's hands, you'd better listen. You must stop thinking of your tape as a music demo. Start thinking of your tape—your music—as the solution to a problem. Audiovisual producers know the power and impact of music in their work. Show them that your music can help them achieve the results that they want and need.

Next, ask yourself: What is the purpose of this demo? Do you plan to use it to make direct sales? Are you just using it to generate qualified leads? Or is its purpose to close sales? It is perfectly acceptable to have different demos for different situations. Once you decide the real purpose of your tape, then you can proceed. For example, my sample tape (explained later in this chapter) is only for lead generation. I send it out with clever offers to get people to contact me. Once I'm contacted, I can control the sales process through traditional marketing and sales techniques, including using different music to close a sale. Yes, you can—and probably should—have more than one demo!

WHO IS YOUR TARGET MARKET?

There are essentially three buyers of original music composition services:
- Advertising agencies
- Production companies (video, film, radio and TV stations, etc.)
- Client end-users

Ad agencies typically commission scores and jingles on behalf of their clients. You work directly with the agency to produce the music they need for a particular project or ad campaign.

When working with a production company, you and the director discuss the various music cues and other technicalities. You may never meet the actual client, because the production company works directly with them and you are the music subcontractor. Often an advertising agency hires a production company that in turn hires you.

Rarely will the actual client commission you to write music for their projects and ad campaigns, but it does happen, especially when you're writing jingles for local clients.

The point is, you must target your demo to the specific audience. If you plan to sell jingles, put lots of short jingles on your tape. Try for a variety of styles, singers, and genders. If you plan to sell to other music houses or directly to production houses, you must grab their attention and show your versatility.

You can also prepare custom demos for your super hot prospects, but stick to a generic demo for mailings and when responding to inquiries.

WHY YOU NEED A DEMO

It is very good advice to believe only what an artist does, rather than what he says about his work.
—DAVID HOCKNEY

Before you can start selling your music to clients, you must demonstrate that you can do the job. That means a demo tape. What goes into a good demo? Good music! Well-recorded, clean, solid tracks with a neat package—not fancy, but definitely professional.

Your demo must be very high quality, feature your composition skills, demonstrate your originality and versatility at covering many styles, and it must do all this in less than ten minutes, preferably less than five! You may have personal preferences when it comes to music, but the purpose of your demo is to show clients that *you can do the job.* Even if you don't have exactly what they are looking for on your tape, your skill must convince them that you can give them the music they need.

Here is one single piece of advice that will ensure the success of your demo: grab attention, hold on to it, and keep the energy up. The next most important tip is to use contrast. Unless you are targeting a specific niche, it's crucial that your tape showcase your talent range, and that means many styles and many instrumentation variations. Mix it up! I've heard too many tapes where the music sounds the same from track to track. Part of this is the single synth/sampler syndrome that results in a certain "sound" to all tracks. The solution is to bring in real musicians. An all-synth track is OK, but real guitars, horns, and such add a new dimension to your music and make your demo tape much stronger.

Also, avoid soundtrack background music tapes. Most movie music is boring on its own because its purpose is to be complementary to visuals or a story. If you write music that needs the visual adjunct to work, put together a video demo. Otherwise, your music demo must contain very strong soundtrack music of the opening title variety. Listen to Bernard Herrmann's opening for *North by Northwest,* John Carpenter's *Halloween,* John Williams' *Star Wars* (specifically the "TIE Fighter" sequence), or Maurice Jarre's "Building the Barn" sequence from *Witness.* This is strong soundtrack music.

Consider preparing several different demo tapes, such as a jingle demo, a dramatic underscore, and a commercial score, which will showcase your particular strengths, and a sample tape with free music you give away as a promotion. Though there are many approaches, here are three methods that work consistently:

• Five complete tracks
• Montage of several tracks
• Free sample tape

DEMO FIVE

The demo with five complete cuts on one tape seems to work well. I recommend you include a rocker; a jazzy track; an orchestral piece (synth orchestra is OK); something unusual; and an ambient, new age piece. In other words, include the most popular music styles.

Always lead with your best track and style! The slow track that takes two minutes to get to your ripping sax solo has no place on your demo reel. While not every track needs to be commercial, it helps if they have impact and make a good, strong first impression. If you specialize in one particular style, you can limit your tape to just your specialty, but you'll also be limiting your clients. Most are looking for versatility. Show them you can cover a variety of styles, and you'll be more successful.

DEMO MONTAGE

This innovative method works in most circumstances. In fact, it's becoming the de facto standard for general music demos. Here's how it works: Put a montage of short snippets from several songs on one tape. For one of my demos, I wove twelve songs into an eight-minute montage. What is especially good about it is that you include only the best parts of each track on the tape, so it's the smartest way to present all of your skills. A two- or three-minute montage of your best music grabs attention, makes a solid impression, and helps you stand above the crowd. However, there is a drawback to this method. Many music buyers want to hear longer pieces to see how well you can sustain a listener's interest. To accommodate this request, include a few longer pieces after the opening montage.

If you decide to use the montage format, I suggest you compose a specific montage sequence. While you should draw from your best existing tracks, you may need to write pieces that bring the montage together into a seamless whole. For example, use the cymbal crash on a rock track to serve as the opening to an orchestral piece. Remember how the chicken squawk on "Good Morning, Good Morning" matches the guitar note introduction to the "Sgt. Pepper Reprise" on the Beatles' landmark album? The best tactic is lots of little snippets (including jingle stingers such as a station ID: WFCG!) carefully woven together into two or three minutes of high-powered music with impact. After the montage, you should include a few longer pieces to finish out the tape.

SAMPLE MUSIC TAPE

This last option is a somewhat radical idea. While I recommend that you have a cassette of your latest, greatest music, I also suggest that you prepare a sample music tape. This is not a demo; it is a music sample. In other words, you are giving away a few music tracks to anyone who requests your tape, just as a cookie store will let you try their latest culinary delight. They hope that you'll come back for more. Try the same approach with your prospects. Here's how to do it right.

One of my promotions (a very successful one, I might add) was a free cassette with five music tracks that anyone who requested the tape could use. A demo screams, "Here's what I did," while a sample says, "Here's something for *you* to use to make your work better. If you want more of this, just call." The demo gets listened to and then sits on the shelf. Your sample gets used, stays on the prospect's mind, and gets you the jobs.

Face it. People just aren't interested in your music. They're only interested in what your music can do for them—how your music can make their project better. You must position yourself to help them. Show how your music solves their problems. This is how you get work. Understand? Sell the sizzle (better video, more effective message), *not* the steak (music).

To make this sample work, you need a few music cuts in different styles. This must be music you own all rights to and are willing to give up completely to the world. Make sure you are *very* clear about how people can use your music. It's a good idea to invite them to contact you and tell you where and how they used your tracks.

Are you seeing the difference? Instead of giving them a tape to listen to, you are giving them music they can *use*. Yes, you are giving your music away for free. But you hope they like what they hear and come back later to *pay* you for more.

The sample music tape makes an ideal offer for ads and direct marketing. Consider how you can grab attention with an offer like, "Get *free* music for your projects." When people respond, send them your sample music tape. This concept is unique and creates lots of interest, so be prepared for the phone calls. Make sure you have enough demo tapes and marketing materials on hand to fulfill the demand. In the "Samples" section of this book is a letter that consistently generates an 8-10% response for me. I use this piece to promote the sample music idea. In fact, one mailing to only 20 prospects generated four leads (20%) and one client, a terrific return!

You might consider using the sample tape idea periodically. You can offer the first one for free and then charge a nominal fee for subsequent tapes; it's sort of a music subscription. What you are really doing is building a buyout music library that you can use to get custom music jobs. You can also use this library as a separate profit center in and of itself (more on that later).

JINGLE JANGLE OF MONEY

How about you jingle composers out there? Here's how you can use the same principle. You'll still need a demo tape of your best work. Additionally, write a few jingles that are somewhat generic. Make it easy to slip in a different company or product name.

Next, listen to the radio or watch local television for advertisers who don't use jingles. Visit those businesses and get some of their promotional material. Write the words to your generic jingle and slip in important points about your prospective client. Add a new vocal track and make a demo cassette. Contact this client and ask for the marketing or advertising manager. Tell them you've heard or seen their ads and wondered if they ever considered using a jingle. Tell them you have prepared a sample jingle especially for them. Set up an appointment to play the jingle.

In other words, you compose a jingle specifically for the client, customized to their needs, and use this speculative work to secure the project. Or you can write several generic jingles that can be easily customized and updated through new lyrics. Offer to do a custom jingle or, for a cut-rate price, rewrite the generic jingle just for them. Only grant a "local" license to the jingle. This frees you to sell the music many times over across the country, which is the secret to jingle syndication.

Instead of calling, you might try sending one of the letters from the "Samples" section. You need to customize it to the particular client, but that's about it. Print it on your letterhead, throw in a brochure and business card, and if you don't hear from them, follow up by phone. There's more information on promoting your services later in the book. Stay tuned.

TO NARRATE OR NOT

Often music houses add narration to their demo tapes, for example:

You know original music makes a difference in your productions, and you shouldn't have to settle for something that almost *fits. Now, you don't need to compromise your creativity. You get the music you need—music with impact, music that works—at a price you can afford. Just listen . . .*

While it's not necessary, the narration can reinforce your marketing and sales message, help guide the listener through the tape, introduce sections, profile different services, make an offer (call now to get the music you need), and provide the necessary follow-up information (address, phone, e-mail, etc.).

HOW MANY TRACKS?

The rule is to include as many as you need to demonstrate your skill, but my gut says no more than five songs of about a minute each on the standard demo. If you go for the montage, cram it full of tracks—as many as you can fit—and plan to hit the two- to three-minute mark. Don't let a single track last more than 15 seconds in the montage, and any single longer piece should certainly be no longer than a minute. It's crucial that you grab attention and hold it for the entire tape. A demo is not music as art. Don't try to impress your prospects with your music prowess. Go for the jugular and connect emotionally with impact and contrast.

WHAT FORMAT?

Without a doubt, put your demo on cassette. You may think that DAT is the big thing, but stick to the plain old cassette. If you want to pay the money, you could drop your demo on CD, but it's probably not worth the expense unless you are considering marketing your own music library. If you are, your CD can serve as your demo. Then you can interest prospects in your music library by letting them hear one of its CDs. Or you can leverage the contact for your original commercial music services.

WHAT ABOUT A VIDEO DEMO?

If you have several video clips that use your music, a video demo is a terrific idea. I've stayed away from this format for the simple reason that most of my video work is nonbroadcast, and music under the narration to a software training film just doesn't have the impact that a demo needs. If you choose video, the same rules apply. I suggest a short montage followed by longer sequences from as many different sources as possible. The downside to a video demo is the expense of putting together the production. While most of you can create an audiotape demo in-house, you'll have to pay to create the video demo. Maybe you can trade services with one of your video produc-

tion houses by giving them some music or a discount in exchange for helping you produce your video demo reel.

KEEP YOUR DEMO UP TO DATE

Don't prepare just one demo and use it forever. Once you get the first tape down, start on your second. As you get some clients under your belt, you'll have new music to add to your reel. Try to have a new tape each year, and make sure you send your newest reel to all your previous clients. As soon as you complete your new demo, start sending it to new prospects. You can shelve the old tunes or use them as supplementary material for client meetings or when you need a demo in a particular style.

PACKAGING YOUR DEMO

Now that you have picked and recorded the right music, it's time to duplicate and package your tape. Don't spend too much money duplicating your tape. *Put all your money into making it sound great.* You might want to handle all your duplicating in-house, using two cassette decks. If your demo is on DAT, spend an afternoon making about 50 tapes. When the stock runs out, duplicate more. This way your inventory doesn't get unmanageable, and you're not out much money up front.

Use your demo package to promote the main attraction: your music. Remember that this is not a retail sale, so graphics and so forth are not mandatory. Keep your package neat and clean with a good, clear message. Once you get your music on tape, package it nicely with a printed label, a J-card, and quality tape. If you go to a duplicator, they can usually handle all this for you. I recommend using a local duplicator. That way, if you have any trouble, you can complain easily. You can find duplicators in the telephone book under Audio/Video Duplication.

If you have a computer, use it to print your labels and J-cards. My typical demo is a C-20 chrome tape with label and Norelco box. I pay about 65¢ for the tape and about $25.00 for 1200 blank labels. You can buy offset sheets, laser compatible sheets, and fan-fold labels. I use the J-card to give information about the tape, including the crucial follow-up information (name, address, phone). Remember to print your name, telephone number, and the appropriate copyright information on the label as well as the J-card. Be sure to keep some blank labels around for special projects, too. You can get blank labels, card stock, chrome tape, boxes, and all your duplication supplies from Polyline. Ask for their free catalog by calling them at (847) 390-7744.

BEWARE OF SPECULATIVE DEMOS

Often clients will ask you to compose specific music for them, saying that if they like what they hear, they'll hire you. This is in addition to your usual music demo. It's up to you whether you want to put time and energy into such a speculative venture when there is no guarantee you'll get the gig. While it is common practice in the jingle industry for music houses to get paid for their demos, it's usually only a token fee to cover production costs and little else. The catch-22 of this situation is you can't cut back on either the composition or the production quality. The whole job hinges on how good your speculative demo is and you are judged by the quality of this single composition, so you must do a first-class job.

Put your money into your regular demo and make sure it stresses your talent and versatility. If a client wants music for their project, they should be able to determine your suitability from your regular tape. However, if they insist on a speculative demo, quote them a token fee that covers your basic costs. To sweeten the deal, tell them you will deduct the demo composition costs from your full fee when they *hire* you for their production.

DEMO TRICKS OF THE TRADE

Do not send metal tapes and do not encode your demo with Dolby C, DBX, Dolby SR, or any exotic noise reduction. Use chrome tape and Dolby B noise reduction for your demo, but tell your clients to play the tape back on normal, not chrome. Print this on your label, too. When you record on chrome and play back on normal, there is an increase in presence to the cassette. Also, duplicate in real-time and not high speed! People are accustomed to hearing CD quality, so you need to make your tape shine. These little tricks will help you do just that.

It may surprise you how rudimentary, even crude, most production houses are. Many just have boom boxes, or worse, some crummy mono-cassette player. Some newer houses have DAT players, but don't count on this being the case. Make your mix work on a variety of systems, and you will be safe. Also, purchase a good quality boom box to take to client meetings. Don't rely on their having a cassette deck or even a remotely decent system. You want your music heard at its best, don't you? Take fresh batteries, too. It can be embarrassing searching for an AC outlet. I use a boom box with auxiliary inputs and actually mix to it, using its speakers for reference. If you can get your demo to sound great on a boom box, it'll sound great anywhere. Remember always double-check your tape's sound anywhere and every-where you can—your car, a Walkman, a home system, your boom box, and of course, your studio monitors.

For crucial client presentations, I use a special enhanced demo mix that absolutely kicks on my boom box. Even if the client has a decent system, I still insist on playing my boom box mix if possible. It makes a powerful impression and presents my music at its best. Most clients will listen to your music either in their car or on a Walkman. Make a good mix that works on a variety of systems and give that version to clients. My special boom box version stays in my briefcase, because it really only sounds good on my particular system. I give a different mix to clients to keep and listen to again at their leisure.

LAST WORD ON YOUR KILLER DEMO

Good music resembles something.
It resembles the composer.
—Jean Cocteau

Don't save money on your music. If you must cut corners, cut out other things, like stationery, fancy packaging, full-color brochures, and so forth. *Always record and present your music in the best possible light.* It's your lifeblood. And remember this: You never get a second chance to make a first impression. So make sure your music knocks their socks off!

CHAPTER 4

Your Typical Gigs

Film music should have the same relationship to the film drama that somebody's piano playing in my living room has to the book I'm reading.
—*Igor Stravinsky*

Composing to visuals and under narration is *very* different, both technically and stylistically, from other forms of music composition. Surprisingly, the majority of projects are not locked to picture. Most use freeform composing or rough timings, and a few just guess. At some point, though, you'll probably need to lock videotape and music together through SMPTE time code. Don't invest in that equipment, though, until a substantial job warrants the investment.

HOW DO YOU SCORE?

In some cases, you work with the director in charge of the production. Other times, your clients will have their clients to satisfy. When writing jingles, you almost always work directly with an advertising agency and rarely with the client. Often you won't ever meet the people who are actually paying your fee. Don't worry about these layers of bureaucracy. All you need to do is find out who approves your music and concentrate your effort at working alongside and pleasing that person.

Usually the project is finished or nearly complete when the composer is called, and you'll do a post-score to picture. The first time you see the tape is during a spotting session with the director or producer. Here you examine each scene, choose the style of music, decide where to place it and for how long, and determine the total amount of music needed. Take extensive notes and get a copy of the video to take back to your studio.

Approach your scoring projects by capturing the essence and emotion of the whole work. Don't worry about the specific events in a given scene. This way, you can adopt a more freeform approach and not worry about matching everything exactly. If you do compose for every little screen action, your score turns the scene into a cartoon. This is called Mickey-Mousing in the trade, and it's only effective if used sparingly.

Next, you should rough-time the cues and write sketches. Sometimes I sync the music to the videotape; other times I run it wild and rely on the math. All you need for this step is a stopwatch and a click book that shows time, tempo, and bars so you can see what tempo will get you to what point in a scene. This method takes a little getting used to, but it's worth the effort and works fine for most short cues.

Once you finish the sketches, run off a quick cassette and give it to the director for approval. After changes, start fleshing out the music and recording the final master tape. When it's complete, deliver the final tape and your job is over. The process described above can take days or merely hours.

Occasionally, you'll pre-score your music, especially if you're writing a jingle. This means that you provide a specific track style and length that the production house uses to edit their visuals or put under sales copy for a radio commercial. Often you'll provide a scratch track that consists of mostly rhythm and maybe a basic melody. Next, the director will cut the footage to your music. You'll get a copy of that tape and use it to post-score the finished track, adding elements to correspond to the visual sequence.

YOUR SCORING OPTIONS

There are essentially four methods used to score soundtracks and jingles:
- Pre-score
- Post-score
- Hybrid
- Master cue

Let's discuss each in greater detail.

▶ PRE-SCORE

As the name implies, pre-scoring means you compose music and deliver complete mixes before the project is produced or edited. Your music is added during production (and is sometimes used for lip synching or choreography at the shoot) or during editing. Often the project is cut to your music. The style, instrumentation, and timing are worked out with the director in advance. Virtually every jingle uses this method.
- Advantages: Fast turnaround, the production doesn't need to wait for the music, and the track is easy to change or augment.
- Disadvantages: Limited hits, subtle changes and shifts in music are not possible, hit or miss timings, and not very different from using library music.

▶ POST-SCORE

This is the traditional method of soundtrack scoring. Here you compose to a finished, or nearly finished, cut of the project. By synching the picture to a multi-track tape recorder or MIDI sequencer, you compose directly to and while watching the images.
- Advantages: Flexible shifts in score are easy; matching action, drama, timing, instrumentation, volume, and more are always dead on.
- Disadvantages: More costly; time pressure is high; and inexperienced scorers mimic every screen action, turning sequences into cartoons. Also, because the project is almost complete, there is a tendency to put unrealistic time constraints on the composer.

You'd think that post-scoring would be more predominant, but my experience shows that the hybrid method is used more often.

▶ HYBRID

This technique combines elements of both pre- and post-scoring. You provide a rhythm track to be used when editing. Then you post-score, building around the basic music track, once the project is cut. For example, you compose an upbeat tune with bass, drums, and piano. You get the edited piece back with your basic track cut in and sync the music to the edited master and flesh out the score by adding solos, drums fills, etc. Then you replace the basic track with the more complete piece. This hybrid is becoming *the* main method of scoring soundtracks today.
- Advantages: Combines the best of both worlds. The score is easier for the composer to write, and the director gets the subtle changes needed to make the project come alive.
- Disadvantages: None, really.

▶ MASTER CUE

While at first this may seem similar to pre-scoring, it's not. This technique requires better planning and relies on composition and orchestration rather than math. Here's how it works.

You compose a long, fully orchestrated musical theme and use it throughout the project. By stripping away the pieces of the master cue and creating alternate mixes of varied tempos, lengths, and musical styles, much more music is available from a single composition. Usually this method means you produce several alternate mixes for the director to choose from. Plus, all the music follows the same basic thematic element (repetition of the theme creates dramatic continuity), but there's enough variety so that it's interesting in different situations.

You write one full piece with many parts. Next, you cut, paste, and change parts to create and mix several other cues based on and part of one main theme. MIDI technology makes this a snap. The result? You get versatile, flexible, and affordable music! You can pass the savings on to your original music clients. This master cue method saves time and money and produces a thematically rich score with a unique character and style all its own.
- *On the Track: Guide to Contemporary Film Scoring*, Fred Karlin and Rayburn Wright. Schirmer Books; 866 Third Ave., New York, NY 10022. This is an enlightening book. You'll learn all about the stylistic and technical aspects of scoring to picture as well as cues, hits, Mickey-Mousing, and more. There are pages and pages of example scores, all of which you should recognize (rent the movies at your local video store for further study). You also get a complete click book at the end. Use this to time beats and frames; it's a mandatory reference. This book carries my wholehearted endorsement and recom-

mendation. If you are serious about scoring soundtracks for a living, you definitely need it.

SMART MUSIC

It might be helpful for you to see how a typical scoring assignment comes together. Writing the score for
Street Smarts: Straight Talk for Kids, Teens, and Parents
was challenging and rewarding. Not only did we need
a great deal of music, but we also needed it fast. From
the time the director and I talked to the day I hand-
delivered the master tape, only ten days elapsed—but
what an exciting ten days!

▶ TUESDAY
I met with J Marc Group for the first time to discuss
music for their latest project, *Street Smarts*, a documentary for PBS. First we discussed the style. Since
this video would deal with crime prevention and how
children can protect themselves, the score had to be
dark and ominous. The ending, however, had to be a
somewhat more positive closing theme—upbeat and
hopeful.

Next, we discussed the placement of the music.
They wanted seven cues: opening and closing themes
and five specific cues to complement the video's
dramatizations. After viewing the rough cut, I suggested several other cues. The video features interviews with children as they describe their experiences
with drugs, gangs, and crime. I proposed adding
music under these sequences to enhance these vivid
accounts. The director agreed. Some mechanical discussions followed (timings, format, etc.), and then it
was time for me to translate these ideas into a coherent music score.

▶ THURSDAY/FRIDAY
I spent these two days composing. It was 54 hours of
coffee, various junk foods, pen, paper, several floppy
disks, my trusty Ensoniq SD-1/32 keyboard, and me.
By late Friday afternoon, I had recorded over 25
minutes of music on tape. These were just sketches,
mind you, but they captured what I thought was right
for the score. I sent the tape via overnight mail for
review.

▶ SATURDAY/SUNDAY
I used these two days to flesh out the music sketches,
re-record some parts, and do some general MIDI
housecleaning. At this point, I had no idea which
tracks would be approved and which would be
scrapped, but in the name of time (the online edit
was seven days away), every minute of music had to be
ready for mixing to the final master tape. I was hoping to get approval of the work-in-progress by Monday

so I could improve the recordings and concentrate
on mixing.

▶ MONDAY
I spent most of Monday tracking down a ¼-inch quarter-
track reel-to-reel mastering deck with 10½ inch NAB
hubs. This was not easy to locate, but eventually I
found a nearby rental house that had the right deck.
At first I didn't think this was the right format (doesn't
everybody use ¼-inch half-track?). So I took extra
time to make sure it was what was needed. A call to
the editor reassured me that we were on the same
wavelength.

▶ WEDNESDAY
After a day of telephone tag, the director and I talked
again. He decided which cuts he liked best. I agreed
with most of his choices, but there wasn't time to fight
about (er, discuss) why I disagreed with his other
choices. We had a score to finish! The director made
several suggestions to the master cues. This included
adding a heartbeat rhythm to the main track used for
the dramatizations and adding a bell to the opening
title stinger. These were good ideas and really helped
make the tracks stronger. The opening, though, was
not working. We needed something sweet and innocent that turned dark and ominous in exactly 15
seconds. It was back to the drawing board (or is it keyboard?) to compose a new opening sequence.

Suddenly a violent thunderstorm blew in and a
nearby lightning strike knocked out the power to my
studio. Ah, the perils of the electronic musician. So, I
played acoustic guitar and tried to find a solution.
After an hour of trying, unsuccessfully, I put that idea
to rest. I was just about to play the opening riff to
"Stairway to Heaven" when the lights came on. Saved
by Com-Ed.

Well, it must have been the break, because I
immediately came up with a possible musical solution. After a few minutes, the idea was in presentable
form and I was soon playing it over the phone. We
finally had our opening. I worked well into the night
orchestrating all the parts; tweaking sounds; recording guitar, bass, and percussion parts to tape; and
preparing for the final mix.

▶ THURSDAY
I got up early—a rarity for me—to begin mixing the
final master. It took most of the day to mix the cues
and their several variations. They wanted some extra
flexibility in the editing suite, so I made alternate versions of all the final pieces. This way they could
choose the right cut for any given situation. Since the
dramatizations used one basic track, the variations
were just different enough to make each sequence

interesting. This was also true for the interviews. The same basic underscore was used repeatedly, so these variations made each sequence different and more memorable. I finished recording and mixing too late in the afternoon to make the Federal Express truck. Since I was leaving for Florida on Saturday and the director was going to Dallas for the final edit session, I decided to hand-deliver the master tape. It helped me sleep better that night.

▶ FRIDAY

I returned the tape deck to the rental company and started downtown, tape in hand. We had a rough cut of the new opening, and I wanted to see how the music fit, because we still had time to change it. We popped in the backup cassette I had made and pressed play. It took me a second to realize the tape had jammed and that a spaghetti of chrome tape was pouring out of the boom box. Don't you hate that? Thankfully, we saved the tape (it was a safety copy anyway, not the original master). Pressing play on the VCR and boom box again, we leaned forward in our chairs with at least one of us crossing his fingers.

A soft, bell-like piano filled the room. It played a simple melody, almost childlike, while scenes of 1950s America dissolved into titles expressing the innocence of that era. A playful string arpeggio lightened the mood. And then: today! Cops, arrests, sirens, drugs, and violence fill the screen. A rich, dark texture swelled up and overpowered the piano and string motif. It continued, ominous and powerful, underscoring the violent and haunting images. The piano disappeared as the images faded to black. Suddenly, a heavy, almost ripping sound swelled to full volume. It was punctuated by a loud bell ring as the opening title, *Street Smarts,* faded in.

Everyone seemed to like it and thought the sequence worked well. I had a rather hard time hiding my exuberance! We replayed it again several times and it just seemed to get better. We had our opening and our music score. It was handshakes all around, and in minutes I was on my way back home. The results: Over 15 minutes of music with variations and alternate mixes extending the count to about 25 total minutes. It's not easy to write that much music in ten days, but it's well worth it!

If you ever see *Street Smarts: Straight Talk for Kids* on PBS, let me know your thoughts about the score. You might not even notice my music because they did such a terrific job with the whole program. That's fine. If my music helps complement the message, I know I've done my job. This is good television; it's a very important and helpful piece about a subject that affects us all. I'm proud to have been a part of it, and I hope you get as much from it as I did.

Self-confidence is the first requisite to great undertakings.
—Dr. Samuel Johnson

Audiovisual producers are creative people. Their work can be very demanding and can require them to use every ounce of their physical, mental, and creative faculties. When they hire a composer for their project, they want to make sure they get the best music possible. This can mean that they'll be relying on you for every aspect of the music composition and recording process. Therefore, you must have a collaborative relationship based on mutual respect and trust. Here are guidelines for establishing this rapport. When you use these strategies, you and your clients will share a long-standing and fruitful relationship that results in music that makes productions better.

▶ HAVE YOUR CLIENTS DESCRIBE EXACTLY WHAT THEY WANT

Before you write any music, ask your client to describe the project in detail, including its ultimate message. Have them discuss exactly what they want musically in the most specific way. Chances are, they won't be very musically inclined. Tell them not to worry about the musical or technical terms and just describe how they think the music should be and what it should sound like.

John Lennon was notorious for describing music in abstract terms. Beatles producer George Martin recalled that during the recording of "Tomorrow Never Knows" (from *Revolver*) Lennon said, "I want to sound as though I'm the Dalai Lama singing from the highest mountain top, and yet I still want to hear the words I'm singing." Maybe your client won't use such vivid description, but you should encourage them to try to be as precise as possible. (By the way, Martin's solution was to send Lennon's vocal through the Leslie speaker in the old Hammond organ and record it to tape. You can hear the effect about one minute into the song.)

If it helps, have your client refer to or use specific examples from previous recordings. Hopefully, they'll avoid obscure examples. If they have the recording, ask them to play it for you. Make sure to tell them not to expect the exact track that they're citing as an example. Ask them if you can interpret the music without copying it directly.

▶ BEWARE OF TEMP TRACKS

Many directors start editing before any music is written. Some like to use temporary music tracks and cut their visuals to them. Unfortunately, many get hooked on these temp tracks. When you deliver your score, the director loses all objectivity. It happened to Stanley Kubrick during *2001* when he used the "Blue Danube Waltz" for the space station docking sequence. It also happened during *The Year of Living Dangerously*. Maurice Jarre's wonderfully atmospheric score is heard throughout the movie except when Vangelis' "L'enfant" survived to the final release print.

When you present your music, listen along with the director or creative team. To make the music review session a positive and constructive experience, I let all my clients know how I expect them to review my material. Here are a few suggestions you can offer to your clients.

▶ LISTEN AS AN OUTSIDER

They must put aside all their preconceived notions and listen to the music as if it were the first time and they know nothing about it. Ask them to let go of expectations and imposed limitations and just listen to the music as it is. It may help to wild sync the music to the visuals and see how they work together. After this first hearing, rewind the music and listen again. This time, have them pay closer attention to specifics and begin to evaluate the positives and negatives of the piece. When the music finishes, begin to discuss it together.

▶ START GENERALLY, GET SPECIFIC, AND BE HONEST

Usually it is best to start with a general comment about the music. Don't allow your client to jump right to the details. Constructive criticism benefits both of you and makes for a better project. Hopefully, they'll treat you the way they themselves expect to be treated in such a situation. Make sure to ask for reasons for any objections and suggestions. Don't let them just nit-pick. State the problem and then work together to find the right solution.

▶ ASK FOR A REWRITE

If the piece completely fails their objective, then tell them not to be afraid to ask for more if necessary. Proper planning up front should prevent this from happening, but if it does, don't apologize for it. You could waste valuable time trying to massage a dead horse when it would be easier to try another way and start fresh. You will appreciate their candor when clients are honest and have specific objections. I know I do. It makes me work twice as hard to come up with the ultimate musical solution.

▶ THEY MUST BE HAPPY

Primarily, the music must satisfy them. If it doesn't work, find the reasons why and then work to correct it. If it does work, be content that you've made another project better and more effective.

Establishing a good working relationship between director and composer is vital. If you follow these simple guidelines, you'll deliver the exact music your client needs and deserves.

EIGHT STEPS YOU MUST TAKE TO IMPROVE YOUR COMPOSING

The artist who aims at perfection in everything achieves it in nothing.
—EUGENE DELACROIX

You want your musical skills to get better and better, don't you? Of course you do. If you are nowhere close to reaching your peak performance, it's because you don't understand the *process* that helps you produce your best music all the time. Here are some steps you must take so you'll constantly be improving your talents.

▶ COMPOSE SOMETHING EVERY DAY

In order to compose, all you need to do is remember a tune that nobody else has thought of.
—ROBERT SCHUMANN

Composition is, for the most part, an effort of slow diligence and steady perseverance, to which the mind is dragged by necessity or resolution.
—DR. SAMUEL JOHNSON

The best way to make sure you get the most from your talents is to use them. This is simple advice, yet it's crucial. Write a piece of music every day. It doesn't have to be extravagant or even complete, just put your first thoughts down on paper, tape, disk, etc. Make composing part of your daily routine. Not everything you do will be good, but the exercise will yield some bits and pieces that you can later turn into something special.

Too many people believe they must be in a creative mood to compose. It's infinitely easier to procrastinate than to just start working, but you must not be seduced by this unfortunate fact. You must banish those "ifs" and "buts" and start writing. Don't worry about style or if you are composing something worthwhile. Write first to please yourself. If you let your inner voice of judgment interfere with your creative flow, you severely inhibit your work as an artist. Turn off the messages in your head and let go.

The toughest part of writing commercial music is, by far, learning to be creative on demand. You can't always write just when you feel like it. You must write when you're asked. You must get instant inspiration and be able to orchestrate, play, and record quickly. Music is both art and craft. You can learn and practice the craft aspects. Personally, I save up all my energy for when the muse is especially strong. This way I can sit down cold and write a score from scratch. If I composed and recorded all the time, I would find it difficult to create on short notice.

Get into a routine. Write at the same time each day. If you are especially strong in the morning, get up a little earlier and start composing. Late night your strength? Set aside an hour before going to sleep just so you can capture your energy in a musical sketch. You must find the method that works for you.

Regardless of your working method, make sure you practice, too. Don't confuse doodling around with being serious and truly creative. You must expend some energy and use this time to sharpen your skills. I play and goof around all the time, but I also set aside time to seriously compose. I go back and listen to my doodles and transform them into stronger, more structured pieces. This keeps me fresh and original. And my clients get my best work first!

If your well of creativity temporarily dries up, you might enlist some help from your computer. Art Song is a terrific algorithmic music composition program that helps you create original MIDI sequences. This unique program produces musical passages by tracing a path over any Windows bitmap file; it converts pictures to music by turning colors into MIDI notes. I've found the program to be inspiring. Though you get lots of unusable material, you do get the occasional bit that is very clever. I've generated few stand-alone sequences, but I've used bass lines and chord sequences as the basis for other songs. A little tweaking here and there, an overdub or two of my own, and soon I've written some new music. When you use it to help you generate an idea or two that you can transform into your own musical creation, Art Song is worth the investment.

- Digital Expressions. W6400 Firelane 8, Menasha, WI 54952; (414) 733-6863; strohbeen@aol.com

▶ LISTEN TO MUSIC EVERY DAY

Take a music bath once or twice a week,
and you will find that it is to the soul what
the water bath is to the body.
—OLIVER WENDELL HOLMES

Make sure you do take that oh-so-important music bath every single day. If you're like me, you have tons of music in your collection, from Aztec Camera to ZZ Top. Don't just play it in the background, though. Take time each day to really sit down and *listen* to the music. Study it carefully and apply what you learn to your own work.

Will this affect your appreciation of your favorite tunes? I doubt it. You will gain a keen awareness of music composition and a greater respect for other artists. For this to be a truly useful tool, you must scrutinize every note, every phrase. First, ask yourself "why," and then apply the answers to your own work: Why that progression? Why that instrument? Why a counter melody there? Why slapback echo here? Next, ask yourself how the composer used a certain technique, instrument, or phrase. Make sure you recognize what is art (why) and what is craft (how). If you record music too, listen first to the music, then concentrate on the recording techniques.

Personally, I don't make a distinction between composing music and recording music. I think composing and recording are integrated and synergistic, not mutually exclusive. I can't write without hearing how the final version will sound.

Finally, listen to a particular piece repeatedly until you've exhausted every possibility. Then put it away and don't listen again for a few weeks. When you eventually go back to it, see if you hear or feel anything new.

▶ IMITATE OTHER COMPOSERS BY WRITING IN THEIR STYLE

When people are free to do as they
please, they usually imitate each other.
—ERIC HOFFER

This is a natural extension of the listening step above. The easiest way to grow as an artist is to get inside another composer's head, first by listening and second through imitation. Many musicians learn by copying their favorite songs. This is useful toward improving your *mechanical* skills, but imitation is also critical to improving your *composition* skills. Pick artists you admire and compose in their style. Don't just copy their songs. You must try to write a piece as if you *were* the artist. To imitate without directly copying is harder than it sounds. This assignment will teach you much about music, how other composers think, and what this means to you.

I admire Patrick O'Hearn, and at one point, I found myself trying to figure out his songs. I've never been adept at playing by ear, so I settled for trying to compose like him. I wrote pieces that sounded much like his work. After a few weeks, my own interpretation began to emerge. I was able to shake his influence and concentrate on my own style. Elements of O'Hearn were intact, but overall, the music was distinctly my own. I've also explored David Torn's approach to guitar loops, and it revealed both positive and negative aspects of my musical prowess. After that, the trick was to use what I learned to grow as a composer and artist.

Don't ignore this exercise. Learn from the masters: first by listening, second by playing, and last by imitation. Then let go and use what you've learned to discover your own music. This won't happen overnight, but your critical study will pay off in time.

◗ TRY OTHER STYLES AND FORMS OF COMPOSITION THAT YOU USUALLY IGNORE

Classical music is the kind that
we keep hoping will turn into a tune.

—KIN HUBBARD

OK, so you're a rocker. Nothing wrong with that. But have you considered composing for a string quartet? No matter what your level of talent is, try choosing a simple tune like "Row, Row, Row Your Boat" and writing multiple versions in various styles, such as rap, jazz, orchestral, new age, etc.

Choosing a simple, familiar tune means not having to worry about the melody. You are free to experiment with structure, chords, counter melodies, and so forth. Just because you don't like or aren't comfortable in a particular musical genre, doesn't mean you shouldn't give it a whirl. Also, try playing an instrument you don't normally play. If you play keys, take up guitar. You'll gain useful new perspectives.

Creativity means looking outside the boundaries. Don't stay tied to a single way of doing things, try many different approaches. You'll find the solution if you open up your mind to all the infinite possibilities and the true creativity within you. Leaving your comfort zone is the doorway to your best work. Do you really want to risk shutting out this world and stifling your musical talent? Then what are you waiting for?

◗ PLAY YOUR PIECES FOR FRIENDS AND ASSOCIATES AND ASK FOR CRITICISM

In giving advice seek to
help, not to please, your friend.

—SOLON

Find someone whose opinion you trust and ask for their help and candid, constructive ideas. You don't need a judge; you need help! When you get ready to debut your newest music, don't apologize for it and don't interrupt while it plays. Let your music play all the way through and then ask open-ended, leading questions. Next, play the track again and analyze it in detail. If you chose someone with musical knowledge, you can discuss the track on the same level.

The opinions of wives, husbands, girlfriends, boyfriends, and your mother will be worthless for this exercise. No offense, it's just the truth. Try to find someone you don't share a deeply personal relationship with. Because they don't want to upset you, many people will not be brutally honest. To combat this, use the same ground rules you do with clients as discussed earlier. Once you get opinions and advice, go back to the drawing board and put all you've learned to work and repeat the process again.

◗ SEEK ADVICE FROM A RECOGNIZED EXPERT

Your manuscript is both good and original;
but the part that is good is not original, and the
part that is original is not good.

—DR. SAMUEL JOHNSON

Find a mentor to review your work. Objective opinions and useful suggestions will really open your eyes and give you insight into your work. Once again, you are looking for constructive criticism. You don't need someone saying, "That's good." You want *specific* information about how to make your work better and stronger, and you want to learn from your mistakes. Take advantage of expert knowledge and benefit from professional, objective expertise.

There are many ways to get this valuable information. You might try professors at your local college or university. Maybe there's a musician in your area whom you admire and who might evaluate your work. A songwriters group might be another alternative. Consider sending your tape for review in magazines such as the *Transoniq Hacker* or *Recording*. Or consider a professional critique. Some services review your work and make suggestions for a fee. It's a service I offer to fledgling commercial music composers. If you're interested, drop me a line for complete details on this service designed to make your demo and sales material stronger and more effective.

Now, many books and articles say you should never pay money to have someone listen to your demo, and I agree with that advice . . . to a certain extent. You should *never* pay an agent, lawyer, or record company (or anyone for that matter) who claims they will get your music published, recorded, etc. in exchange for a substantial fee. However, I know it is useful to have a professional review your work and make useful suggestions. This professional should have no claims on your music or a vested interest beyond a desire to share their expertise with you, and this kind of third-party opinion could save you mistakes you might make unknowingly. It's like having an accountant prepare your taxes. Sure, you can do it yourself, but you may benefit from a professional's experience, and it's almost always worth the price you pay for the services.

❧ PRODUCE YOUR DEMO AND SEND IT INTO THE MARKET

There are no wrong notes.
—THELONIOUS MONK

Once you follow the above steps diligently, you will be ready to put together your killer demo tape and start marketing your music talents and services. This is the real test of your skills. Don't fret about rejection. Use your worries to your advantage and make your work stronger.

❧ EVALUATE YOUR PAST WORK

Life can only be understood backward, but it must be lived forward.
—KIERKEGAARD

Don't let your old music fade away. Dust it off and give it a critical listen. I once discovered an old song on a long-forgotten tape; I reworked it, recorded it, and turned it into a jingle for a major advertiser. Once you've let music sit for some time, the warts really stick out. Most of what you find will be coal, but sometimes you unearth a gem. Use this distance from your work to improve your past, present, and future music.

❧ FINAL TIP

I've never known a musician who regretted being one. Whatever deceptions life may have in store for you, music itself is not going to let you down.
—VIRGIL THOMSON

The best guidance I can give you about unleashing and controlling your creativity is this: Look outside the boundaries. Don't rely on a single way of doing things. Try many different approaches. Find the solution by opening your mind to all the infinite possibilities. Here are a few other thoughts to consider:

• Think positive thoughts. Try to do your best all the time.

• Take time to relax.

• Ask questions. Listen. Be committed to constant improvement. Stay interested in your life and your life's work. Most of all, be enthusiastic about everything you do.

• When you reach a major milestone, treat yourself to something special. After completing a new score or jingle, I usually buy a book or CD and curl up on the couch for some well-deserved R&R.

You must follow this eight-step process throughout your musical career. This crucial advice is essential to making sure you grow as an artist. That's what you want, isn't it? This is how you do it.

• *A Whack on the Side of the Head*, Roger Von Oech. Warner Books; 666 Fifth Ave., New York, NY 10103. This is my favorite book about unleashing your creativity. It tells you what it takes to be a creative artist.

You've organized your studio, streamlined your composition techniques, created your demo, and learned the basics of how the commercial industry works. Now it's time to find original music buyers and discover how to contact and sell them your music.

CHAPTER 5

Finding Prospects Who Buy Original Music

You can automate the production of cars but

you cannot automate the production of customers.

—Walter Reuther

Finding the people to sell your music to is a lot easier than you might imagine. Turning them into clients, well, that's the hard part. But if your music is good quality, your price is fair, and you always deliver more than you promise, your tracks will earn you some cash. First, be aware that your competition falls into two different groups:
• Other musicians and small music companies
• Production library tracks

I don't consider the big music houses—those that score for McDonald's and AT&T—to be your main competition. These groups only work on big budget projects. It's the smaller, budget-conscious companies that you should approach first. Business and special interest video is the fastest growing market today. Computer-based multimedia is close behind. Eventually, the big guys will have to jump in, but you should beat them to the punch. Cut your teeth on this market segment, earn a reputation, and build your success before you pursue bigger projects. Plus, many novice producers who go on to bigger and better projects will bring you along as they move up the ladder. Building relationships now will pay off for you down the road.

How you choose to proceed is up to you. There are enough small productions and local commercials to keep you busy, but you can easily apply this information to land the big accounts, too.

In smaller cities, there will usually be only a few small music companies or other musicians trying to supplement their income for you to worry about. You, however, have one distinct advantage. You have this book and access to other resources that put you far ahead of your competition.

In big cities (like Chicago, where I live), the competition is fierce. But there's more work to go around, too. Still, it seems that many people mistakenly believe if you have a synth, you are a composer. Only those with true talent and business savvy make it. I can't really help you with the first, but I can show you how to succeed with your business.

If you live in a remote area, don't be discouraged. There is plenty of work within a one hundred mile radius of your home, and there is less competition than in the big cities. You may just need to widen your market somewhat. You might find one or two production companies who will give you all their work.

Finding a few production companies willing to use you for all their projects is the real secret to this business. Once you convince them that you are a better deal, you will become their one-stop music source. This is what I have done, and it has worked well so far. Your goal is always to find a few clients and work hard for them. Don't think that your prospecting should stop there, though. You must keep expanding your client list. When you use the techniques that follow, you will do just that.

HOW TO BEAT THE BIG MUSIC HOUSES

He who thinks everything is easy will find everything difficult. He who regards everything as difficult will meet with no difficulties.

—LAO TZU

Small companies like yours can outwit the bigger music houses if you do the following.

- Exploit niche markets. Go after the smaller budgets and companies that the big guys pass up. Diversify your service line to offer a variety of music and recording services to people who (wrongly) think they can't afford professional work. Carve out a position in your market and promote your particular strengths.
- Get close and personal. Stay in contact with your clients and be available to meet their needs. Don't put barriers between you and them. Answer your own phone, follow up promptly, and concentrate on their locally based needs and desires.
- Use technology. Today's computers will give you a distinct edge. They can become the "staff" of your company and allow you to store, monitor, and use vast amounts of data. They can handle your routine duties, freeing you to market and create.

YOUR REAL COMPETITION

In this market, you should consider your real competition—the enemy—to be library music. Although I must admit, the quality of royalty-free music has improved over the years, it still has major drawbacks:

- It is nonexclusive. A producer can use a theme for Al's local body shop and then hear it as some movie of the week theme.
- It is never exactly right; never exactly what the producer or director wants.
- It never "hits" the specific dramatic points or follows action (unless the project is edited to the music—easy for a visual montage, not so easy with dialogue).

Unfortunately for you and me, library music is very cheap. Some companies can sell 60 minutes of music on CD for under $60. It's impossible to compete on that price level. So, you must capitalize on the library track's shortcomings. Since you can't possibly compete on price alone, you must offer something more:

- Your service
- Your composition skills and versatility
- Your ability to write the exact music (both styles and timing) that your client requires
- Your convenience and fast turnaround
- The unique value your original music adds to projects

- The way your music enhances visuals, makes them more exciting and memorable, and therefore, more effective

Believe me. This is what every producer wants!

CHECKING OUT YOUR COMPETITION

Want to know what your competition is doing? Just listen to the radio, TV, and cable. Check out educational and business videos and CD-ROMs from your local library. Get demo tapes from production music producers and from your competitors.

Once you know what your competition is doing, you can position your music composition services accordingly. The best way to find this information is to ask for it. I'm not advocating lying and misrepresenting yourself, but you may need to use a little competitive deception to get the information you need.

Call your competition and request their latest demo tape and marketing materials. Tell them you are new in the area and are interested in their services. Some may catch on to your story, but others will give you what you need. If you don't feel comfortable asking for this information, have a friend or colleague do the dirty work and get the information sent to their office. Study what your competition is doing and learn from their mistakes. After collecting a few samples, you'll know exactly what you need to do to compete in your market.

Most importantly, ask your clients and prospects what they are specifically looking for in music. What styles do they use or prefer? How much music do they need? These questions are useful for both you and them. The answers will help you sell more of your music. Once you find out what your clients need, you are in the ideal position to give it to them. Make sure that you do.

LIBRARY MUSIC SUPPLIERS

If you want to learn more about library music, use the same tactics. Once you hear some of this stuff, you'll know why good original music is a much sought after commodity. To be fair, library music is not all bad; there is some fine work. Here are a few companies that supply buyout library music to the audiovisual industry:

- Firstcom Music. 13747 Montfort, Suite 220, Dallas, TX 75240; (800) 858-8880; www.firstcom.com
- Manhattan Production Music. 355 W. 52nd St., Sixth Floor, New York, NY 10019; (800) 227-1954; mpmusic@aol.com

- The Music Bakery. 7522 Campbell Road, Suite 113-2, Dallas, TX 75248; (800) 229-0313; www.musicbakery.com
- Signature Music. P.O. Box 98, Buchanan, MI 49107; (800) 888-7151

An important point: Buyout music is *not* copyright free. The copyright holder has chosen to make the music available on a nonexclusive basis. Users pay one fee and can use the music within the boundaries of the license agreement. The music copyright still belongs to the music supplier.

NOTE FOR RURAL COMPOSERS

Because of today's technology, including telephone, fax, e-mail, and overnight mail, you can compose music for clients located virtually anywhere in the country. Although it won't be as easy (some people just refuse to work this way), you can do it.

Don't forget that it is your music that matters, not where you live. Do you really need to meet face-to-face with your client? In most cases, probably not. They can send you a videotape of the project, you can watch it, discuss the music with them by phone, write, and deliver their score. You can do this as easily by mail as in person. Plus, you don't waste time in endless client meetings.

I live near Chicago (a thriving music center) and have written scores for clients in exactly the way described above. Don't lose hope just because you don't live in a major metropolitan area. You may need to work a little harder and expand your service area, but you too can build a strong commercial music business.

CLIENTS: WHO TO LOOK FOR AND WHERE

So, who will you sell your music to and make money from? You're looking for names, addresses, and telephone numbers of producers, directors, and other creatives at audiovisual, multimedia, video, film production, and cable companies; advertising agencies; and radio and TV stations in your area.

Use these many resources to get the information you need. I've never had any trouble compiling a list of prospects to contact. If you follow this advice, you won't have any trouble either. You are creating a marketing database to use to contact music-buying prospects through the promotional programs described later. Take extra care when compiling your list. Be thorough and complete. What's the easiest way to get these names? Start with a directory.

▶ THE TELEPHONE BOOK

The Yellow Pages are a good first source. Look under Audiovisual, Video Production, Post-production, and Advertising Agencies. You'll get the addresses and telephone numbers easily, but you won't get a name. You'll need to call each place listed and ask to whom you should send your demo and promotional materials. It's that easy to get off and running. When you call, simply say:

> Hi, this is [your name]. *I run a music production company in town and am preparing to send out my latest demo of original music. I'm calling to find out who usually buys music for your company.*

▶ CREATIVE DIRECTORIES

A better resource is a trade directory. In Chicago, there are two such directories, the *Screen Production Bible* and the *Illinois Film Guide*. Not only do they list every production company, but they include names, addresses, and telephone numbers of the principals. Most major cities have a directory of creative talent or resource of some kind. Contact your local Chamber of Commerce or Advertising Council (get their numbers from your phone book) to find out how to get your copy. Also, contact your state's film office. Your local library can assist as well. Here are some helpful resources:

- *Audiovisual Marketplace*; R.R. Bowker; 245 W. 17th St., New York, NY 10011; P.O. Box 31, New Providence, NJ 07974; (800) 521-8110
- *The Shoot Directory for Commercial Production + Postproduction*. 1515 Broadway, New York, NY 10036-8986; (212) 536-1430
- *Hollywood Reporter Blue-Book Directory*. Hollywood Reporter; 5055 Wilshire Blvd., Los Angeles, CA 90036; (213) 525-2150
- *Screen*. 16 W. Erie, 2nd Floor, Chicago, IL 60610; (312) 664-5236. This is the Chicago and Midwest industry guide.
- *The Producer's Masterguide*. 330 W. 42nd St., 16th Floor, New York, NY 10038; (212) 536-1400. Covers 3000 listings in 200 categories, including motion pictures, broadcast TV, commercials, cable, and video industry in the U.S.
- State of Illinois Film Office. Illinois Department of Commerce and Community Affairs; 100 W. Randolph St., Suite 3-400, Chicago, IL 60601; (312) 814-3600

CABLE TV

To find a prospect at your local cable company, just call them and ask for their production department. These people always need music for commercials, local shows, etc. A cable company is a great training ground for a novice. It's how and where I started. Other sources for the information you need are in the next section.

RADIO/TV

You can find radio and TV outlets in a creative talent directory or the telephone book. Contact the production department and then ask for the person who buys original music for the station. Other sources for this information include:

- *Bacon's Radio/TV Directory*. Bacon's Publicity Company; 332 S. Michigan Ave., Suite 900, Chicago, IL 60604; (312) 922-2400
- *Broadcasting and Cable Marketplace*. R.R. Bowker; 121 Chanlon Rd., New Providence, NJ 07974; (800) 521-8110. Find all the radio, TV, and cable data you need using this resource.
- *College Media Directory*. Oxbridge Communications; 150 Fifth Ave. #302, New York, NY 10011-4311; (212) 741-0231. This directory lists college media, including radio programs.
- *Film Directors Guide*. Lone Eagle Publishing; 2337 Roscomare Rd. #9, Los Angeles, CA 90077-1851; (310) 471-8066
- *Radio, Television, and Cable Directory*. Bacon's Publicity Company; P. O. Box 2015, Lakewood, NJ 08701; (800) 753-6675
- *Film/TV Music Guide*. Music Business Registry; 7510 Sunset Blvd. #1041, Los Angeles, CA 90046-3518; (800) 377-7411; mbr@pacificnet.net
- *Who's Who in Entertainment*. Reed Publishing; 121 Chanlon Rd., New Providence, NJ 07974; (800) 521-8110. Features pros in the entertainment industry.

SONGWRITER'S MARKET

Another source for companies that buy original music is the annual *Songwriter's Market* (Writer's Digest Books; 1507 Dana Ave., Cincinnati, Ohio 45207; [800] 289-0963). They have a complete section devoted to audiovisual producers. But be forewarned: The competition is fierce. I've heard horror stories about a single listing getting over 500 tapes! Go for it if you have the chops. But getting these jobs requires more than skill alone; you also need luck. After about a hundred "Don't call us, we'll call you" letters, you'll think twice about wasting your money on this resource. I suspect that most who list here just like getting tapes in the mail. In my experience, they never respond to any of them. Lest I seem too jaded, let's just say that for me, it has been a dis-

couraging experience. There are other people who will gladly buy your music and appreciate your hard work, too.

ADVERTISING AGENCIES

These companies buy scores and jingles for commercials. Find them in all the same places listed above and the *Red Book* listed below. It's an expensive book, so check it out in the reference section of your local library.

- *Agency Red Book: Standard Directory of Advertising Agencies*. National Register Publishing Co.; 121 Chanlon Rd., New Providence, NJ 07974; (800) 521-8110
- *Madison Avenue Handbook*. Peter Glenn Publications; 42 W. 38th St., Room 802, New York, NY 10018; (212) 869-2020. This is another source for people and companies in the advertising field, mostly on the East Coast.

SEEK AND BE FOUND

The best part of a local directory of creative talent is that you can (and should) list there, too. I'm listed as a Composer and Producer in the "Music and Sound" section of both directories. Listings in both *Screen* and the *Illinois Film Guide* are free, but even if a listing isn't free, it is usually very affordable. Contact your local directory to see how to list, when, and how much it costs.

NEED MORE HELP?

These resources can help you find vital information about music buying prospects.

- *Directories in Print*. Gale Research; 835 Penobscot Building, Detroit, MI 48226-4094; (313) 961-2242. Having trouble locating a directory in your area? Try this guide. If you can't find it here, what you need probably doesn't exist.
- *Encyclopedia of Associations*. Gale Research; 835 Penobscot Building, Detroit, MI 48226-4094; (313) 961-2242. There are over 22,000 associations listed in this huge resource that you can join or otherwise use to find music buyers.
- *National Directory of Mailing Lists*. Oxbridge Communications; 150 Fifth Ave. #302, New York, NY 10011-4311; (212) 741-0231. For mailing lists, consult this resource.

STAY UP TO DATE

It's a good idea to subscribe to any and all industry publications in your area, as well as a few national ones. They tell you what you need to know about the corporate, commercial, and film production community, and you'll gain valuable insight into all aspects of the commercial music world. Here are the best:

- *Mix.* 6400 Hollis St., Suite 12, Emeryville, CA 94608; (510) 653-3307. Also publishers of the *Mix Master Directory.*
- *Film and Video: The Production Magazine.* 8455 Beverly Blvd., Suite 508, Los Angeles, CA 90048; (213) 653-8053

◗ STILL CAN'T FIND IT?

Can't find publications that only serve your area? My advice is to ask around. When you visit a client or prospect, look around and see what they're reading. Or just ask them outright. Often local business publications have sections devoted to advertising and audiovisual production. Put on your Sherlock Holmes hat and start researching. You'll soon have what you need. And don't forget that your venerable local library is always a wealth of information, too. So, *use it!*

CHAPTER 6

Reaching Prospects and Turning Them Into Paying Music Clients

Everyone lives by selling something.

—*Robert Louis Stevenson*

Marketing is the most important part of this business. Sure, you must have talent, but if the world doesn't know about it, you'll fail miserably. You must always promote. Period. In good times and in bad, you must constantly market and sell your services. I probably spend 40% of my time marketing, 20% running my business, and only 40% actually doing my business. That may shock and amaze you, but it is nevertheless quite true. When you start out, you may spend almost all of your time marketing. I did, and I learned one very important lesson: Your next client is always three months away. Can you afford to wait for the phone to ring?

Many people believe that marketing and advertising are synonymous. Nothing could be further from the truth. Advertising is only a small part of marketing (granted, it's usually the most expensive), but it's not a panacea. Marketing is not very complex. My Business Success MAPS break down this concept into four chunks: Marketing, Advertising, Publicity, and Sales. While these individual functions all fall under the marketing banner, it's often easier to understand them if you separate them. Just remember that everything you do as part of conducting your business is marketing. And that means:

- How you answer your phone
- What you say at meetings
- The look of your stationery and business cards
- Your promotional material and how you present it
- The quality of your music demo tape
- How you follow up
- Your prices
- Your company name
- Your market niche and how you fit in
- Your advertising: print, direct marketing, etc.

All this is marketing. Some methods cost money, but others are absolutely free. I mean, what does it take to say, "Hello, Jeffrey Fisher. How may I help you?" when you answer the phone? Believe it or not, this is marketing. Sadly, many people don't get it.

One day I called a rental house and the owner picked up the phone with, "Yeah, rental house here. Whaddya want?" When I asked whether he had a certain piece of equipment to rent, he replied, "Uh, I think so. It's 50 a day plus delivery. When d'ya want it?" He wasn't the least bit interested in my needs, so I hung up. Needless to say, his dubious phone demeanor cost him all of my business.

Don't run your business this way (the poor fool). Be polite, understanding, and genuinely interested in everyone who calls. Give your clients exactly what you expect others to give you. Most of all, make sure you are sincere. You do want to help people through your work, don't you? Make sure this comes across with everything—and I do mean *everything* you do.

THE TOOLS TO USE

You need several different marketing and promotional weapons in your arsenal to turn prospects into paying clients and keep satisfied clients buying more and more:
• Telephone marketing strategies
• Direct marketing sales letters
• Postcards and flyers
• Classified and small ads
• Free music samples
• Free consultations and estimates
• Prospect and client sales tactics
• Articles, booklets, and books
• Free client newsletters
• Promotional kit and other marketing materials

Whatever methods you choose to reach your prospects (and at some point, you'll probably use them all), please remember this: Your prospects are *not* interested in you. They are only interested in themselves. To succeed, you *must* make sure every marketing opportunity, meeting, and document focuses completely on your prospects and clients— their needs and their desires.

Before you develop letters, postcards, ads, marketing kits, and so forth, pay close attention to this next point. Don't send out a thing until you read the sections about preparing promotional material in this book. This advice will save you tons of money that you would otherwise waste on materials that don't sell your music. If you don't think you are capable of producing your own documents, then please hire a professional. It may cost you some money, but the return is often well worth the small investment.

YOUR ROAD TO SUCCESS

Victory belongs to the most persevering.
—NAPOLEON BONAPARTE
- -

The plan you must follow to be successful in this business is deceptively easy. (Simple, practical, and realistic advice often is the best and the most effective.)
• Identify your target market. Discover what they need and adapt your services to meet those needs. First, think about the kind of music you want to write. Do you want to write jingles? Long-form scores? Next, look for the places your music fits, such as commer-

cials, dramatic films and videos, computer games, and so forth. Finally, find the people who create these productions and let them know you can solve their music problems.
• Create a name, address, and telephone list of people who make up the market you identified in the previous step. Go back to the last chapter and use its many resources to help you compile the list of ad agencies, productions houses, et al. that you need.
• Develop a sales letter to mail to these people that shows how you can help them. How will you make these people aware of both the needs you uncovered and your ability to meet those needs? Convince them that your music can help them reach the goals of their audiovisual projects. This step is so important that this chapter and the next detail precisely how to create winning sales presentations.
• Call these people as a follow-up to your mailing.
• Send your marketing kit and demo tape to the most promising prospects.
• Once again, follow up by phone on the material you sent.
• Schedule a meeting, either in-person or by phone. Meet with the leads you generated to close a sale with your first client.
• Send a thank you note following your meeting.
• Get hired to compose and do a good job for this client.
• Send your contract and get one-half of the payment in advance.
• Write a rough music sketch and send it to the client.
• Get approval of sketches.
• Write, record, and deliver the final master.
• Invoice for final contract payment.
• Receive payment.
• Parlay the success with this client to get more clients.
• Solicit a testimonial from the satisfied client.
• Send a thank you note or small gift after you get the testimonial.
• Keep in touch with this client regularly via phone, newsletter, letter, etc., and work to get more business from this happy client.
• Bring this success (and each subsequent success) to the attention of others who would benefit from your music through another mailing and then follow up by telephone.
• Send a news release to your local and trade press about your success.
• Keep highlighting your ongoing triumphs to other potential clients through additional mailings and telephone calls. Use the promotional ideas contained in this book and let all your prospects know that you can meet their music needs, why they must take advantage of your services, why they should

choose you, and exactly how you can help them.
• Repeat from the beginning.

Although we will add details to this framework, it is the basic plan you must follow because it works. You won't reach every step with every prospect, but still, you must persevere. If you truly want to make it in business, there is an important work worth adding to your bookshelf: *How to Make at Least $100,000 a Year as a Successful Consultant in Your Own Field* (Dr. Jeffrey Lant. 50 Follen St., Suite 507, Cambridge, MA 02138). It will teach you how to get clients, work with them successfully, build long-term relationships, and profit from their needs. Your ability to solve problems through music, sound design, recording, and such is really what you sell. Use this resource and score.

YOUR CRUCIAL INSIDE MARKETING TIP

Don't send out your demo tape unsolicited. Repeat that phrase ten times out loud.

Advertising agencies, video production companies, and the like get assaulted by audio and video demos every day. It's hard to stand out from the crowd, so you can end up getting buried alive. *Screen* once reported that a single call for resumes resulted in a small production company getting *over 400 tapes in one week!* Good luck. There is only one exception to this rule: Do send new music to past clients along with a short note. Heed this advice or suffer the consequences.

Sadly, most unsolicited tapes are *not* listened to or at least not with much attention or enthusiasm. My mailbox gets filled with tapes from singers, musicians, and would-be composers all the time, but unless I have an immediate need, the tapes get filed away. I listen to many of them while I'm doing something else, and they rarely get the attention they deserve. Why? Because I didn't ask for them. If I listened to every tape I received, I'd have precious little time left for running my business. Such is the fate of most, if not all, unsolicited tapes. It might not seem fair, but it's the harsh reality of the commercial music world.

Here's another reason why I hate unsolicited demos. Those who send them don't take the time to see what I really need, and they don't position themselves to help me. They just send me their tape and hope I'll figure it out myself. Guess what? It just doesn't work that way. To me, every unsolicited demo says this: "I'm great. This tape proves it. Listen to it right now—you've nothing better to do—and then hire me. You can't be without my talent, that's why I sent you this tape." Right.

Case in point. Recently I received a tape from a singer with a handwritten Post-it™ note attached that said: "Next time you need a great singer, you know who to call." Oh, really? He wasted his money. I believe in portraying yourself as successful (you really are or you really want to be, don't you?), but arrogance will get you nowhere. Saying you are great is not the same thing as *proving* you are great.

I once produced a slide show for a client that cost about $4000 to make. It brought in $80,000 in sales. This is a tangible success story. I could write to another prospect and simply bring this success to their attention and then show how I could do the same for their company! The singer illustrated above comes across as selfish, foolish, pompous, and just plain stupid. He didn't take the time to find out what I needed and what was in it for me. He didn't translate his skill into a tangible and provable benefit for me. Don't fall into this trap.

YOU MUST GET PROSPECTS TO REQUEST YOUR DEMO!

Why? Because *you* control the sales process. You take the active role of converting casual interest into a tangible client. You're not just sitting by the phone, fingers crossed, hoping the damned thing rings. This business requires a proactive approach, not a passive attitude. When you are in control, you can print on the envelope, "Here's the information and music *you* requested." Then you can send follow-up information along with your demo and do that again and again and again until they become your client.

People rarely buy something after being exposed to it only once. You must hit your market and prospects regularly. Someone who requests your demo is a warm, or qualified, prospect. When they make the first move, they will have expressed a specific interest in your work and will be looking forward to your tape. You can fully control the selling process from that point on. If you get a meeting after the prospect listens to your tape, you have a hot one on the line. Time to reel this one in. You have a better chance of converting warm and hot prospects into clients than anybody else. Do you see the importance of this strategy?

Ever get junk mail (an unsolicited tape) and throw it out? Ever called or written for something; waited for it to arrive; and when it did, put everything you were doing aside just to investigate it? The former gets very little time from you, while the latter gets your full attention. Case closed.

The advantages are simple. First, you'll save a bundle of money by not mailing hundreds of demos that probably won't even be listened to ("Hey, I didn't ask for this"). Second, those you do send the tape to are expecting it and are more likely to listen to it intently . . . and then buy. The universe is your potential market, but only qualified prospects buy your services. While you must often market to cold prospects, you should quickly separate them from better sales leads. This way you spend the majority of your time, energy, and money on the warm and hot prospects you uncover, as well as on your past clients.

HOW TO QUALIFY PROSPECTS

At this point, you now have the names of potential soundtrack and jingle music buyers. There are two ways to transform your cold list of possible prospects into a strong list of warm and hot prospects (and then into clients):

- Telemarketing. Call people on your lists and ask if they'd like a demo.
- Direct marketing. Send a sales letter to the list and ask them to request more information.

I hate cold calls. They're very hard and, if you can't deal well with rejection, not for the squeamish. I prefer direct marketing. It can be just as personal and just as effective. And when you follow up your letter with a not-quite-so-cold telephone call, it's almost unbeatable. That said, let's discuss how to use the telephone.

COLD CALL TECHNIQUE

The purpose of a cold call like this is to generate initial interest and whittle your list down to the best prospects. It's *not* to sell your music outright. With this method, you need to ask if the prospect buys original music, and if so, are they interested in hearing your work. If they are, you can mail them your most persuasive marketing kit and killer demo reel. Again, don't try to sell your music on a cold call. Get the client sufficiently interested in hearing more first. When you follow up later, you can begin the sales process. This way they'll know more about you (from your promotional material and music demo) and will be in a better position to discuss details at length. Call up and be firm but polite:

This is [your name]. *I'm an independent composer in town, and I'd like to take just a minute of your time to introduce myself and my music composition services to you. Who buys the music for your productions?*

Once you get a name, ask to speak with that person directly. If they can't take your call right then, don't leave a message. Find out a good time to call that person and call back at that time. Once you get through, introduce yourself again and explain a little about what you do:

I am calling to see if you'd like to know how you can save money while getting the exact music you want. Would you like to get my demo and information packet? It shows you what you need to do to get affordable original music for all your productions.

or:

Would you like a sample of my music? You can keep and use it; it's not a demo tape. This is royalty-free music you can use to make any of your productions better right now. Of course, it won't have the same impact as music scored specifically for your project, but it just might help you out when you need some good music fast. And it will give you an idea of how I can help you with your original music needs.

At this point, it's essential that you lead the prospect to the next step:

I'll send my information kit to you by first class mail today. You should have it in three or four days. I'll call back in a week or so to answer any questions. Thank you for your time.

Again, don't try to set up meetings with your initial calls. Get people interested in your service, let them hear what you can do, and then ask for a meeting when you call back later.

USING DIRECT MARKETING TO GENERATE LEADS

Just like the telemarketing example, don't expect to sell your music with just one mailing. The purpose of both of these marketing strategies is to generate leads of warm and hot prospects you can then turn into paying clients.

I adore direct marketing. When people respond to my sales letters, there is a better chance of giving them the right information, custom-tailored to their specific needs. By providing exactly what they want, I come across as more helpful and genuinely interested in them. I'm not just sending out tapes to see what happens, and my client prospects know it. This is the ideal situation because you are in control.

If you decide to use direct marketing, your package is crucial to your success. It must be persuasive, loaded with benefits, and make client prospects an offer they can't refuse. The average response to a well-written sales letter is 3-5%. I rarely get less than 7% or more than 15%. You'll learn how to duplicate my results a little later.

Many people think that direct marketing is expensive. It's not. The most costly part is the postage (yes, it *must* go first class!). A two-page sales letter and brochure or flyer doesn't cost all that much to produce and mail (about 45-65¢). Let me put this another way: Any promotion that fails to produce a response or a customer is expensive—even if it only costs a buck. And marketing that costs $1000 is cheap if it brings in $20,000 in business.

HOW DIRECT MARKETING SAVES YOU MONEY

If you mail 500 letters (a big mailing in your immediate area, by the way) at about 50¢ apiece (postage, paper, and printing), your cost is $250. If 25 people call (5%) and request information, and you send them your tape and marketing materials at a cost of $2 each, that costs you an additional $50. You need only one small sale to recoup your investment. If you mail 500 tapes and materials at $2 each, you'd spend $1000. And my experience shows that *still only 25 people will respond.*

Since you can't expect most people to respond to just one letter, you must hit them repeatedly with different packages and offers. The rule is that a person must be exposed to you several times before they even consider buying. It makes more financial and promotional sense to mail several letters, not three or four tapes. You could easily get four letters out for the price of just one single tape mailing, and your chances of making sales will be much higher. Actually, you'd probably do several different things to connect with people beyond just mailing sales letters and tapes. You might choose postcards, small ads, publicity, newsletters, and more.

YOUR STEP-BY-STEP MONEYMAKING MARKETING PLAN

Don't think that a single letter, single mailing, single telephone call, or a single success is sufficient enough to ensure the profitability and longevity of your business. Businesses are built slowly, steadily, through your patience and your continuing ability to identify the problems of a highly targeted market and solve them.

—JEFFREY LANT

- -

The following is not a theoretical model. It is *exactly* how to sell your commercial music composition services. This is good, practical, proven advice from someone who knows what it takes to succeed. So you can, too! You must connect with prospects several times and in several different ways before they become your clients. You must also consider specific strategies for getting more business from existing clients. This outline is essentially a carefully controlled series of sales letters and follow-up telephone calls combined with various other promotional gambits. The details of the plan follow this section.

▶ GENERATING LEADS FROM COLD PROSPECTS

- Using the list of your market that you've accumulated, call each company and verify the prospect name, title, etc. Do not use this call to pitch services; only say you are updating your files for a mailing.
- Mail direct mail package number one as an introduction. This should be a personal letter with an enclosed brochure or flyer. In the letter, say you will be calling to confirm its receipt and to answer any questions.
- Call to follow up ten days after this mailing. Use this call to determine the status of the prospect: cold, warm, or hot.
  - Cold prospects are only vaguely interested in your service. Plan to contact them again in two months. Don't give up on these people yet!
  - Warm prospects show immediate interest. Make sure you send more information (probably your complete promotional kit and music demo tape) to these prospects.
  - Sometimes a hot prospect may have an immediate need. This is rare, but timing is critical. Schedule an appointment with all hot prospects immediately and proceed to the meeting plan described later. When you schedule meetings with hot prospects, call to confirm your appointment the day before the meeting. You may need to fax any information this prospect requires before the scheduled meeting.
- Call to follow up ten days after mailing the package to your warm prospects. Use this call to confirm the receipt of your information, answer questions, and determine whether you should upgrade the status to hot or downgrade it to cold. Schedule an appointment with the most promising prospects. Plan to contact the cold prospects again in two months.
- After two months, mail your second direct mail package to your list of cold prospects. This package should stress more benefits and make a different offer.
- Once again, call to follow up this second direct mail package ten days later. Determine this prospect's status and follow the same steps as outlined above.
- Mail a third sales package to your dwindling list of cold prospects four months later. Stress even more benefits and make yet another new offer.
- Call to follow up this package and divide the responses again into cold, warm, and hot prospects. Continue the plan as before.
- In six months, send the cold list your fourth and last plea. Call to follow up the package ten days after mailing. Indicate the final status of this prospect.

Deal with warm and hot prospects accordingly. Retire the cold prospects to a semi-permanent dead cold file and pursue them again from the beginning of this plan in 18 to 24 months. Reactivating this prospect at that time can bring new information to light (staff, situation, and other changes).

At this point, a prospect has received four mailings and four follow-up telephone calls within a year. With the other promotional exposures (explained later) that you will use, this prospect has heard enough about you to make a buying decision. If this prospect still doesn't convert to a client by the end of this plan, they probably never will. Rather than open up new markets all the time, concentrate on the same group again and again until you become the inevitable choice or not.

▶ AT THE PROSPECT MEETING
- Make sure you are prepared. During this initial client contact, there are several crucial pieces of information you should discover.
  - Do they need your service?
  - Can they afford your fees?
  - Do they have authority to purchase your services?
  - Based on what they tell you, can you deliver what they need, meet their deadline, and for the agreed upon fee? Don't be afraid to say no if a project is beyond your skills. Just make sure you explain why you are turning the project down, and then help them find someone who can deliver what they need.
- Take additional sales materials, another promotional kit, and new music not included on your current music demo tape. If a prospect asks for more information, supply this, too.
  - I always take a copy of my booklet, *How to Get Low-Cost Original Music for All Your Productions*, to client meetings. It explains how I work and acts as a primer to my services, my music, and me. It also brings me some extra prestige and makes a strong impression on clients by showing that I want to help them realize their goals. I'll talk further about why you need this kind of material later.
- Identify the personality type of your client (explained later) and slant your presentation accordingly.
- Vary your speech pattern and pace to follow your prospect.
- Listen and take notes.
- Follow up all meetings, whether they result in immediate work or not, with a thank you note. If you get the gig, send your contract within a day.
- When meeting with this prospect at a first appointment, you should once again determine whether this person is still hot or should be downgraded to warm or even cold. Try to convert your hot prospects to clients at this or a second meeting. Get them to sign a contract or an agreement. Hot prospects are close to a sale. I suggest you start treating them like a client and follow the plan for keeping in touch with clients as explained below. Move the warm and cold names back to your original plan and keep contacting them accordingly. Send direct mail packages and follow up as outlined above starting from where they left off in the plan.

▶ WHEN A PROSPECT CALLS YOU
If at any point a prospect responds to an offer or calls you following some promotion, here's the plan for contacting them:
- Fulfill the offer with your promotional kit and music demo.
- Follow up with a telephone call to check on their receipt of the package, answer questions, and ask for a meeting.
- Determine if they're cold, warm, or hot, and keep marketing to this person accordingly.

▶ OTHER MARKETING METHODS
In addition to these strategies, other elements must occur simultaneously.
- Determine the media servicing your target market. This media should include radio, TV, cable TV, Internet, and print outlets.
- Place articles in the media reaching your market at least once each quarter.
- Advertise in the media occasionally, but only if you swap ad space for an article or if the rates are low (under $75).
- Update your music demo at least once each year. If you have several demos targeted at specific music needs, keep them updated regularly, too.
- Distribute news releases highlighting your activities to the media at least once each quarter. Alternate this material with articles and ads so that your name appears regularly, almost monthly.
- Send reprints of all articles, advertisements, and publicity to clients and hot prospects. These can be included with your newsletter mailing to conserve postage.
- Participate in local trade shows, offer to give talks to area service and business organizations, and use networking regularly.
- Diversify your services to reach other markets. Supply clients and prospects with music library recom-

mendations, other services, and experts who can help them solve their problems. Not everyone desires or can afford your service. Work to help them on a different or lesser level.

◗ MATERIAL NEEDED FOR THIS MARKETING PLAN

You need to develop specific sales material for this plan to work. This includes:

- Four or more compelling offers or ideas to use in your initial sales letters and other appropriate support material. Start thinking of ways to attract buyers and to sell your music. We'll explore this in greater detail later. You will not be successful if you just rely on promotions that simply say, "I do music. When you need some, call me." Only the following are the real offers that get people to respond:
  - Free consultations
  - Free sample music
  - Free planning or information kit
  - Free booklets or reports containing musical how-to and problem solving information
  - 10% off your first original music order
- When using letters follow these basic tips:
  - Identify what you do and how you can help the prospect.
  - Cut to the chase and don't waste time on useless background material.
  - Push the benefits and results you achieve.
  - Make sure your letter has an offer of some kind.
  - Include other marketing and promotional material that relates to your benefits or offers.
  - Follow up all contact initiated by a letter with a telephone call.

You need:

- Various pattern letters to meet routine situations. Automating your follow-up is the key to handling promotion efficiently and effectively.
- A general brochure about your services
- A company fact sheet, background, history, and philosophy
- A flyer that answers all sales objections. The Q&A or Internet FAQ format is best. It should present a simple, logical progression of questions and answers to inform your prospects about your business.
- Short case histories, client profiles, and project listings to share with prospects. These are success stories in which you say, "So-and-so benefited from our help, and we can do the same for you!"
- News releases as needed for publicity
- Biographical narrative feature story of you, your people, and your company
- Several clippings of previous ads and publicity

- Photographs of the composer, both a head shot and some action shots

◗ CLIENTS MUST ALSO RECEIVE REGULAR ATTENTION

For your clients and hot prospects, use these keep-in-touch techniques regularly:

- Make sure you alert all your clients, hot prospects, outside advisors, staff, and others associated with your business to any media coverage of your work in print, radio, and TV.
- Prepare a simple monthly or quarterly newsletter. This can be nothing more than a letter you send out regularly highlighting achievements and special offers. Call two weeks after each newsletter to check on any new projects.
- Send birthday cards and appropriate holiday greetings.
- Provide special facts, updates, information sheets.
- Occasionally send friendly letters or make just-saying-hi telephone calls.
- Send article and publicity reprints.
- Send clippings of vital client information and interest.
- Hold a client-only seminar or an open house.
- Ask for referrals from all clients or consider providing them with suitable materials to pass along to other people. Let them network you to more business!
- In the event of negative publicity about your business, make sure all clients are informed before the negative story appears.
- You might prepare a letter to do informal market research. Send this to hot prospects and present clients and ask their opinion about music issues. The response will give you valuable insight as to how you should market your commercial music.

This plan may seem intense, even overwhelming at first. Don't fret. Follow this road map slowly and steadily, and everything will fall into place. It's not designed to be handled all at once. It's better and easier to manage if you concentrate on five to ten prospects each day and coordinate the follow-up using a client log to track progress.

The purpose of this exercise is twofold. First, you're trying to discover potential original music buyers. Second, you're seeing if you can work together successfully. By carefully selecting clients, you avoid many future problems. Not everyone is a buyer. Understand this advice and save yourself tons of heartache. Your letters, ads, calls, and such must perform this crucial screening and separate the cold fish from the ready and willing—and paying!—original soundtrack music and jingle clients. Plus, if marketing, promoting, and selling were so easy, we would all be millionaires. Right?

TRACKING CLIENTS AND PROSPECTS

Keeping track of all the details of your burgeoning commercial music business can be a formidable task. I suggest you develop a basic questionnaire or log. Use a single sheet of paper for each prospect lead and store them in a binder or on your computer. Use this information to keep track of prospects and clients and the various details of your dealings together. Each sheet should carry this basic information:

• Client name, title, company name, address, telephone number, fax, and e-mail address
• Kinds of music they use
• Typical music budget
• Names of others who have supplied music in the past
• Client's evaluation of past music used
• Other comments

Next, keep a detailed listing on the same page of all your contact:

1/7	Mailed marketing kit and demo
1/14	Telephone follow-up to mailing
1/16	Meeting to discuss projects
1/20	Sent contract
2/5	Finished score for ABC Widgets
2/18	Follow up to ABC project
3/1	Mailed newsletter

Use this log to coordinate your follow-up and track your progress. Arrange your binder by months. Once you fill out the sheet and enter your first contact, file the log based on your next action. If you said you'd call next month, move the sheet to the next month in the binder. As you keep contacting clients and prospects, enter appropriate data on the log sheet and file it in the next place in the binder. After that, it's easy to determine where each prospect is on your marketing plan. Plus, you can include specific information about a client and refer to that as you make subsequent contact. Don't rely on your memory; use this method instead. By the way, there is also software available that you can use to automate this plan. And always remember this vital equation: **Leads + Follow-up = $ales.**

While most companies are happy to generate the leads they want, sadly, most are not prepared for the prospects they do get. Make sure you don't fall into this trap. Do everything in your power to manage your leads and convert them into a sale. First and foremost, be ready in advance. Before promoting yourself, prepare for the possible response your efforts may produce. Get the proper mental attitude, take care of necessary technical matters, prepare the needed documents, and refine your follow-up and sales procedures.

SELLING YOUR MUSIC SERVICES ON FIVE DOLLARS A DAY

There are two crucial keys to building and sustaining your successful music business:
• Generating and contacting new business leads
• Bringing your business benefits to current and past customers

You should always work hard to keep your name alive and deliver your message to those who need what you offer. Unfortunately, most of us have precious little time and often even smaller checkbooks. Here's a tip that I use to promote my commercial music business.

Rather than sending out huge bulk mailings all the time, it's easier to spend a little time each day marketing. One way to do this is to use what I call five-dollars-a-day marketing. The basic strategy is to contact ten clients or prospects each day, five days each week, contacting five by mail and five by phone. This is very easy to manage, especially for the one-person shop, and with a targeted list of prospects, this method is both inexpensive and potentially lucrative.

Each day, send out sales letters and brochures to five prospects or customers on your list. As outlined in the plan above, use a series of sales letters, brochures, newsletters, thank you notes, special offers, and postcards to hit the same list three or four times each year. Next, follow up each mailing ten days later with a telephone call to check on the receipt of the direct mail package and answer any questions. Use these opportunities to keep in touch with past clients and hunt down new prospects.

So, on any given day you will mail five direct mail promotions and make five telephone follow-up calls. That's it. With this plan, you'll put your name in front of prospects many times in a short period. Your marketing will be better and more profitable if you keep plugging away, bit by bit, day in and day out.

Your cost to print and mail five letters is about 75¢ each, for a total of $3.75. The telephone calls cost about a quarter each, for a total of $1.25. This is how you can promote your products and services for $5 each day. That's only $1250 a year that you pay one tiny morsel at a time. Every single business can benefit from this simple, effective strategy. It's easily managed, lets you build your prospect and client database steadily, keeps expenses low, and brings your benefits to the attention of your market several times in a carefully controlled, methodical way.

WHEN YOUR PROSPECT CALLS

You've finished your mailing and have some qualified, hot prospects who actually contacted *you* and requested your tape. Do not delay. You must get the material to them right away. Strike while the iron's hot, I say. Here is a sample script to follow when prospects respond to an offer:

Thanks for calling about my special offer. Yes, I'll send you the music sample. Don't forget, this is not a demo. You can keep and use this music for any of your productions. Please give me your name, address, and telephone number.

I'll send you the music and a detailed information kit today by first class mail, and you should have it in three or four days. Is this OK? The kit shows you how to get low-cost original music for every program you produce. And you'll be getting some good, useful music you can start using today as my special bonus. If you don't receive this package after a week, please call me and I'll make sure you get the facts about low-cost original music overnight.

I'll follow up in about a week to answer your questions. Thanks for your interest in my offer and for your call. I'm looking forward to talking with you again after you have a chance to review my information kit and music. By the way, is there any music in particular you're looking for at this time? Do you have a current project that I can help you with?

I once received a call from a tape duplicator who said they were updating their mailing list (another good tactic when making first contact by telephone, by the way). They asked if I was interested. I told them yes and that I would like to see their catalog. Then the caller said they would send it in a few weeks and I should have it in *four to six weeks!*

Can you believe that? Why did they bother to call? To be honest, I only remember the phone call. I don't think I ever got the catalog. If I did, it went the way of the circular file. When I get requests for my material it *always* goes out the same day. Providing superior customer service is vital to building and sustaining your business. Make sure that you do.

WHAT TO SEND TO YOUR HOT PROSPECTS

Obviously your tape, whether it be a demo or a sample, is going to be your main marketing piece. However, supporting documentation is vital to reinforcing to your prospect that you can do what you say. A generic brochure about your services is one thing you can include with your tape, along with a cover letter and business card. Here are your promotional options:

◗ SALES LETTER

This is always the best way to introduce yourself to prospective clients. You can be as detailed or brief as you want. Follow some of my examples or apply the information in this book to your own situation. Use simple language and fill every line with compelling benefits and a strong offer.

◗ THREE FOLD BROCHURE

You don't have to go far to find an example. Everybody uses one, or something very much like it, to promote their business. Usually this is one sheet of 8½x11 paper folded into thirds and inserted into a standard #10 envelope. Add a benefit-rich sales letter, a business card, and a demo tape, and you have a strong, effective promotional package.

◗ SELF-MAILER

This is usually a brochure or flyer mailed without a letter, envelope, or tape. It's ideal for making special offers, sending your newsletter, or announcing new products or services. Make sure you understand the real postage costs involved. You can usually mail four or five sheets in an envelope for one first-class stamp. Why waste all the postage on a single sheet? You decide.

◗ MARKETING KIT

Instead of a single brochure and cover letter, you include lots of promotional material in a presentation folder. These items should include press clippings, client recommendations and testimonials, project listings, and so forth. Make sure you add a detailed cover letter that introduces each item and explains its significance. You might consider calling this a "music planning kit" filled with the material music buyers need to plan, budget, and select original music for their productions. This makes it sound like a useful tool, not the promotional piece it really is.

A single brochure can be impersonal and is usually incomplete for selling music services. So I send lots of information, probably more than necessary. I want my hot prospects and clients to know *how* I do business by answering their questions with my marketing kit. The impressive attention to detail also adds value to my services. Don't just pop a tape in the mail with a sticky note. Instead, include material designed to promote and sell your services in a presentation folder, add your tape, and mail the package the same day you get a request.

Using an organic, ever-changing marketing kit also means information is always up to date. A brochure is fixed, and if you change something, you either have to reprint (expensive) or cross things out (yuck!). And yes, on the outside of the envelope be sure to type: Here's the music *you* requested!

WHAT TO INCLUDE IN YOUR MARKETING KIT

Please understand this important distinction. Your marketing materials have only one purpose: to sell your music. Don't simply dump your tape and information on your client prospects. Take a minute to *describe* each piece to your client prospects, what it means to them, and how it will benefit them. My music planning kit contains:

- A personalized cover letter that thanks the prospect for responding and draws attention to all the information in the packet. I also try to address any points brought up during our conversation.
- A one-page flyer that details the services I offer
- Another flyer specifically about my music composition services, costs, rights, etc.
- A simple contract showing how easy it is to do business with me
- A list of testimonials and recommendations from clients I've worked with in the past
- Details about the music on my tape (what it was used for, instrumentation used, recording techniques, etc.)
- Reprints of ads and articles published in the past
- A flyer about *How to Make Money Scoring Soundtracks and Jingles* with an order form so they can get their own copy
- My *How to Get Low-Cost Original Music* booklet. However, I often wait and send this out as a follow-up premium or as an offer in a later letter or newsletter. It creates another reason to call: "Say, did you get my special booklet, showing you how to save money when you order original music from me?"

I send this information packet to every prospect who responds to one of my offers. It makes a good impression and is easily updated and quite inexpensive. Whatever you decide to send, make sure that exactly ten days later you call to see if they received the information and answer any questions. Assess their needs (immediate or future) and set up a meeting. Take additional information and music to the meeting, and then follow up with a brief thank you note. If they haven't hired you, add them to your keep-in-touch program. And so on and so forth, as specified earlier.

HANDLING SUCCESSFUL CLIENT PROSPECT MEETINGS

No passion so effectively robs the mind of all its powers of acting and reasoning as fear.
—EDMUND BURKE

Far too many service providers and other professionals believe selling is beneath them. They conjure up visions of used car dealers or Herb from *WKRP* and say they don't want to be like that. While there are plenty of hucksters out there, there are also plenty of good, honest people selling their services.

Ultimately, you will need to sell your music and yourself. That thought may scare the daylights out of you, but let me assure you it shouldn't. You won't need to become some high-pressure, pushy stereotype. You will, however, need to practice consultative selling. That means you will talk with your client prospects, determine their problems, find out what they want and how they want to solve their problems, and then show them how your music and ancillary services will solve these problems. Or put simply: Find out what they want and give it to them.

Creative people require patience, respect, and more than their fair share of hand holding. I believe most truly creative people are rather insecure and thus are always looking for recognition of their work. They need validation that what they are doing is good—whatever that means. "Do you like it?" I hear that all the time, putting me in the precarious position of judge, jury, and firing squad. Honesty truly is the best policy, but watch it.

Be interested in your prospects' work and be sincere. Ask questions. Listen. The real key to selling success is active listening. Don't take this point for granted. Concentrate on what your prospect is *really* saying. Read between the lines and you will get the insight you need. Once you know what they need, you can show how you could help them achieve what they want to achieve.

Also, don't brag, boast, or drop names. Although you must demonstrate your previous success, you don't need to be pompous about it. Phrase your answers to reflect the *benefits* your past clients received, not *who* your past clients were. Here's an example of what you might say:

> *If your budget is small, perhaps you might consider something several of my clients have taken advantage of. I can write a single theme for you, perhaps only two to three minutes long, and then produce several alternative mixes. You'll get a variety of music, all based around a single thematic concept, and a price that fits your budget. Let me play you an example of what I mean.*

Recently I was asked the secret to sales psychology. I didn't need to think about it for very long. "Benefits," I replied. From the buyer's perspective, it's simple: "What do I get?" Therefore, it's your job to show and tell them precisely what that is. After benefits comes value. Notice I said value, not price. Are the benefits and results you promise offset by the fees associated with your product or service? People don't look for low prices; people want maximum value for their money. It's a subtle shift in perspective, but it's crucial that you recognize this. If what you offer gives them what they want and need, the sale is easy. If you don't close the sale, it's because you didn't promote benefits and provide maximum value.

Making sales is not some crazy formula. Simply stress the benefits and results of using your products and services. Show the value of your offer and how the expense (whether it's money or time expended) outweighs the advantages. Don't sell your music. Instead, solve your client prospect's problems through your commercial music services. How do you get to the root of the problem? Ask leading questions. Open-ended, probing questions force your prospects to spill their guts—and they should do most of the talking. If your mouth is open more than 30% of the time, you're talking too much when you should be listening. So shut up and sell!

SEVEN LEADING QUESTIONS THAT STIMULATE CLIENT PROSPECTS TO TELL YOU WHAT THEY REALLY WANT

When in a meeting, you need to focus solely on your client. These questions make sure you don't dominate the conversation. You want to get the information you need to close the sale. Let your prospect tell you what they want and then tell them how your music fits in. Phrase your questions like these examples:
• What is the message of your production?
• How do you see the message or problem?
• What role should the music play?
• What is the purpose of the music?
• How do you see the audience responding?
• What should the music sound like?
• What I understand is that you . . . *[summarize your prospect's answers]*

If you're ever not sure about something or you're not getting enough information, just ask, "Can you tell me more about that?"

USING ACTIVE LISTENING EFFECTIVELY

You must practice your active listening skills in all selling situations. Here are some tips to help you.
• Try to avoid distractions and time constraints when meeting with prospects and clients.
• Face your prospects, lean toward them slightly, and look them straight in the eyes.
• Stay relaxed and open. Don't cross your arms or legs.
• Watch body language and listen for the *real* message.
• Pay attention. Don't let your mind wander or be distracted. Concentrate on what is being said. Repeat and rephrase each sentence in your head.
• Don't interrupt your prospects.
• Indicate you are listening and that you understand what is being said. Nod your head, take some notes, or answer that you understand by uttering a simple, "OK."
• Don't rush or ramble. Before giving your answer, pause for a few seconds and collect your thoughts. Even if you are excited or nervous, take a deep breath, think about what you're going to say, and then begin.
• Summarize what your prospects say in your own words and ask them if your understanding is correct.
• Smile and be friendly. Let your enthusiasm shine through.

UNDERSTANDING PERSONALITY TYPES

There are essentially six personality types that you'll encounter in the creative world. Virtually everyone falls into one of these categories. And while some may cross over into other types, each person typically exemplifies one main attitude. You must learn to recognize these types quickly and tailor your presentation accordingly.
• Leader. Always in control, dominates conversations, makes quick decisions, and follows through all projects from start to finish. These people tend to be all business and are only interested in results.
• Supporter. Likes being with and relating to people and is often a bit talkative. Usually seeks approval from others before making final decisions. These people are always quite friendly, casual, and relaxed.
• Optimist. Always full of energy and creativity. Likes to discuss myriad possibilities, most of which are completely outlandish and impractical. These people can be very energetic and prone to quick, spontaneous decisions.
• Bean Counter. Brings highly structured and thorough analysis to every situation. These people look for accurate, logical solutions.

- Adversary. Always sees the negative side of things. Can never find the good and tends to nit-pick. Completely the opposite of the optimist, adversaries tend to be very conservative and realistic.
- MOR. The middle of the road person tends to go with the flow. Never caught making their own decisions, MORs tend to work better in groups where individual thought is not cherished.

This may be oversimplifying human behavior, but in many sales situations there isn't time to fully understand someone. You need to uncover their tendency and use it to your advantage. With the leader, be the consummate music business expert. Ask about moods, feelings, and such with the supporter. Discuss wild ethnic percussion with the optimist. Go through the budget and other details with the bean counter. Carefully balance the up and down sides with the adversary. Take charge of the MOR. Use these as a guide only. We are all complex human beings, after all.

VITAL TELEPHONE TIPS

The telephone is one of your most important means of contacting prospects and clients. Practice what you're going to say, write scripts, and learn to be personable, helpful, and enthusiastic on the phone. Here's another sure-fire tip: Just before you pick up the receiver, take a deep breath, exhale slowly, inhale again, and smile. Your relaxed, friendly smile comes through during your call. Here are more ways to use the telephone effectively when contacting clients and prospects.

- Have a reason to make the call. Are you generating leads, following up mailings, responding to requests, and so forth? Prepare a brief outline of the major points of your call.
- Make sure you will not be interrupted during the call.
- Use your voice to project confidence, and be polite.
- Vary your speech pattern and pace to match your prospect.
- Listen and take notes.
- Many people may try to get you off the line by asking you to send them your tape. Hold on a minute. You are here to help them through your music services, not just send out demo tapes. Don't be put off by, "Send me your demo." Ask them if they use original music, if they have any projects coming up, and so forth. This can get a conversation started and allow you to show how you can help them better.
- If you can't seem to talk to the person you need to, don't ignore whoever you have on the line already. Tell this person how you can help, such as, "Mr. Producer uses original music, doesn't he? I'll bet he pays far too much for it. I can show him specifically how to save money on his next production. Would you see if he's interested in knowing more?"
- Make sure you rehearse your technique. You might find it helpful to script your calls or at least the answers to your prospect's most frequently asked questions. Having your notes in front of you can help you get over the anxiety of phone calls. Don't forget your benefits. Put your services and offers in perspective and build some anticipation, like, "There are three ways I can save you some money fast. First . . . " Next, elaborate on your offer. Also, consider recording a few calls and then listen to them again later. You'll see where you succeeded and perhaps where you may have failed. You can learn quickly from this method.
- Talk only a small part of the time, under 30%. Listening to your clients and prospects is essential. If you give them the chance, they will tell you their problems and concerns. Now it's up to you to use this information to position yourself and show how you can help.
- Make sure you use verbal cues while you listen. Say things such as, "I see," "I understand," "very interesting," "really," "tell me more," and other phrases that suggest your interest. This is the verbal equivalent of nodding.
- If the prospect says they don't need your services now, counter with a statement that reflects you're ready when they are. "You have my material. Why don't you keep it with your budget files, and the next time a project comes your way, call me and I'll quote you my best price for original music services. Just because we can't work together right now doesn't mean I can't help you in the future."
- Some prospects may tell you they are already satisfied with their present music supplier just to get you off the phone. Don't be discouraged. Ask them how or why they are happy. How has their current music house earned their business? Perhaps you'll discover a niche or service you provide that they are not getting right now. That gets your foot in the door and can lead to bigger projects.
- If the prospect sounds interested or almost interested, but you don't feel comfortable springing too much on them, try simply asking, "What's next?" or "What do you need from me right now?"
- Even if they request your promotional material, don't just drop it on them. If they persist, trying to end the call, tell them you need more information to better tailor your presentation. Try to set a meeting. "Instead of mailing my tape, how about if I come by on Friday, say 3:00, and we can go through it together?"
- Follow up any telephone contact with a letter. This

letter should outline the points discussed during your telephone meeting. Also, provide any other answers or sales material you promised the person during your call.

• Not every call will result in a sale (duh)! Every time you dial, you are moving one step closer to selling your music. Don't stop or give up. Get a tough skin, persist, pick up that phone, and start selling. And should you get discouraged, remember these immortal words from Sir Winston Churchill: "Never give in, never, never, never, never."

While on the phone, use the active listening techniques described earlier. Pretend the person is right in front of you and talk to them directly. You'll probably have many telephone meetings, so practice using the phone. The best resource to help you improve your skills is *99 Ways to Sell More by Phone* (Art Sobczak. Business by Phone Inc.; 5301 S. 144th St., Omaha, NE 68137; [402] 895-9399). I love this little booklet. Though the title says telephone selling—and you will sell your music by phone—the advice is applicable for most face-to-face selling situations, too. I keep this resource in my briefcase and review it before *every* client meeting.

CLIENT KEEP IN TOUCH

Getting new clients is difficult. Keeping your current clients is crucial to your success. Businesses lose customers every day, and the major cause is lack of attention on the part of the seller. What this means is that you must build a strong relationship with your clients from the very beginning, and you must continue to reinforce your commitment to them through carefully controlled promotional efforts. By keeping in contact with and responding to client demands, you will win their loyalty. If you don't do this, they will walk. It's a sad fact of life, but it's true.

Follow the program outlined above and continue using it on hot prospects and clients as long as you are in business. This plan works. It keeps your name alive; reminds client and prospects of your work; and keeps them informed about what you are doing, your successes, and how you can help them.

You must work very hard to gather names, interest the individuals sufficiently to turn them into prospects, and further interest them to turn them into paying clients. Then you must motivate them regularly so they buy from you again. Selling additional products and services to current clients is far easier than getting new business.

You must do exceptional work and make sure they know it. You must tell them that you're always ready to help them on a moment's notice. Keep your clients and your hot prospects happy. Always! Once you get clients, you want to do two things:

• Keep them for life.
• Use them to get more and better clients.

Don't forget to invite hot prospects and clients to keep in touch regularly as well. Give them special offers and discounts, and always send them your latest, greatest music (update that demo at least once each year!). I also make it a point to send them reprints of my articles and copies of my booklets. And, individually, if I see something that might interest a hot prospect or client (like an article about them, their latest advertisement, or some information they'd find useful), I send it to them with a note simply saying: *Thought you'd find this interesting. Keep in touch, Jeffrey.*

I do everything—whatever it takes—to keep my clients satisfied. It is a way of doing business that I recommend to you. Why? Because it works. It's how you make the really big money in this business. Care about your clients and do everything possible to make them happy and keep them forever. Make sure you focus on what your clients really need. Handle as much as you can using your personal resources; compose solid, quality music; be dedicated to your clients; and supply them with complete, one-stop service packages at reasonable prices.

IF YOU HATE TO SELL

He who undervalues himself
is justly undervalued by others.
—WILLIAM HAZLITT

Many people are shy about selling. Being in front of an audience is the number one human fear (death is seventh on the list). Nobody likes to make cold calls, and certainly nobody cares for rejection. If you diligently follow these plans, strategies, and develop the proper promotional materials, *people will call you.* That's the whole idea of doing all this preparation. Make sure you promote and market yourself and your music relentlessly. Prospects will seek you out or at least know you when you do call. That makes life easier, and it makes more sales, faster.

Don't worry too much about selling. While I can't say you'll never be in a selling situation, I can say that selling music is not as bad as it sounds. You do good work, don't you? Your demo does demonstrate your talents and abilities, doesn't it? You are passionate about your skills, aren't you? If you answered yes to all these questions, you will have no trouble presenting your music and persuading your prospects to give you work. These are the skills you must master:

- Get comfortable with who you are and what you can do.
- Prepare all the materials you need (tape, brochures, and so forth) in advance.
- Practice making your case. Script your answers to basic questions and rehearse.
- Relax and listen. Your prospects will tell you what they want and need. They either have a problem or want a specific result. You solve that problem or you provide results through your music. When you look at selling this way, it's easy!

NO TRACK RECORD?

Don't worry about not having a track record when you're just starting out. If you're careful, this point rarely comes up in conversation. *Make sure you focus your sales presentations on your prospects.* Don't go in saying I've done this, I've done that. Look them straight in the eyes and say, "Tell me about your latest project and how I can help." If the prospects press for credentials, give them a sample of your work and say, "Here's a record of my skills. I'm currently building relationships with production companies and ad agencies in town and would welcome the opportunity to serve you."

Make sure you bring other music and material to meetings that clearly demonstrate your skills. If you ask questions in advance, you'll have an idea of what your prospect has in mind. Or perhaps you'll feel inspired and whip something up for your meeting. Say: "After we talked on the phone, I composed a rough sketch of what I thought you wanted for this project. May I play it to you?" Get the idea? Position yourself as the consummate professional, ready, willing, and able to help prospects and clients.

CHOOSING YOUR MARKETING OR SALES ASSOCIATE

By now you know many of the tasks you must perform to make money scoring soundtracks and jingles. Maybe you don't possess the skills or have the time to oversee all these marketing functions. Or maybe you just want someone else to handle your sales. There are several ways you can pass on the marketing and selling so you can concentrate on music.
- Try adding a partner who complements your skills. You compose and record while your partner markets, sells, and runs the business end.
- Taking on an employee is a big step; consider an independent representative to promote your business instead. This person would market, promote, and sell your music for you in return for either a salary, commission, or both. Commissions can range from 15-25% or more. While you might wince at

such a fee (that's why I suggest you do everything yourself), it is fair for the work they do.
- Create an informal network. Invite people to recommend you. Supply them with the materials they need to promote you—several copies of your demo and marketing kit are best. In return for a commission, they do all the selling. This differs from the single rep above in that you can have several people working for you at the same time. Most independent reps will not like this situation; they don't like competing in small markets. However, friends, associates, and others may enjoy helping you while making some money at the same time.
- Make a deal with a production company or ad agency. If they recommend you to all their clients, you give them a discount or commission when you deliver the tracks. This is an ideal situation. As your business gets going, you will find a few people who adore your work and who will give you every original music opportunity that comes their way. Cultivate these clients and give them something (a discount) in return for their loyalty and confidence.

Make sure you get a contract with all your independent reps and dealers. Model it after the concept presented later in the "Taking Care of Business" chapter. It should cover what they do, what you do, what they make, how you determine their fee, etc. You should also add independent contractor language and maybe even a noncompete clause to prevent your reps from selling for other music houses.

FINDING YOUR INDEPENDENT REP

Before hiring an outsider, try handling your own marketing and sales. You'll gain valuable insight, and you'll learn what you must do—and exactly what it takes—to sell your music services. That knowledge will help you choose the right associates who can assist you in reaching your goals. Make sure you read the "Choosing Your Advisors" section (also in the "Taking Care of Business" chapter) before adding any advisor, especially a sales rep, to your business network. Meanwhile, here are some guidelines for you to follow:
- Ask your other business colleagues to recommend someone. Most reps have several (noncompeting) clients they sell for. Some even provide package deals by representing a production company, a writer, a post-production facility, and a music house all at once.
- Ask local professional associations such as your Musician's Union, Chamber of Commerce, or Advertising Council for names of possible sales representatives.

- Your local college can sometimes provide you with student interns who want to learn more out in the real world. Contact the business or student resources department.
- Take out an ad in the trade or local press:

  Sales rep wanted for growing music house. Must be master promoter, publicist, and salesperson. Industry contacts a big plus! Commission only. Contact [your info here].

MORE MARKETING HELP

Knowledge is of two kinds. We know a subject ourselves, or we know where we can find information upon it.
—DR. SAMUEL JOHNSON

Learning what you need to market and promote your music services can sometimes seem overwhelming, but it is vitally important to your inevitable success. Don't take it lightly. Thankfully, there's plenty of help out there for you. First, a good chunk of this book is devoted to helping you organize, start, and continue your promotional efforts. Study it carefully and refer to *How to Make Money Scoring Soundtracks and Jingles* periodically. Second, here are several resources to consult that are absolutely the best books written on the subject. They are not dry textbooks, either. These books are fun, practical resources that will start working for you the minute you pick them up, and they'll serve as essential references for many years to come.

- *Guerrilla Marketing, Guerrilla Marketing Attack, Guerrilla Marketing Weapons,* and *Guerrilla Marketing Excellence,* Jay Conrad Levinson. Houghton Mifflin Company; 2 Park St., Boston, MA 02108. Though this series is filled more with what to do than how to do it, I still recommend it for the exhaustive lists of inexpensive, creative, and proven marketing tools that you can use to promote your commercial music business.
- *Finding Your Niche: Marketing Your Professional Services,* Bart Brodsky and Janet Geis. Community Resource Institute Press; 1442-A Walnut St., Berkeley, CA 94709. Here's the ideal primer to marketing any professional service. I recently discovered this helpful book and adore its basic, practical hints.
- *No More Cold Calls: The Complete Guide to Generating—and Closing—All the Prospects You Need to Become a Multimillionaire by Selling Your Service,* Dr. Jeffrey Lant. 50 Follen St., Suite 507, Cambridge, MA 02138; (617) 547-6372. This is a general business book, but I assure you that the information contained in these pages is completely applicable to selling music and music-related products and services.

You now know *what* you must do and *how* to turn your music into cash. Next, you will learn how to bring this material together into the moneymaking promotional material that helps you sell your soundtrack music and jingles.

CHAPTER 7

The Secrets to Moneymaking Sales Letters, Brochures, and Other Promotional Material

No man but a blockhead ever wrote except for money.

—*Dr. Samuel Johnson*

Why is writing sales copy so important? Because you will communicate to both your prospects and your clients through the written word. Learning these secrets will greatly improve your chances for success. Plus, if you're smart, you'll apply these principles to all your sales situations—on paper, in your ads, on the phone, and in person—and use them to sell!

This chapter concentrates on preparing promotional documents and writing the kind of copy that gets results. This book, the only one of its kind, will tell you precisely how to present your music services in ways that get people to respond. No theory here, just proven methods from my successful campaigns that *work*. These methods, of course, are applicable to all your communications. Remember, everything you do is a marketing opportunity—even a thank you note. Read this carefully and consult the other resources I recommend; you won't regret it. You'll stop sending out promotional communications that fail, and you'll start bringing in clients that pay you for your music.

COPYWRITING ESSENTIALS

Like you, I get tons of marketing and advertising material every single day. Sadly, most pieces are disappointing and useless. Why? Because they don't do what they are created to do: sell. There is no other reason to produce a sales letter, brochure, ad, flyer, or newsletter other than to motivate people to take some action. That action is usually to buy something, specifically, to buy your music products and services.

The fundamental flaw is often the copy. Every day I see copy that offers no clear benefits. It concentrates on the seller, *not* the buyer. Or it's confusing, which makes it difficult to buy, and on and on. The industry is filled with amateurs who copy what others are doing. Since 99% of marketing fails to produce any results, these people are perpetuating a system that only wastes money and fills the world with hype and egotistical images. It's easy to spend your money on an expensive ad that says: "We're great, buy our product or service." I see this all too often. I've found there is no shortage of ego or bottomless checkbooks to produce the marketing we see every day.

But not you, right? You have this guide to show you how to prepare promotional documents and write the kind of copy that gets results. Stop sending out letters and other communications that fail. Start bringing in clients that pay you for your original music. If you want to motivate the largest number of prospects to buy what you offer and spend the least amount of money doing it, follow these specific guidelines.

PREPARE TO WRITE

The key to success in your promotional communications is to focus only on your prospects. This means you must write benefit-rich copy that speaks to your prospects and answers their questions. Far too much marketing centers on the seller (you), when it should be focusing on your prospects (them). Your clients aren't interested in you or your goods and services. These people simply don't care about you; they care about themselves.

Their attitude is simple: "What's in it for me?" It's essential that you provide the answer in your sales letters, brochures, postcards, proposals, contracts, ads, articles—indeed, every promotional piece you use. Good sales copy convinces people to take the next step. To do that, it must be about your prospects and what they want to achieve. Talking solely about yourself is foolish, arrogant, and wasteful. So stop it!

Here's how to master the copywriting process. First, ignore all the features of your products and services, because your clients don't care about features. They are only interested in benefits and results: *their* benefits and *their* results, not yours! You must sell benefits, not features. People don't buy shampoo; people buy silky, smooth, manageable, beautiful, and clean hair, like the model in the commercial has. What are your client prospects looking for? Benefits and results are what people really buy.

I bet right now you're saying, "But I just want to sell some music and make some good money doing it!" Of course you do. And I want to help. But you must realize that people don't just buy your music. *They buy what your music does for them!* If your music makes their production better, if it helps deliver their message more effectively, if it helps them sell more products and services, if it helps them achieve the results they want, they'll be happy to sign the check. When you help make their program a success, they achieve all these benefits and more. That's why you must turn every feature into a tangible benefit. Do your sales letters, brochures, ads, and such promote these tangible benefits? Or do you waste money droning on and on about features?

Another important tactic is to shift your position to, "You have a problem (or a need) that I understand. By working with me, we can solve that problem (or fulfill that need) together. Here's precisely how . . . "

Do you see the difference? Hear the difference? Feel the difference? Begin thinking about your clients. What do they want? How does your music benefit them? Follow this advice and you will save tons of money that you would otherwise waste on promotional gambits and materials that don't work and won't sell.

Never forget this next point. Marketing is about action and motivating people to take action. Ultimately, the action you want—the only reason to develop promotional copy—is to get more people to buy. Your objective is to sell and nothing more. Though it may take several steps before they dig deep into their pockets, load each step with benefits designed solely to motivate your clients and prospects to take action, to move one step closer to buying.

If your marketing documents don't do this, you need to fix them so they do. It's not enough to say how great you are. You must prove it by showing your client prospects how they can benefit from using you. You also need to motivate your client prospects to do something right away (either call, ask for more information, or buy). When you simply list the kinds of things you do and don't explain what they really mean to the client, you're creating the worst kind of marketing drivel. Don't follow what you see others do. Most marketing communications produced by so-called professionals fail miserably to do what is necessary. The world is filled with bad marketing. It's easy to spot the poor pieces, but the good examples are rare.

FOUR ESSENTIAL STARTING POINTS

There are four essential starting points to every promotional piece you create. They are:
- Turn every feature into a benefit.
- Create a compelling offer.
- Tell them to do something, to take action right away.
- Tell them what will happen if they don't do that something.

◗ TURNING FEATURES INTO BENEFITS

Features are descriptions of things. Benefits highlight what people get and the results they achieve by using your music services. Benefits sell. The easiest way to illustrate this point is with concrete examples.
- Feature: We have low prices. **Benefit:** You save money.
- Feature: We offer fast turnaround. **Benefit:** You save time.
- Feature: We use digital audio recording. **Benefit:** You get clear sound that's free of those annoying clicks, scratches, and hiss that interfere with your message.
- Feature: We are a full-service studio. **Benefit:** You

save time and money! And you get exactly what you need to handle every facet of sound for your project. Right here. Right now.

Don't say, "We have state-of-the-art equipment," because the best answer to that statement is, "So what?" Ask yourself why your client cares. What does having this mean to them? How do they benefit? What are the results? The easiest way to turn any feature into a benefit is to add two words: "so that." Case in point:

We use an electronic orchestra to produce any sound, real or imagined, so that not only do you save money, but you also get the original music score you need to enhance your production and deliver your message effectively.

Do you hear how a simple rephrasing shifts the focus away from the feature (electronics) to both the benefit (saving money) and the result (delivering the message effectively)? Moving the focus from you and your work to your client prospect's point of view is essential. Now, to really make this paragraph shine, switch the benefit and the feature and tighten the copy.

You get the original music score you need to deliver your message effectively. Enhance your project using my electronic orchestra to produce any sound, real or imagined.

You must put your music services in perspective by changing "we have" and "it has" descriptions to "you get" this benefit and "you get" these results. Banish the self-centered marketing, and focus only on what your clients and prospects want to achieve. And then give it to them! You must carefully define your benefits, give them credence, and provide tangible results. For example:
• Bad: "We compose quality music." Huh? Quality what? How? Why? Prove it!
• **Better**: "You get exactly the music you want or your money back!" See the difference? Feel the difference?

Don't think for one minute that this applies only to your advertising and promotional material. This approach is mandatory for creating effective marketing documents. You must do this all the time: in letters, on the phone, in brochures, as part of your publicity, and so forth. Remember everything you do is a sales opportunity. This attitude must prevail in all your communications, written and oral. It's crucial to successful marketing and your profitable business.

The best word to use in any marketing document is "you!" Talk to your client prospects one-to-one. If your marketing sounds like a letter to a friend

from a friend, it's on its way to being effective and getting prospects to respond. And avoid the innocuous "we." Write: "You get this" or "I can help you"!

♦ CREATE AN OFFER

You must have a reason to produce any marketing piece. Your sales letters and brochures shouldn't just sit around and die a slow death. Make them interactive and require some sort of action. Ask yourself what the purpose of each is and what you want to happen next. It is essential to make an offer if you want your promotions to generate business. Offers can be hard (buy now) or soft (more info). Have the client prospect call for a free price quote, a product sample, a free information kit, or a copy of your latest how-to booklet. Stress the benefits of having that item, not the item itself. Make your offer something that motivates further action.

And please don't send out a piece that whispers, "We're here, call when you want." That's a waste of your prospect's time and your money. Your documents must scream, **"You get this benefit now!"**

♦ TELL THEM TO DO SOMETHING AND EXPLAIN WHAT WILL HAPPEN IF THEY DON'T

Make sure you include a call to action in every promotional document. Don't rely on your prospect's knowing what to do. Explain precisely what you want to happen next:

When you want this result, pick up the phone and call me right now and get what you want today.

Those who want what you offer will call. At that point, you can ask questions and position yourself to help. You control the marketing and selling process. You're in the driver's seat at all times. That is how it *must* be.

Also, you should say what will happen if they don't respond to your offer. Make sure you tell your client prospect that unless they act right away they will lose something or fail to get your benefit:

Stop paying too much for music. Call right now and I'll send you my booklet, How to Get Low-Cost Original Music for All Your Productions. *It's a $12.95 value, yours FREE if you call now. Hurry—this offer expires soon! Don't spend another penny on music until you read this money saving book."*

Do you see the benefits? Do you feel the push? If they act now, they get this premium and the benefit it promises. If they fail to respond, it will cost them money.

◆ THE MEANING OF FREE

You can never rely on the word "free" alone to motivate prospects. The free thing must have value—a defined and explicit benefit. Such as this:

> Save money when you use original music for all your productions. My FREE tape shows you how. A $12.95 value, yours free if you call today.

Understand the difference? Which would you rather get: A free demo or the secret to saving money? It's simple: Sell the sizzle (what's in it for me), not the steak (free tape).

COPY MAKEOVERS

Here are a few bad examples and how to correct them into copy that sells.

> Introducing the new X10 Clean Air Machine. Johnson Heating and Air is proud to announce our newest product.

The ad goes on to describe every X10 feature. It's not until the last paragraph that we get even the slightest indication of a benefit:

> Eliminates bad odors, pets, and cigarette smoke.

Despite the grammatical error (the writer probably meant the X10 eliminates pet odors, not pets), this is the only benefit of the X10. So tell me: Are you interested in the X10 or are you interested in eliminating offensive odors? Unfortunately, the writer of this ad forgot the copywriting fundamentals: Sell the benefit (eliminate odors), not the feature (the X10). So another tree was wasted on useless marketing.

Here's another bad piece that typifies exactly how *not* to grab attention. Instead of concentrating on a sure attention grabber like benefits, many amateur copywriters resort to futile, manipulative devices. Here's the headline for a video equipment dealer:

> FREE BEER!!

The rest of the ad has absolutely nothing to do with beer or how to get it free. This stupid, misleading headline doesn't catch attention, it's just insulting. This clever copywriter decided to ignore the first rule of moneymaking ad writing: offer a clear benefit and you always get your prospect's attention. Focus on features or try stupid tricks, and your marketing will fail and waste your money. It's that simple. Substituting a real, tangible benefit will increase response:

> Save money! We'll beat anybody's price . . . or it's free.

I hope you see the difference. Marketing is about action: save money, close sales, stop wasting time, etc. Get attention by offering these benefits in your headlines and throughout your printed pieces. Create interest by showing every benefit your prospect gets. Stress limited availability by telling them they must act now to get the benefit they want. And make sure you say *exactly* what they need to do next. Tell them to pick up the phone and call *now.*

Which do you think is more persuasive? Pain or gain? The loss of a negative (paying too much) or the promise of a positive (saving money)?

> Stop paying too much for original music.

or

> Save money on your next music package.

Pain is *always* the better motivator. We are emotional human beings, after all! Grabbing attention through price (saving money) or greed (making money) is a sure-fire way to motivate.

I recently opened my mail to find a brochure from a copywriter. On the cover was only his name and the words "freelance writer." Opening the first flap, my eyes focused on the first word "I." The entire piece was devoid of benefits and never addressed my needs or concerns. After laughing my way through this waste of paper, I declared his drivel to be the prototypical, "I'm great. Just look how great I am. Hire me," so-called promotional piece. What's in it for me? Nuthin'! And to the circular file it went.

Every marketing document needs clear benefits, an offer, and a call for action. Don't forget this. Stop talking about yourself and start talking about your buyers. Stop selling features and start selling benefits and results. Stop this insanity now or you are wasting your money. Heed this advice and you will sell more music. Follow these guidelines and thrive; ignore them and suffer. You must master this skill; it is crucial to your success.

YOUR BASIC FORMAT TO FOLLOW

When you prepare a sales letter, brochure, or other promotional piece, direct it at your prospects and make sure it follows this simple format:

- You need original music or you hate library music.
- You can get the solution we provide right now.
- This is the ideal way to get what you need. (Include your many benefits.)
- Getting the results of original music is well worth the money.
- Our track record proves we can help. (Include third-party validation in the form of reviews, recommendations, testimonials, etc.)
- Here are the methods we use to help you. (Include

details of how you work and any other useful information your prospects need to make their buying decision.)
- Make an offer that motivates immediate response.
- Tell them to act now and get all these benefits.

CRUCIAL PARTS TO EVERY MARKETING DOCUMENT

There are seven major parts to every promotional piece:
- Headline
- Problem statement
- Solution
- Benefits of solution
- Offer
- Time limit
- Post script (P.S.)

Use the headline to grab attention. Place it big and bold in the upper right-hand corner of the first page or on the cover of a brochure. State the problem and propose your solution (your music services, of course). Explain all your benefits and make an offer. Put time limits on all offers to encourage prospects to respond quickly. Use the post script (the most read part of the page) to restate all that came before in a concise summary. Keep in mind that when your prospects look at your document, they usually read the headline and then the post script. These two items must work in tandem to tell the whole story with just enough prodding to get the prospect to look at all the other words in the letter. Use italics, bolding, and uppercase letters to emphasize important sales points, too.

Here's a hint: Your best weapon is a personal letter from you to your prospect printed on your letterhead. See the "Samples" section for more specific details. Read the copy carefully to understand what I mean. The example letters are warm, alive, pulsating, pushing, and prodding; they motivate the prospect to action and are, of course, loaded with benefits . . . your client's benefits! You would do well to follow these models.

PUT YOUR CREDENTIALS IN PERSPECTIVE

Confidence is a plant of slow growth.
—WILLIAM PITT

- -

Throw out your resume! They're useless. Most only highlight the past and usually in ways that are dreadfully meaningless. While your credentials are important, you need to give them some significance. People who buy your music don't care what you've done or where you've been unless you put your credentials in

context and tell them *exactly* and *explicitly* how they benefit from your experience and skills. All that matters is what you've achieved for others and how your success with one client can possibly bring success to the next. Your formal degrees and your client list do little to impress, let alone motivate, prospects. These facts are features; they're important but not crucial. Only compelling benefits persuade prospects to buy what you sell. Commit yourself to translating all features into benefits and supplying significance to all facts.

Let's say that you have an M.A. in Music. How do you transform that to a benefit? You don't. The fact is superfluous. You have a degree. So what? What does that mean? How does your client benefit? While it's a nice feature, don't lead with it. By all means, *include* your credentials, but don't let them be the main focus of a promotional piece. Use your background to support and complement other more tangible benefits. Your track record of success is more important than any credential.

Being easy and convenient to work with, meeting deadlines, staying on budget, keeping clients (and clients' clients) happy, writing solid music tracks, following instructions, delivering what you promise, charging fairly—these are the credentials that matter. Of course, simply stating that you are creative is not the same thing as proving your originality. Your demo must show that you are competent and creative, and your marketing kit and promotional efforts must reinforce this message. Repeatedly. Client recommendations that highlight these elements will always serve you better—get you more cash for your music tracks—than any single credential.

Here's an example of a so-called marketing letter that relies on "me" marketing. Compare it to the "you" promotional materials in the "Samples" section. This is a real letter that arrived in my mailbox. Of course, the names were changed to protect the innocent.

Dear Jeffery [sic]:
Let me introduce myself. My name is Cole. I have an MA in Music from Bookhouse University. I can play flute, violin, drums, and keys. My background is writing music. Maybe you need some for one of your projects. I'd be happy to send you my demo. I hope you understand that being right out of school, my tape doesn't have any professional experience on it. This is mostly some rock songs I did with my band. It's probably not the kind of thing you usually need, but let me tell you I can write just about anything in any style. I hope you give me a chance to prove myself soon. Give me a call if you want to hire me to compose for you. Here's my business card for you [sic] *files. If you have any questions, just call.*

Did you count the number of "I"s and "me"s? Would you be persuaded by such an amateur letter? Unfortunately, I see examples like this all the time passing for promotional literature.

THE WORST FORM OF ACCOUNTING

History is bunk.
—HENRY FORD

History is often useless. Wait, hear me out. What happened in the past has absolutely no significance, *unless* you apply the knowledge gained to the present and future. Case in point: One cold February afternoon, my accountant informed me that I had underpaid my taxes and would have to pay the endearing IRS nearly $4000! After the initial shock, my answer was: "Where the heck were you in September when I could still have done something about this?!"

That was my introduction to something I like to call the "worst form of accounting." This is when someone says, "You lost a million bucks last year," instead of, "If things continue as they are, you *will* lose a million bucks this year." The former is fixated on the past; it's reactive. It's someone making everything up as they go along. The latter plans accordingly and uses information to make informed decisions—before it's too late! Collecting information and then doing nothing with it until it is too late to do something about it is the worst form of accounting. This theorem applies to everything you do, not just financial matters. Make sure you are proactive.

Learn, friend, learn. Learn as Scrooge did in Dickens' classic tale. Don't worry about how things might be. Focus on how things could and should be. There is nothing more unfortunate than history you do not use to your advantage. You will make mistakes. Count on it. Chalk them up to experience and learn from these misfortunes. Dedicate yourself to using your knowledge to improve your business, music, and life. And never be seduced by the worst form of accounting.

AT YOUR MOST PERSUASIVE

As you already know, grabbing attention through either price (saving money) or greed (making money) are sure-fire ways to motivate. However, there are other compelling arguments you can use to sell your original music.

◗ UNIQUENESS
Audiovisual producers love being creative and the first to do something nobody else has done before. Original music adds a special edge to their project.

◗ ENHANCING IMAGES
From the earliest days of film, music has accompanied images. Sound is one-half of every audiovisual presentation and music obviously plays a very important role in every soundtrack. Using music effectively makes productions stronger. Dave West, *X-Files* lead mixer, recently said in a *Mix* interview, "Music is king. And truly music can add more to a picture in any case than a gunshot ever will."

Jingles also add a musical identity to products, services, and companies. Sadly, many producers don't take as much care with their soundtracks as they do with their visual images.

◗ PERSONAL STAMP
When directors choose original music, they personalize their production. Most recognize that when composer and director share the same vision, the resulting music—indeed, the project as a whole—is that much better.

◗ POWER AND IMPACT
To quote the American composer Aaron Copland:
- *Original music creates a convincing atmosphere of time and place.*
- *Original music underlines elements of character and situation.*
- *Original music provides a neutral background filler and helps bridge scenes.*
- *Original music creates a sense of continuity.*
- *Original music helps build to dramatic finality. (Even a corporate documentary has inherent drama, dramatic continuity, and resolution.)*

◗ OTHER ADVANTAGES
Here are benefits you can use to persuade your prospects to buy your services:
- Original music adds a unique and exciting musical identity to every production.
- Original music is flexible, versatile, and conforms to the project's exact needs.
- Original music precisely matches screen action, drama, and emotion.
- Original music enhances and supports visual imagery.
- Original music increases the impact of every production.
- Original music makes the message more memorable.

Original music plays a very important role in today's audiovisual presentations. Great music won't save a bad production—it's not a panacea—but it can do what no other soundtrack element can do. Producers want your help, through your original musical contribution, to make a positive difference in how their audience responds. And that means a better, more effective production!

Most audiovisual producers simply don't care about drum beats, MIDI, equipment lists, and all that stuff (they're just more "me" marketing features). They want a feeling. They want a certain mood. They want to entertain, amuse, motivate, sadden, persuade, induce, titillate, depress, scare, annoy, educate, and, often, **sell!**

Can your original music fulfill these requests? Do your marketing materials promote these benefits? These strengths are what you must emphasize when you sell your music.

Also, don't talk about styles too much. Despite the clichés, the distinctions are getting narrower everyday. What is jazz? What is rock? Is it instrumentation? Or is it attitude? For example, your client says, "Give me dark and ominous."

- One composer writes for cello and bassoon
- Another writes analog synth bass drones
- Yet another writes heavy drums swimming in reverb
- I write a children's lullaby—innocent and light—a complete counterpoint to dark and ominous and maybe even scarier. In the right context, this approach may just work.

THE MOST IMPORTANT CLIENT CONCERNS

Why do people buy? This is better put as: *What* do people buy? They buy:

- The merits of your music products, services, and company as a whole. Do you possess the musical skills they need?
- How responsive you are to their needs and what you do for them before, during, and after each project. How you provide outstanding customer service, ongoing support, and stand behind your music services with a guarantee that you will deliver what you promise.
- How fast and efficiently you deliver your products and services and meet deadlines.
- Your benefits outweighing the cost. Price is not as important as the value of what you produce. Are you the best deal?
- The dependability of your music products, services, and company. Do you deliver as promised? Don't forget trust. Your marketing must promote your reputation.
- How easy it is to work with you, your convenient location, hours, etc. How ready you are when they need you.
- The diverse service, product, pricing, and payment options you offer, including musical styles and rights.
- Your past successes, years in business, testimonials, and recommendations.

- Your attention to details and specific requests. Being friendly and understanding. Don't forget: People patronize a business they are familiar with. While you don't need to be friends, you should be personable.
- Other intangibles. Some clients just have a gut feeling. It can be an overall impression or a subtlety. Make sure you build relationships, act professionally, and make a difference in your client's life. Give them what they want. Always.

As you develop your promotional material, you must provide tangible benefits that address these concerns.

TIPS AND TRICKS TO IMPROVE YOUR COPY

I forget the actual source, but someone once said that you should write to *express* not to *impress*. That is very good advice. Here's some more:

- Talk *to* your prospects, not at them. Use simple, everyday language; and write short, action-packed copy that moves from one place to the next.
- Cut to the chase. Don't spend too much time on useless background material. State your case up front, make your point, and present your argument. Remember, your job is to motivate further action, not educate or pontificate.
- Be specific, realistic, and accurate.
- Use action words and simple words over their longer counterparts. Take heed and follow the words of Sir Winston Churchill, "Broadly speaking, the short words are the best, and the old words best of all."
- In the battle between intellectual, rational thought and emotion, emotion always wins. Emotional appeals are always stronger and more effective than logical pleas.
- People would rather remove a pain than potentially gain something. Address that with a strong headline: "Stop wasting your money on music that bores your audience. Get original music that excites and motivates."
- Avoid hype like the plague. If you can defend your claim, it's not hype. If you can't defend your claim, it's not hype either—it's lying.
- Don't exaggerate, try to impress, criticize, use clichés, or ridicule. Also, use humor carefully, because it can backfire and ruin your intentions.
- Marketing and promotion is about "when" not "if." Use it this way: "When you want to save money on your next jingle, call me . . . "

Follow these copywriting guidelines and thrive; ignore them and suffer. You must master this skill—it's crucial to your success. Here are the resources you need to use before you write another word:

- *Cash Copy: How to Offer Your Products and Services So Your Prospects Buy Them . . . NOW*, Dr. Jeffrey Lant. 50 Follen St., Suite 507, Cambridge, MA 02138. I *highly* recommend this book; it is the best book on copywriting. If you are struggling to create the marketing documents you need to run your business better and more profitably, this has exactly what you need.
- *The Copy Workshop Workbook*, Bruce Bendinger. The Copy Workshop; 2144 N. Hudson, Chicago, IL 60614. The second edition was just released.
- *Words That Sell*, Richard Bayan. Contemporary Books; 180 N. Michigan Ave., Chicago, IL 60601. A useful thesaurus of strong copy.

ALL INITIAL DOCUMENTS YOU NEED

Here is a partial list of all the marketing documents you need to develop:

- Introductory sales letter
- Sales letters with different offers
- Basic sales brochure
- Success letters or project listings highlighting your recent accomplishments
- Cover letter to those who respond to your initial contact
- Thank you notes to follow up meetings
- Letters of agreement
- Contracts
- Marketing kit with biography, client list, description of services, pricing guide, article samples, and your demo tape
- Other information designed to help your clients recognize their problems and promote you as the solution to those problems

A WORD OR TWO ABOUT PRESENTATION

Your promotional material often makes the first impression *before* your tape can go to work, so present it well. Make sure everything you send is neat, organized, and well-written. Keep your presentations simple and uncluttered and use clean, readable typefaces. Avoid fancy typefaces that are difficult to decipher. Dot matrix printing can look shoddy—get a better printer. Don't send handwritten letters; use a typewriter until you can afford the computer. Have brochures and so forth professionally typeset. Laser printing is fine—anything else looks unprofessional.

Print all marketing materials on your letterhead (unless you opt for a small brochure). Make sure you include your complete address and telephone num-ber on *every* piece (don't forget your area code). Make every item tidy, professional, and focused on your client's needs.

Don't worry about having some fancy four-color brochure. You want your material to be read, kept, referred to, and used. Many corporate accounts expect a brochure of some kind; the marketing kit fulfills this requirement and much more.

Don't forget to include your killer demo, of course! Spare no expense making your music sound fantastic. Your promotional materials must tell and sell, but the ultimate seller, the bottom line, is you and your music. Remember that good music and a great price don't sell, per se. Prospects must see the value of your service and that you can live up to what you promise You must instill confidence that you can do the job right. Sometimes that means explaining in detail. This is why you need other materials to accompany your tape.

One bit of caution. It's very easy to look good in print. With preprinted papers and design software, even the smallest business can get a Fortune 500 image. But don't neglect the most important—dare I say crucial?—element: strong copy. Stunning design and vibrant colors will never miraculously turn boring words into dazzling sales copy. Use these tips diligently or get help from a professional copywriter who can transform your promotional communications into ones that increase your leads and sales significantly.

PUTTING ALL THIS TO WORK

Since this chapter is about writing promotional copy successfully, let's apply what you've learned to some real documents. In the "Samples" section are the ready-to-use marketing and promotional documents you need for your commercial music business. You will find this material helpful, useful, and profitable. Notice that the tone speaks directly to prospects; each item makes an offer and asks for a response. The essentials are here, along with some good strategies for making your services attractive. Feel free to use these formats as a guide for your own letters and marketing materials, but don't use them word for word. Make them your own. Adapt this material to your particular situation. Add your personal information, customize as needed, and print on your letterhead. Once you've been scoring soundtracks and jingles for some time, you will have much of your own material to use. Meanwhile, these examples will get you started. Use them!

CHAPTER 8

Overlooked Promotional Opportunities

All publicity is good,

except an obituary notice.

—*Brendan Behan*

We've talked about marketing and sales, now let's concentrate on the middle parts of my Business Success MAPS.

USING PUBLICITY EFFECTIVELY

To make your commercial music business successful and profitable, you must master publicity. That means taking steps to present your business image, people, products, and services to the world, usually through free media exposure. However, publicity's ideal function is to position you as a leader—*the* recognized expert—in your field. Establishing and using your expert status is a certain way to make your business boom. Use publicity to demonstrate your problem-solving skills, increase awareness, and add prestige to your name, and it's all through free promotion. Here are the methods that build your credibility and expert status:

• News releases
• Articles and columns
• Reports and booklets
• Newsletters
• Speaking at and conducting seminars
• The Internet. The Web is, by far, the perfect marriage of publicity and advertising. Here you can both promote and sell your music services. This is so important that I've devoted a whole chapter just to this subject.

There are two kinds of publicity: The stuff you send to clients and hot prospects and the information you release to the industry. Publicity is the soft sell part of marketing. You use it to say what you've been up to, detail the results you've achieved, and imply that you can do the same for others. What you are actually doing is packaging your knowledge into several different formats. A speech you gave might make a fine report that could be published as an article and then excerpted in your newsletter.

You have a responsibility to help your clients in any way possible, and that means giving them advice and solving their problems. Use your media releases, articles, columns, newsletters, reports, booklets, speeches, and more to show your clients that you can help them. That is the mark of a true expert: YOU!

LET THE MEDIA PROMOTE YOU

Use the media to promote your products and services by issuing news releases regularly. Ideal topics are new products and services, staff changes, equipment purchases, problems solved, and projects completed. You can also piggy-back on national, state, and local coverage of your topic by being quoted as the expert on the subject. Don't forget to help the media by letting them know you welcome their calls.

There is only one road to success in this arena. The media want problems and solutions to problems. (Some want entertainment, but even most entertaining pieces are slanted at exposing problems or offering possible solutions.) For your promotions to work, you must either expose a problem or offer a solution to an existing problem. To reap the most benefits, you must bring your triumphs to the attention of your market often. Send media releases to your local and trade press a few times each year. Send news, not shameless promotion. For example, send a short bit like this:

> *JEFFREY P. FISHER recently scored the music to XYZ Film's latest documentary about the plight of the homeless. Fisher and other area talent contributed their expertise to the project free of charge.*
>
> *"I saw it as a chance to give something back to the community," said Fisher, who wrote and recorded the score at his project studio. "I hope, in my own little way, that I have helped bring awareness to this very real problem."*

or:

> *FISHER MUSIC SCORES FOR PBS*
>
> *Jeffrey P. Fisher Music got the nod to score the PBS documentary,* Street Smarts: Straight Talk for Kids, Teens, and Parents, *adding theme and dramatic underscore to the crime prevention program, featuring Chicago Police Detective J.J. Bittenbinder. Fisher said this was his favorite musical style to work in and described the score as "dark and ominous."* Street Smarts *airs nationwide on PBS.*

WHAT MEDIA TO APPROACH AND HOW

Unless you are sending an opinion piece or short bit, you should contact the media source before sending any article. Request a sample issue, writer's guidelines, and advertising and subscription information. Once you get this information, you will be able to quickly determine the publication's suitability.

Next, send a query letter to the editor. Describe your article idea, why it's important to the media source's readers, and why you are qualified to write it. Follow up this letter in about ten days. If your article is accepted, the editor will let you know more details about deadlines, format, etc. Instead of payment, you might try swapping the article for ad space. Get your ad to run in a different issue than the article, and you hit your market in two different ways at two different times.

For opinion and news releases, just type the information, double-spaced, on your regular letterhead. Add the title FOR IMMEDIATE RELEASE at the top of the page, and make sure your name and phone number are on the first page.

Whenever you send material for publication, include some of your standard marketing materials, such as your brochure, biography, project listings, and so forth. What you are doing here is creating a media kit comprised of pertinent information about your business. This is similar to your marketing kit for prospects, but it's slanted specifically at the media. Explain in your cover letter that you are open to being interviewed about your work and that you are including this additional material to help the media outlet write or edit a better story. The purpose is to get these people to feature you in an article. This third-party validation of your work is the kind of favorable publicity that money just can't buy.

Remember that the idea is not to write articles and get interviews—you are doing this to generate leads and to make money. You must let the world know you exist, that you have successfully provided music services for others, and that you can and will do the same for others if they'll just pick up the phone and call. This is what effective publicity is all about and what your goal must always be. Here are the best resources for finding possible media to feature you and your work. These are big, expensive books so you should check your local library first.

- *Gale Directory of Publications and Broadcast Media.* Gale Research Inc.; P.O. Box 33477, Detroit, MI 48232; (313) 961-2242. This directory profiles 25,000 magazines and newspapers and 10,000 broadcasters.
- *Standard Periodical Directory.* Oxbridge Communications; 150 Fifth Ave., Suite 302, New York, NY 10011; (212) 741-0231. Simply exhaustive.

WRITING ARTICLES AND OTHER HELPFUL INFORMATION

> *The best way to become acquainted with a subject is to write a book about it.*
> —BENJAMIN DISRAELI

- -

It's very important to help your clients in many different ways. Writing articles and providing helpful (and useful) information to your market serves two purposes:

- You show your knowledge and expertise.
- You get some free publicity and promotion.

The best, most effective articles provide solutions to your client's problems. Each article will show your expert knowledge and position you to help those who need your music. If you have lots of information to share, you might consider becoming a columnist. Having a monthly column in a trade magazine that serves your market adds instant credibility to your name and can set you apart from your competition.

This is an effective way to stay in contact with your prospects. I'll often write an opinion piece to the trade press or a letter to the editor. As long as you're not too cantankerous, you have a good chance of getting your opinion on an issue printed, especially if the subject is relevant. Or I'll write a helpful article about some problem I've solved. I've condensed my booklet, *How to Get Low-Cost Original Music,* into several articles and sent them to be published. The goal here is not to get paid for the article, but to make sure the editor includes your name, address, and telephone number in the article. This way readers can easily contact you.

Since there's no guarantee that your article will be published, it pays to build a good relationship with your local trade press. When you get any media coverage, use reprints in your marketing kit. Add the line, "As seen in *[name of magazine].*" You'll seldom get *direct* work from an article, but it keeps your name alive, builds awareness, shows your expertise, and adds prestige to your name. And the reprints strengthen your promotional material.

WHY PAY FOR PROMOTION WHEN YOU CAN GET IT FREE

Remember, you only have that space because some advertiser wouldn't buy it.
—HERB CAEN

You want your articles, news releases, and other activities published in local and national trade press, major newspapers, small community papers, Chamber of Commerce newsletters, and any other media outlets that serves your target community. There is an amazing amount of free media available to you that you can use to promote your business. You can find the contacts you need by visiting the reference section at your local library or taking a trip to your favorite newsstand. You might want to write for the music press, such as *Transoniq Hacker, Keyboard, Recording, Electronic Musician,* etc. If you have information, tips, techniques, and other music-related activities to share, these magazines can generate some terrific and profitable publicity.

Think of angles and short bits for your stories. For example, "Local composer scores music for PBS special," or "Author donates book to new library." You might want to try opinion pieces like the "Fisher Music Goes Digital" piece in the "Samples" section. Also, "Better Working Relationships" in an earlier chapter was adapted from a problem-solving piece written for clients. Use these examples as the basis for your articles and news releases.

WRITING: ONE STEP BEYOND

The sage never tries to store things up. The more he does for others, the more he has.
—LAO TZU

You may take article writing to the next step by developing a line of reports and booklets designed to help music users achieve the results they want. Nothing builds instant expert status and prestige more than being a published author (I speak from experience). These pieces need not be extravagant. Most reports and booklets are easy to produce. All you need to do is pick a music-related subject that you know and write about it. Use the examples I suggest as guidelines for your own work.

The choice to sell this information or give it away is up to you. Reports and booklets make ideal offers in sales letters and small ads, and they can also give you a reason to issue a news release. Use them as offers, rewards, and premiums to prospects and clients. This strategy is most effective as an incentive when generating prospect leads. You show your expert knowledge while giving away some valuable information. Through your articles, newsletter, reports, and booklets, you *can* help them. But don't forget that talking about music is not the same thing as composing good tracks. All this is in vain if you don't have the chops to do the job right!

PROMOTING THROUGH A FREE CLIENT NEWSLETTER

Sending information to clients and hot prospects through a quarterly newsletter is an ideal sales strategy. My *For Score* newsletter is a two-page letter that talks about my latest projects, gives information about how I can help clients save money, and mentions any special offers, such as discounts, that may be coming up. Throughout the year, I collect material for each issue and use it as a follow-up to clients and hot prospects. It may take a while for you to write, print, and mail something like this, but if you keep it short and simple, it's well worth the effort.

You can easily produce a simple newsletter. This kind of newsletter is nothing more than a personal letter that you send out regularly. Just write a few stories about a recent project or two, add some helpful hints or other pieces of information you've discovered along the way, and do some outright promotion for your work. You can print it on your letterhead and mail it first class to your client and prospect list. Or you can get a little fancier and use desktop publishing to produce a newsletter as I do. I use Microsoft Publisher and my laser printer to create and print my newsletter. I only make as many as I need, and I mail them quarterly. There's an issue in the "Samples" section of this book.

Make sure you include your general service brochure, business card, reprint of an article, or other promotional flyer with the newsletter mailing. You can mail about five sheets of paper for the price of one stamp—that's *ten pages* of information. I don't suggest you send that much material to your prospects, but make sure you have extra promotional material in the envelope anyway.

Your newsletter makes the perfect vehicle for your keep-in-touch program. You can highlight one of your projects and show the *results* you achieved. Be sure to mention that you can get those same results for any client that you work with. For extra credibility, list all the work you've done. You might also include a testimonial or two from satisfied clients (more on them later). This newsletter takes some commitment on your part, but it will work for you if you let it.

USE THE PODIUM TO PROFIT

Public speaking and conducting seminars are both terrific ways to reach your prospects and develop your reputation. You should start small at Chamber of Commerce meetings, work your way into music stores, and graduate to trade shows. Use these speaking engagements to promote yourself as the leader in commercial music production in your area.

A WORD ABOUT WORD OF MOUTH

Do your best work for those who buy, and they'll become your best sales representative. They will go out of their way to tell others what you did for them. Don't go for the quick sale. You should be building clients for life. Work hard to cultivate healthy, long-standing relationships with your clients. Help them in any way you can, and they'll help you in return—by recommending you to other prospects. My friend and *How to Make Money Scoring Soundtracks and Jingles* alumnus, Mary Brooks, offers this piece of advice: "I cannot stress enough the importance of developing long-term relationships with clients. This is where the gigs come and keep coming from. Mailing sales letters and such are the best methods for *starting* discussions, but your business will only prosper when people begin to know and trust you." Thank your clients publicly for their business. Be their best advocate. And let your other promotional gambits—news releases, sales letters, newsletters, ads, etc.—reinforce this message.

Also, ask clients if they know of others who could use your services, have them write testimonials and letters of recommendation for you, and ask if you can use them as references. Give clients incentives, suitable promotional material, or even a few extra business cards to hand out on your behalf. Make sure you foster and encourage this behavior. When they send business your way, thank them with a letter or some other token, like a booklet, article reprint, or discount on a future purchase. Word of mouth marketing is the best there is—it can sustain your business. Of course, you need to get to the level where word of mouth works. Start by using these guidelines and you are well on your way.

GETTING AND USING CLIENT TESTIMONIALS

Inducing clients to say good things about you and your business is essential. A few words from an industry leader will work quite well for you, and you can use these quotations in other promotional documents. But how do you get your clients to write about you? It's simple: Ask them. Just remember that you need *business* references, not personal ones. Specifically:

• Letters of recommendation from past clients
• Testimonials and other useful quotes for including in promotional material
• Past clients that your prospects can call to verify your skills

After you've achieved something significant for clients, ask if they wouldn't mind putting their comments down on paper. Make sure they give you permission to use what they say, and use these words to promote your success to others. I ask my clients to write a letter of recommendation and then use copies of them in my marketing kit or quote specific passages in other sales letters and brochures. You should do the same. This third-party validation of your work is important to easing the fears of prospects who haven't purchased from you before.

Also, to guarantee satisfaction at the end of each project, you should ask the client's opinion about your services. You might consider sending a short survey to past clients asking for feedback about your music, services, and company. This can give you valuable insight. Clients will happily tell you what's right with what you are doing so you can keep on doing it. And they'll tell you what's wrong with your approach, so you can improve, too.

You can fool all the people all the time if the advertising is right and the budget is big enough.

—JOSEPH E. LEVINE

Ads are expensive. And in this business, they rarely pay off. Yellow Page ads are especially worthless. Who looks for a composer in the Yellow Pages? The trade press is your only good advertising place, but often even display ads there don't generate enough response to justify their cost. I'm not a fan of paid advertising, especially when you can get publicity for free and (usually) with a better response, too! I highly recommend using the mostly free marketing avenues already discussed. Why do people continue to waste their precious capital resources on advertising? I suspect there are several reasons:

• Ignorance. Some people don't know any better. They see the big advertisers plopping down millions to sell their gym shoes, soft drinks, cars, and perfumes, so they think they must do the same. Not so, folks.

• Laziness. Advertising is easy. Most other marketing strategies take time and effort. Advertising promises instant results and gratification, but this is a deception.

• Limited resources. A small business must carefully control its marketing budget. When advertising promises a flood of new customers, many (foolishly) put all their money there. Don't be seduced by the dark side, Luke!

Lest you think I'm totally against advertising, I'm not. It has its place, but it's not magic. There are many less expensive, more lucrative opportunities and options for marketing and promotion that work better. If you must advertise, follow these tips:

• Many small ads are better than one big ad. Repetition of your message to your target market is critically important. You must bring your music products and services to their attention repeatedly. You need to repeat your ads to keep your name alive so when prospects need music, they call you first.

• Don't use an ad to sell directly—especially a classified ad. It's hard to sell most products and services from a few lines of copy. Use it to generate sales leads and uncover people interested in your commercial music services. People want complete information before they make their buying decision. Elicit a response from your target market—get them to contact you—and then you can control the marketing process. Once again, focus on your clients and provide them with the results and benefits they will get by using your music services. Advertising works if you use it this way.

The same kinds of offers you use in letters and on the phone will work in an ad. Invite prospects to contact you for more information; offer a free initial consultation; or a free demo, brochure, or booklet. Don't push the item itself; instead stress the benefit of having that item. And don't try to sell your music in an ad. Once you get an inquiry, send your promotional material and do the selling with that. The best ad is simple and packed with benefits. Here's an example:

MAKE BIG MONEY SCORING SOUNDTRACKS AND JINGLES! Turn your music into cash! FREE report: Fisher Creative Group, 323 Inner Circle Drive, Bolingbrook, IL 60490.

This ad is designed to attract people who would benefit from my book. I follow up all inquiries with a sales package. The idea is to do the selling with the subsequent marketing piece, not from the ad directly. A tantalizing benefit (making money) along with a strong offer (free report) creates an ideal small ad. Why do I like classified and small-space ads? They are inexpensive and, when you follow these suggestions, generate tons of leads for your business. Here are the essentials of every good ad:

• Audience identifier
• Main benefit
• Offer
• Necessary details

First start by writing down what you want your ad to say:

Audiovisual producers can save money with their next original music purchase by getting a free consultation with composer Jeffrey P. Fisher. If they call, Jeffrey will provide the details of how to save money and still get original music that works, sounds great, and is affordable.

This ad includes everything that makes a small ad work, but it's too long. So, reduce the needless details to one benefit, the offer, and the follow-up information.

Save money on original music. FREE music planning kit. Call Jeffrey P. Fisher at (630) 378-4109 NOW!

You can skip the audience identifier if your ad appears in a targeted magazine. There's no sense wasting the words "Attention Producers" if the ad is in *Video Producers*. The beauty of regular classified advertising is you can skip most identifiers because your ad will fall under the appropriate classification (business services). That leaves you room to concentrate on benefits. The "Samples" section has additional ads you can adapt and use.

Don't use abbreviations. Whittle down the words to the barest minimum that will present your benefit and make your offer. Don't sacrifice words for clarity, though. And make sure you track all of your advertising. When people call, take a second to ask them how and where they heard of you. Keep a record of their responses so you can see where your money, time, and energy are best spent.

POSTCARDS

What makes a good, strong small ad also makes an ideal postcard. These 3x5" reminders are an inexpensive way to keep your name alive. The postage cost is less than a letter, they're cheap to reproduce, and if they're properly worded, do get prospects to call. Make sure you limit the postcard mailing to a single idea or offer—don't try to cram every last detail into this small space (but don't forget to include your complete address and phone number). Grab attention, state your benefits, and get prospects to take action now.

You might consider the popular double postcard used by many magazines to get subscribers. The double postcard gives you four panels: an outside address panel, two sales panels, and a postcard reply panel. The production and postage costs are less than traditional direct mail and may even work better for you.

NETWORKING FUNDAMENTALS

That's the buzzword everyone uses. The goal is to use casual, personal contact to reach others who could either use your music or know someone who could. As I've said many times before, *everything* you do is a sales opportunity. When you are at music stores, industry events, trade shows, meetings, and more, make sure you have a supply of business cards or other promotional material. It will surprise you when the most mundane circumstance results in a lucrative client. Join local trade organizations and, more importantly, go to the meetings. Talk with everyone you meet and don't be shy about letting people know what you do. It might help if you practice describing your work in 20 words or less:

> *Hi, I'm Jeffrey P. Fisher. I compose music and jingles for commercials and business. What do you do?*

Much of what we've already discussed applies to your networking opportunities. Here are a few more tips:
• Be confident.
• Don't wait for someone to speak to you. Strike up your own conversations.
• Make eye contact and use both verbal ("That's interesting, tell me more," etc.) and nonverbal (nods, smiles, laughs, etc.) cues.
• Carry suitable promotional material, such as business cards or small brochures. Make sure you trade information with the person you're speaking to.
• Use active listening skills and add in humor, kindness, and genuine interest.
• Follow up all business leads with calls or letters. Make sure you allude to your meeting when contacting this lead.

Don't forget family, business contacts, religious affiliations, alumni organizations, schools, civic groups, professional groups, and unions—let *everyone* know you are in business and make sure they know what you do and what kind of clients you are looking for.
• *Power Shmoozing: The New Rules for Business and Social Success*, Terri Mandell. First House Press; 6671 Sunset Blvd. #1525, Los Angeles, CA 90028; (213) 467-2898. Need more help in this important area? Try this wonderful, basic introduction to the fine art of networking.

OPEN HOUSE

If you are in a band or play solo gigs, make sure you invite clients and prospects to your gigs. A great promotional tool that bands and recording studios can really benefit from is to throw a party and invite clients, prospects, fans, family, club owners, and other influential people from your local music market (don't forget the media!). You're the entertainment, of course. Composers, don't despair. You could have a special screening of your latest work. If you work from home, you could rent a hall or hotel banquet room for your open house.

Make sure you have *plenty* of promotional material to give away. Why not make up a gift bag containing your latest music (demo, CD, etc.), printed promotional material, discount coupon or other appropriate offers, and more. Be sure to serve some munchies and libations. You could offer discounts or give away door prizes, but make sure your prizes will result in more business, such as an offer to get four hours free studio time (or 10% off your next original music order) if the winner buys four hours.

HOLIDAY SEASON

Giving tokens of appreciation at holiday time is a tradition for many businesses. Unfortunately all too many people think narrowly about the gift: "Send 'em a tub of popcorn" (usually with a computer generated note card). Hold on a minute. What is the purpose of this business gift? I suspect there are two.

- To thank your best clients for their business and remind them how much you appreciate their support.
- To encourage your clients to buy from you again (and again and again).

So what makes the ideal business gift? Give them a discount coupon. This can be either a percentage or dollar amount toward their next music purchase from you. This strategy meets the criteria above. You thank and reward your customers at the same time. Plus, your coupon is only good for your business, so you automatically encourage them to buy from you again. That can't be bad!

Make this coupon a fancy document. A Certificate of Appreciation motif is a good start. Use it to thank your best clients for their business and tell them you are rewarding them with this special discount. Next, sit down at your computer and write a short letter that offers your sincere thanks for their support throughout the past year. Throw in items specific to each person to remind them how much you care about their success. Include this highly personal letter with your discount certificate and send it at holiday time.

Do this for those clients who have spent the most money with you during the past year. You do keep track of such information, don't you? For others, send a personal note. Even a sentence or two scribbled on a greeting card thanking them and wishing them future success will go a long way toward building loyal clients for your business. Make sure you hand sign and address all the cards.

Need a special gift for your best clients and hottest prospects? Prepare a tape of five holiday or original songs. Your simple, cassette-only release makes an ideal and appropriate business gift. Think of this as a self-published record rather than a demo. Make sure the music fits your usual style and send it wrapped with a holiday wish. The beauty of this idea is that it features your talents in a soft-sell format that's different and pleasant. If you use Christmas carols, make sure they are public domain. It doesn't cost anything to record "Away in a Manger," "Silent Night," or any other old-time favorite. "White Christmas" will cost you mechanical royalties, though!

Another holiday marketing idea is to send a book or booklet related to your soundtrack scoring and jingle business. I recently sent copies of *A Guide to Good Audio* published by the Shure microphone company as a premium to my best clients and prospects.

INSTALL A DEMO TELEPHONE LINE

You might consider adding a demo hotline to your promotional arsenal. You need to get a second business telephone line and hook it up to an answering machine. Better still, get the dedicated voice mail-only line that many local telephone companies provide. Your cost is quite minimal and the potential returns are great!

You promote this service in your ads or other marketing materials by asking prospects to call and listen to a short excerpt of your latest music tracks. Add your sales message at the end of the recording and be sure to keep the music up-to-date. Ask people to leave their name and address so you can follow up easily. This doesn't replace your regular demo; it's just another way for possible music buyers to hear your work *and* your sales message. It's a convenient and relatively inexpensive marketing tool. Here's the kind of message you might add:

Welcome to the Jeffrey P. Fisher Music Hotline. Do you need music that works, sounds great, and is very affordable? Stay on the line and listen to this musical montage of my latest work. I'll be back in two minutes with a special offer just for you.

[Run your short, two to three minute musical montage.]

Thanks for listening. Here's that special offer I promised. Leave your complete name and address after the beep and I'll send you a free copy of How to Get Low-Cost Original Music for All Your Productions. *This shows you exactly how to get the original music you need and deserve, at a price that makes sense.*

Promote your demo line in letters (makes for an ideal postscript), news releases, postcards, and your marketing kit. Add a short snippet at the end of your regular demo that invites clients and prospects to call to hear your latest music, too.

SPECIALTY ITEMS

Don't forget merchandising. If you have a decent business logo design, it can make ideal posters, T-shirts, etc. that you can give away. Otherwise, you might want to consider promotional merchandise—caps, mugs, pens, calendars, scratch pads, etc.—to advertise your business and keep your name in front of clients. There are dozens of ideas, but try to stick to a music theme. Whatever you choose, make sure your name and phone number (with area code) are clearly visible. Also, include an explanation of what you do: scores, jingles, sound design, etc. Try your local printer for information about these products.

Looking for some unique music-related gifts to give away or use for promotions? Get this catalog:
• *The Music Stand.* 1 Rockdale Plaza, Lebanon, NH 03766; (802) 295-7044

SERVICE RULES

Recently I moved and found an interesting item in my mailbox: a clever welcome kit comprised of an address book, coupons for various area businesses, and other general offers. In the address book were the preprinted names and addresses of those who provided coupons in the package. There was plenty of space left for me to add my personal data, but the big bold type on each page always reminded me where the address book came from.

Looking through the coupons, I noticed most offers were for discounts of some kind. A few were for free samples. As you already know, I'm a big fan of samples. Get people to try what you offer, make sure they're happy about what you can do for them, and turn them into a customer for life. It's a terrific promotional strategy, provided you take the necessary steps to get contact information from your customers so you can encourage them to patronize your business repeatedly. Ever the marketing detective, I decided to redeem two free offers and see how these people took advantage of the sales opportunity.

First, a trip to a florist. I walked in, handed a clerk the coupon, and she handed me a bouquet of spring flowers. That was it. No marketing whatsoever. She did not get my name, address, or phone number, so there was no way to follow up. She threw the coupon away, so I'm confident she didn't bother to track her marketing effort. Most importantly, she did not ask for my personal history. A simple survey would have revealed birthdays, anniversaries, and so forth so she could send reminder cards a week or two in advance. That would have been real live marketing, but instead she just gave me a nonchalant, "Come back again." Even that was a hastily ad-libbed line as I exited the store, flowers in hand! This store obviously blew their marketing opportunity. Wasted money. Wasted effort.

Second on the list: a car wash. Once again, nothing. I showed the coupon to the clerk, and my car was washed for free. They did nothing to make me a regular customer. Here I was, new to the town and a ripe prospect for repeat business. I couldn't believe it. Are these people nuts? They spend hard-earned cash to place their ads and coupons in the welcome kit and then do nothing! What a shame.

After this debacle, my wife went to buy some fabric for a craft project. After rummaging through the bins, she found a print she liked. On the bolt was about a yard and a half of fabric. Needing less than a yard, she proceeded to the cutting counter. Then came the surprise. The salesperson told my wife that she had to buy all that was left on the bolt. It was an all or nothing ultimatum. When queried further, she simply replied "take it or leave it." You can guess my wife's refrain as she walked out of the store empty-handed. While I understand it may be troublesome for a fabric store to sell remnants, they lost this easy sale . . . and a future customer!

What is happening here? In a world full of commodity products and services, people just don't get it. *Service* is what it's all about. It's the easiest and often the best way to set yourself apart from the crowd. If you go to the trouble to attract people to your business, the least you can do is get the information you need to either make an immediate sale or control subsequent marketing to get the sale later. It takes time, effort, and money to generate leads. Don't blow it once you get them.

YOUR MUSIC ON THE AIR

While I doubt you will use radio, broadcast TV, or cable to advertise and promote your music business, there is a technique you *should* employ. If your music is appearing on radio, TV, or cable, drop a note or postcard in the mail to your clients and prospects. You could say something like this:

NOW HEAR THIS! Are you still wondering whether Jeffrey P. Fisher Music can help you? Maybe this will convince you: Listen for Al's Body Shop jingle on WXXX radio and other stations in this area. Al claims his sales have increased 8% since starting his new radio advertising campaign. We like to think our jingle has something to do with that. Let us do the same for you. Call now to get started helping you or your clients use music more effectively.

A simple letter, flyer, or postcard like this enables you to reap the benefits of broadcast media without buying advertising time. When your music tracks are easy for your clients and prospects to hear, let them know when and where. Hearing your music from another third party project gives you more credibility than hearing your music demo—even if it's the *same* music as on your demo.

How to Make Money Scoring Soundtracks and Jingles

USE PUBLIC ACCESS CABLE TELEVISION FOR PROMOTION

You may be overlooking a low-cost marketing opportunity that is right in your hometown. Public access cable television is an inexpensive tool you can use to promote your commercial music business. You can use video facilities, equipment, staff, and air time at little or no charge to produce your very own program. Public access is remarkably easy to use. You don't have to pitch a story, convince a producer or host to give you time, or even write a proposal. You can literally walk in right off the street, put your own show together, and air it on your local access station. While this means you'll be producing your own program, you'll also have complete control over its content. It will take commitment, hard work, and time, but producing your own program is often *free* (or very affordable). I've produced over 100 public access programs and offer the following suggestions for taking advantage of free production equipment and air time and using it to successfully promote yourself.

Cable companies are bound by law to provide reasonable access to facilities and air time for individuals and organizations to express their opinions. Contact your local cable company directly and ask for information about public access programming. You'll probably be transferred to the production department. Tell them you are interested in producing your own public access program and want to know what to do. You can also call your local governing body. Most municipalities have commissions, committees, or staff who oversee the cable company's operation in your town. Ask for their public access rules and procedures and the name of whom you should contact.

Most access facilities are supervised by a single access coordinator who is responsible for helping you produce a successful program. This person is usually fresh from college, overworked, and highly underpaid. You need to set up an appointment to discuss the access rules. At your meeting, explain what you want to do and ask how to produce and cablecast your show. Cable companies usually have only one requirement: You must take their production class before you can use their equipment. Take it. You'll learn the basics of TV production and you'll meet other people who are similarly interested. Once you finish the class (and pass their "test"), you are a certified access user. Also, there are some crucial limitations you must understand:

- There is usually no charge for use of the public access facilities and air time (any charges are minimal —class fee, materials, videotape, etc.).
- You can not cablecast any advertising material designed to sell a product, service, or political candidate.

- Equipment resources are usually limited.
- Production expertise is often limited; usually some staff is provided and the remaining assistance comes from an ad hoc volunteer group.

You must be willing to do much of your show's preparation—research, writing, planning, and other chores—yourself. Access is predominantly a volunteer organization. While you will function as producer, coordinator, and on-air talent, you still need help from the access coordinator, staff, and volunteers. Treat them well. Your show will not be successful without them.

Although you'll be using your program for promotion, *you may not advertise.* That does not mean you can't encourage your audience to contact you. Include complete follow-up information throughout your show and send those who contact you more information about how you can help them further. Access, like all promotion, is the epitome of soft sell.

Copies of your finished show(s) make good premiums for client prospects. While you can't *sell* a program made through public access for profit, there's nothing preventing you from giving it away as a promotion. You pay for tape and duplication, but that's it. In most cases, your program airs only in your local area, but it is possible to widen your exposure. Submit your program to neighboring communities (contact the coordinator). Sometimes a single cable company services a larger area. They may have a channel that goes to all their communities. In suburban Chicago, one cable company's system-wide access channel goes to 30 different communities. That's about a half-million subscribers.

I've produced a number of access programs, including several music performances, videos, and other variety programs. When a local band needed some help with their tape, I agreed to help. For the All Night Newsboys demo tape, we decided a straight performance video was too mundane. Instead I set them up in a circle around the drummer, much like the band was rehearsing and trying new material. (The inspiration came from The Beatles *Let It Be* film.) The set was the raw studio with ladders, old set pieces, and other behind-the-scenes matter. We even let the camera and production staff appear in the video. The idea was a relaxed, have-fun atmosphere. So they could have the most control possible, the Newsboys lip-synched to studio tracks that were remixed to be rougher and less produced. We combined these performances with snippets of rehearsals and impromptu jams recorded live on the video set. Once we edited the pieces together, we had a fine program for the access channel, and the boys had their demo tape. The cost? About $100 for videotape and a small pizza party for everyone involved. Not bad for a tape that went all over Chicago and reached a few million homes. It's not MTV, but it sure helped the Newsboys' reputation.

POTPOURRI OF CLIENT NICETIES

Life is like music—it must be composed by ear, feeling, and instinct, not by rule.
—SAMUEL BUTLER

- -

How you are perceived by others is crucial to your business success. Make sure your clients see you as a professional, helpful, knowledgeable, and creative business person. Here are several tips to help you keep in touch with clients, keep them happy, and keep them yours.

- Be neat and thorough. There is nothing worse than hastily scribbled notes, typos, missing pieces, wrong tapes, or other oversights. Use professional and tasteful stationery and have all materials typewritten or typeset. Often your letterhead is the first contact people have with you, so make sure it projects your professional image and makes a good impression. Don't write anything by hand except the occasional note. Check your spelling and grammar. I once received a letter from a composer who repeatedly used the contraction "it's" instead of the possessive "its." Don't make these kinds of embarrassing mistakes.
- Don't forget the telephone. There is nothing wrong with picking up the phone; simply saying, "Hi"; and asking about the work your client prospects are doing. Don't try to get work for yourself, just touch base and make another contact. Be genuinely friendly and helpful. Clients remember these little tokens, so use them to your advantage.
- Practice your helpful, kind telephone demeanor. Smile just before you pick up the receiver. Your attitude will come across to the other person on the line.
- Dress appropriately for meetings. The rule: Dress slightly more formally than casually. If you're meeting a banker, wear a dark suit and subdued tie; if you're meeting with a production company, a tie and sweater or sports coat is fine. Don't ever show up in jeans and a T-shirt!
- Be on time to all meetings. If you are running late, call ahead and explain your delay.
- Be prepared for all client contact. Have the information you need readily at hand. Don't run out of tapes or promotional material. Follow up all meetings—whether they result in immediate work or not—with a thank you note or, if appropriate, a contract. If you can't get an answer out to the client right away, explain why. Return all their phone calls promptly and deliver contracts and quotes within 24 hours.

- Respond to all inquiries promptly. Mail all promotional kits in the fastest medium possible and do it the same day you get the request. Return all phone calls on the same day, too. Use the remote retrieve option on your answering machine or voice mail system if you're going to be away. Even if you don't speak to the person who called, make sure you leave a message to show that you tried. Often I'll send a quick fax or e-mail to those I miss. When they get back to their office, my message is sitting there waiting for them.
- Always meet your deadlines and do exactly what you say you are going to do. If you tell someone you'll call Friday morning, do just that. Should you have to choose between incomplete work and missing a deadline, miss the deadline. Call the client, explain the troubles you're having, and work to a mutually beneficial solution.
- Do your best work all the time. Never hand in shoddy work and never apologize for your work before playing it. Say that this is the best work you've done so far.
- Give your clients more than they expect. It could be something simple, like doing an alternate mix of a score or jingle, making a few extra copies on cassette, shipping a tape by courier or overnight instead of regular shipping, etc. When you work on a project, think of ways you can go the extra mile. Don't charge for it, just do it to show you are working hard to make them happy with your service. Make sure your client knows what you've done, but be subtle: "I took the liberty of creating a mix without the lead guitar, just in case you need some filler under the narration."
- Here's something I've done a few times. Clients invariably call up and ask for a simple job, such as a new mix or dub from DAT to ¼-inch. I go ahead and do the job and then send them an invoice outlining the regular charge. At the bottom, I write NO CHARGE. The client sees what it would have cost them for the work and appreciates the in-kind, extra-special treatment. This adds value to your service. Try it on your next small client request.
- This one's not so unique, but it works anyway. After a major project, send small gifts to the principals involved. Something music-related is best, but I've also sent five-gallon containers of popcorn. The problem with food is that it is eaten and forgotten. Sending a book, CD, or other gift has staying power. They see it and are reminded of you. That's not a bad situation to be in.
- Make sure you mention your clients in promotions. Also, send them copies of your publicity, articles, booklets, new demo tapes, brochures, etc. Think of the many ways you can contact them and make a list.

Divide the list up and start doing these things regularly as the year progresses. At the end of the year, make a new list and start fresh. Also, keep track of what brought in more business and what didn't.

- Listen. Don't dominate conversations. Listen to the full story and then answer in a manner that shows you understand the problem and that you care about solving it. Use all client contacts to gather the information you need to close more sales. Let your prospects tell you what they want and then tell them how your music fits in.
- Ask questions. Don't be afraid to ask for more information. If you don't understand something, ask for clarification. It's better to be thorough than to be ignorant or, worse, to make a costly mistake.
- Be warm, kind, interested, enthusiastic, and genuine. Make sure your client knows you care, and don't put up a fake facade. Be yourself in a straightforward manner. People reflect what they see in you. If you are passionate about your music, you will excite your clients and prospects, too.
- Have fun. Nothing works better or is remembered more than composers who love their work and make that love, commitment, and enthusiasm shine through everything they do. I get more jobs because of my enthusiasm. It's what people remember most. Use it!

RESOLVING CONFLICTS

It happens. No matter how hard you try, something goes wrong, and your client is unhappy about your work. Don't panic. But don't shrug it off or pass the buck, either. No matter what happens, don't shift the blame to someone or something else. Always assume *full* responsibility. Confront the problem head-on and attempt to resolve it. Follow this six step process when a problem arises:
- Take responsibility for the complaint.
- Listen to the client.
- Summarize the client's position.
- Explain what you will do and when you expect to do it.
- Take action right away.
- Follow up to make sure your client is satisfied.

The best approach is to ask the client what the problem is, then sit back and listen. Often the client just needs to vent some anger. I don't think you should stand for any abuse, but you should listen to their side of the story. Practice active listening.

When it's your turn, try to address the points brought up by your client. If there is something you can do right now to fix things: *do it.* If they must wait for the resolution of their problem, assure them that you will drop everything and work to their satisfaction. Make sure you follow up and meet their objections.

Chance is a word that does not make sense. Nothing happens without a cause.
—Voltaire

You must use your success with each client as a springboard to other prospects. Work hard to get a major success, then leverage that success to get more clients, and use that to get still more business, ad infinitum. A satisfactory client endorsement helps strengthen your credibility. Use the road to success sequence to generate leads, get meetings, and close sales. It's your basic strategy; you follow it in a circle. If the prospect becomes a client, keep in touch regularly. And if they remain a prospect, you continue marketing to them until they become a client. Simple, isn't it?

Here's another tip: People buy products and services only from businesses they are familiar with. Therefore, you must concentrate on making yourself known by sharing your successes with possible prospects. Send the newest demo of your latest music. Share the results of your recent assignments. Tell them to listen when your work can be heard on radio or TV. Regularly use direct marketing to your hot prospects and clients with telephone calls, reminder mailings, regular publicity through news releases and newsletters, helpful information, and more—all of this keeps your name alive, builds credibility, and ultimately puts money in your pocket.

Your past work will get you more work because success breeds more success. Make sure you let both clients and prospects know *what* you have done and that you *can* and *will* do the same for them. People want security. If they have confidence that you can do the job, they will buy from you. Of course, your music, your service, and your price all affect sales, too. So have the confidence that you can write the exact music your clients want, need, and deserve, and remember that it's vital that you back up every claim you make with tangible evidence. You must also understand that familiarity breeds confidence, and confidence means sales. Use the techniques we've discussed in this book relentlessly. Most of all, keep hitting your target market with your message, so when they need music they'll call you first.

There is an old business adage that says you must spend money to make money. I heartily disagree. You must spend money *marketing* to make money! Don't think of it as an expense—marketing is an *investment* in your future success. Try many different tactics. Get crazy and be different. Have some fun. And sell your music by spending the least amount of money. In the world of modern marketing warfare, creativity rules, *not* money.

CHAPTER 9

Profit From the Internet

A traveler pays attention to the new culture, as well as to the unavoidable differences, and evolves. The tourist just fills in an agenda . . . So don't just seek information or entertainment on the Internet. Interact. Wander. And wonder.

—*Tim Haight*

As of this writing, the Internet population grows by 10-15% every month. This is a huge and ever-expanding market that offers the most lucrative marketing opportunity available today. Millions of people around the world could be and *should* be getting information about your music products and services through this medium. If you're not online yet, you'd better join soon or you'll be at a severe disadvantage. Internet marketing is the quintessential low-cost, high-involvement promotional strategy. It's very affordable, just pennies a day. If you're smart, you'll jump at the chance and be an active part of this exploding revolution.

What exactly is the Internet? Put simply, it's a huge network of computers linked so that information can be shared. Originally designed by the defense department to decentralize our computer resources, it was soon embraced by colleges and universities. The Internet is made up of several parts: e-mail, newsgroups, mailing lists, and the World Wide Web. Though the first three have been around for some time, it took the introduction of a graphical software system for the Web to emerge as the hot online attraction.

The Internet is an open system. No single company or government owns or polices it. Someone once called the Internet an "exercise in anarchy." That describes it adequately. Just like life, there is good and bad on the Internet. I liken it to a vast library where you can get information, find topics of interest, be entertained, run across material you find offensive, and have some fun. Most importantly, *you* are in control. With the media piping endless messages into our homes, the Internet lets *you* choose where you want to go and avoid the places you don't like.

I'm a big fan of online promotion. Between e-mail, newsgroups, mailing lists, and the Web, there are endless marketing and promotional opportunities. Your basic promotional technique is simple: Offer useful information. Give some of your experience away and help people reach *their* goals. While you're doing that, don't forget to leave information about where they can find additional resources and other information about *your* music products and services.

The very nature of the Internet lets you bring your message to precise audiences. Online marketing is narrowcasting to specific people with similar interests. You can participate in discussions and help other people around the world with solutions to their problems—the problems you're in business to solve! I'm not talking about advertising. Online promotion is the essence of soft sell. It's just another opportunity for you to establish your expert status and add credibility to your name.

Use online marketing to present your business image, people, products, and services to the world; establish your expert status; demonstrate your problem-solving skills; increase awareness; add prestige and credibility to your name; and get some free publicity and promotion. Internet marketing is an ideal way for you to flex your promotional muscles in a number of ways.

- Share your experiences in newsgroups and mailing lists. It's another ideal promotional vehicle through which you can highlight your projects in detail and show the results you achieved. Be sure to mention all the ways you can help your clients, and list all the work you've done for extra credibility.
- Issue news releases regularly to appropriate online forums. Ideal topics are new products and services, staff changes, equipment purchases, problems solved, and projects completed. Also, piggy-back on national, state, and local coverage of your specialty by posting messages that showcase you as the expert on the subject. Often I'll write an opinion piece and post it to the relevant places.
- Write short articles that provide solutions to your client's problems. Through each article you show your expert knowledge and position yourself to help those who need your products and services. The key is to leave a signature that directs people to your Web site or encourages them to contact you directly.
- Here's an important tip: When you can offer something of value, you have a better chance of success. Solid information is a sure-fire winner. Giving something away, like a free tip sheet, report, or booklet, is also a popular tactic. As people contact you about your offer, you capture their name for your mailing list. Now you control the sales process and can send offers for other items you have available.

ONLINE ACTION PLAN

There are two parts to successfully bringing your music products and services to the Internet (I assume you have a computer, modem, and phone line already). First, you need to get access to the Internet; second, you need to become part of the Internet itself. My suggestion is for you to write down what you want to get from the Internet and develop a plan to accomplish that purpose. Here's a start.

- Join a local Internet provider or sign up with one of the national providers: America Online: (800) 827-6364, Compuserve: (800) 848-8199, or Prodigy: (800) PRODIGY.
- Set up an e-mail address. Choose your name wisely. There is a tendency to be cute or cryptic, but I suggest you choose a name that reflects your business image and personality. Product and company names are terrific, obviously.
- Learn how to send, receive, forward, save, and delete your e-mail.
- Learn how to use your Internet software. You need to know how to read and post to newsgroups, subscribe to mailing lists, and browse the Web.
- Add your e-mail address to all your regular promotional material.
- Tell people they can reach you via e-mail.
- Plan and construct your own World Wide Web site.
- Add your Web URL to all your promotional material and begin promoting your Web site both online and through traditional promotional methods.
- Important point: Do not announce or promote your e-mail address or Web site until everything is fully operational.
- Make sure you avoid sending junk e-mail, posting tons of ads in newsgroups (this is called spamming), and other bad habits.

E-MAIL

Once you get your e-mail address configured, you need to *encourage* clients and prospects to contact you via e-mail. It's a very efficient medium. Clients can retrieve their messages at their convenience. I suggest you check your mail a few times each day; it only takes a couple of minutes. Make sure you respond to all e-mail inquiries promptly. I try to get my replies out the same day—often within minutes of getting the message.

It's a good idea to develop some standard replies to cover your most asked questions. I have several generic e-mail messages that contain general correspondence, promotional pieces, proposals, thank you notes, and more. It takes time to gather this material, but in the long run you save time. Once you develop these basic responses, use them repeatedly. Make sure you personalize each piece by slipping in a custom sentence or two.

An important part of your e-mail use is to include a signature or tag line that accompanies all your outgoing messages. Include your name, address, phone, and e-mail address. Also, put in a promotional message or pointer to your home page on the Web. Here's an example:

```
Jeffrey P. Fisher—Fisher Creative Group
         323 Inner Circle Drive
         Bolingbrook, IL 60490
     (630) 378-4109—fishercg@mcs.com
Make sure you stop by my Moneymaking Music
          site on the Web at:
      http://www.mcs.net/~fishercg/
```

I get several e-mail messages each day. Most are questions that come from people who read my posts to newsgroups, visit my Web site, or have read my books and other resources. You should encourage people to contact you as you begin to offer useful information to the Internet community. I work hard to help people to the best of my ability and recommend this practice to you. Here's how a reply might go:

```
To:Stew
Subject: Re: Questions

Stew,
Terrific hearing from you today.
Let me answer your question ...
>>How do I copyright my songs? I'm
>>worried someone
>>might steal my work.
No other aspect of the music indus-
try is more misunderstood than
copyright. Musicians are perpetu-
ally worried that someone, some-
where will steal their creative
work. Unfortunately, most of the
information that continues to cir-
culate is wrong. Check out the FAQ
on my Web site, where I aim to set
the record straight with a simple,
no-nonsense, and ultimately factu-
ally correct description of the
U.S. Copyright Law.
    Contrary to popular misconcep-
tion, there is no great mystery on
how to copyright your original
music and lyrics. According to the
U.S. Copyright Law, as soon as you
affix your music and lyrics in a
tangible medium, it is afforded
copyright protection. In other
words, copyright protection is
automatic. To register your copy-
right (a completely unnecessary
step) requires filing with the
Copyright Office. Check out the FAQ
for complete details.
    Questions? Comments? Just drop
me a note or feel free to call me.

—Jeffrey
```

What's happening here? I commented out the specific parts of the initial inquiry and provided information to answer the question. Of course, this message helped me send the inquiry to my Web site so I could further promote my business, but I was able to do it in a low-key, nonthreatening way. I also acquired Stew's mailing address (e-mail and postal) and can now send him other offers to help make his music career more successful. All this from a single e-mail message.

CLASSIFIED ADS

Another opportunity for promotion is to take advantage of classified ads. America Online lets subscribers post ads for free. Other places are free or very affordable. There are a few Web sites and newsgroups that encourage this practice. Use an Internet search engine to uncover possible places. I've used classifieds to sell gear quite successfully and to promote my music products and services.

```
    Soundtracks & Jingles Needed!
That's right. Movies, radio, TV,
cable, video, slide, multimedia,
the Internet, and other audiovi-
sual presentations desperately
need your original music scores and
jingles. It's a growing opportu-
nity for you. Once you understand
this market and develop a plan to
reach it—this guide shows you pre-
cisely how—you'll enjoy a success-
ful career making money from your
music.
    According to Jeffrey Fisher,
the problem facing musicians and
composers who wish to enter the
commercial music industry is that
they just don't understand the
business. "Making money scoring
soundtracks and jingles for com-
mercial and business audiovisual
presentations requires a specific
set of skills," explains Fisher,
author of How to Make Money Scor-
ing Soundtracks and Jingles. "Mas-
tery of these marketing and business
skills is crucial to your success."
    While there is plenty of mater-
ial available on the subjects of
writing lyrics, hooking up music
gear, and so forth, Fisher says there
is precious little sound business
advice about working in the commer-
cial music industry. "Before How to
Make Money Scoring Soundtracks and
Jingles, many talented people were
left wondering how to turn their
skills into a viable business. Now
my book gives you the tools you
need to make your dream come true—
```

and put some money in your pocket, too."

An accomplished composer with credits for dozens of commercial and business productions, Fisher shares the inside tricks of the trade in his jam-packed resource. Here's precisely what you need to know to make money scoring soundtracks and jingles:

· Essential items every recording studio needs and why
· Eight steps to improving your composition skills
· Dozens of ways to promote your talent and boost your image
· Step-by-step business start-up information, including how to use your computer effectively
· Crucial telephone tips that increase sales
· Guidelines for drafting profit-producing promotional material, using free media, making money from just-in-time marketing, and selling your music on just $5.00 a day
· All this and more, including a complete "Samples" section full of sales letters, ads, contracts, and more that you can start using today to sell more of your music

With How to Make Money Scoring Soundtracks and Jingles, you can stop wondering how to break into this field. You'll learn how to start, build, and sustain your commercial music business. It's all here in easy-to-follow directions with useful, practical details. No beginner or seasoned pro should be without it. Order How to Make Money Scoring Soundtracks and Jingles today!

Send e-mail direct to Jeffrey Fisher at fishercg@mcs.com for more information.

P.S. Make sure you ask for complete ordering information and your FREE one year subscription to Jeffrey's Musician's Business Building Bookshelf newsletter, featuring over 30 ways to make your musical career more successful and profitable.

I've issued news releases, too. Rather than selling directly, use this technique to generate leads or to get people to your Web site:

Moneymaking Music Web Site Debuts
If you need help selling your music products and services, stop by Jeffrey Fisher's new Moneymaking Music site on the Worldwide Web at http://www.mcs.net/~fishercg/

"Every musician can use some help marketing their talents," explains Fisher. "This new service provides specific information about getting your share of the music business profits." Included free at the site are:

· Business Building Tips updated regularly with the latest music business success secrets
· Tips from music business resources such as How to Make Money Scoring Soundtracks and Jingles, Fisher's popular career guide, jam-packed with the inside tips to succeeding with your own commercial music business
· Learn how to get a FREE subscription to Fisher's Musician's Business Building Bookshelf newsletter, your resource of practical, useful, affordable, and proven information on how to improve your music career.

NEWSGROUPS AND FORUMS

You can subscribe to any number of newsgroups and forums. These are essentially gathering points for people with similar interests to get together and share information. People post questions and comments, and other people respond to the postings. Participating in these sessions is a very easy way to promote your music products and services. The big online services have dozens of forums on specific subjects. The Internet has Usenet with thousands of newsgroups. Some of my favorites include:

• alt.guitar
• alt.music.4-track
• rec.music.makers.synth
• rec.music.makers.songwriting
• alt.music.midi
• alt.music.makers.electronic
• rec.music.movies

When someone asks a question, I post a reply to the newsgroup (and also send the author an e-mail message with my reply). Usually I provide direct answers free of blatant promotion and rely on my signature to promote my site. Occasionally I can promote my products and services directly with a subtle approach.

As I said in my How to Make Money Scoring Soundtracks and Jingles *book, promotion is the key to success in the music industry* . . .

MAILING LISTS

Similar to newsgroups, mailing lists are collections of like-minded people who correspond via a common e-mail system called a list server. People post messages and replies to the list just as they do with a newsgroup, except the messages are sent *only* to the list subscribers. It's like a private newsgroup. The same techniques are applicable here, except that these mailing lists are usually sponsored and are less tolerant of blatant promotion and advertising. I suggest you read the group for a few weeks before you start posting. This lets you see what's tolerated and helps you position your presence and offers accordingly. Making a mistake can bring the wrath of hundreds of people down on you. Use caution before proceeding.
• Send e-mail to Filmus-L@iubvm.ucs.indiana.edu for the best list comprising detailed discussion on film and TV music scores.

YOUR PRESENCE ON THE WORLD WIDE WEB

Getting access to the Internet isn't the end of your online promotional strategy; it's just the beginning. Becoming part of the Internet itself is the next step. That means publishing information about your music products and services on the World Wide Web. Essentially you have four ways to get a visible presence:
• Rent space in a virtual mall. Depending on the mall, your cost can be a few hundred to several thousand dollars each month.
• Rent space on a server and start your own storefront. This is often an inexpensive solution, usually only $15-20 a month for a small site.
• Join an Internet provider who also gives you space to publish your own home pages. Essentially, you get room on your provider's server to establish your presence.
• Set up your own Web server. This is the most expensive solution, requiring special computer hardware, software, and phone connections.

The technical aspects of publishing on the Web are intimidating at first but are easily mastered if you're willing to learn a little HTML, Unix, and such. There is now some easy-to-use software that makes getting your site together and on the Web much easier. I recommend you concentrate on the *content* of your pages and leave the technical side to a professional, though. All Internet presence providers will help you design and program your pages. Sometimes this is bundled in your fee, other times you pay extra for consulting time.

WEB SUCCESS SECRETS

Putting your business on the World Wide Web is crucial to your online marketing. It's the one place where you can actively promote and sell. What's nice about the Web is that it's a great equalizer. The biggest and the smallest business have an equal presence. Your pages are right alongside the heavy hitters—and they have no clear advantage. You just need to get people to your site and once they're there, give them something of value.

What can your Web pages contain? Think of your site as a store of sorts. You can include brochures, flyers, catalogs, detailed product sheets, articles, newsletters, samples, pictures—even audio and video clips! The choices are endless, limited only to your imagination and particular skills.
• Plan both what you want to do and what you want to get from your Internet presence. Are you going to generate leads or would you rather make direct sales?
• Take time to cruise the Web and discover how others are using the Internet.
• Make sure there is a reason for people to keep coming back to your Web pages. Provide value by supplying information, samples, useful tips, links to other important locations, and more. Present your best company image in a pleasing and entertaining way. Don't just make your site one long advertisement. Post instant replies to questions that arise. Update your site constantly with new information, perhaps through a Frequently Asked Questions (or FAQ) section.
• Promote your site online and through traditional means. Send news releases; post to applicable newsgroups and mailing lists; send direct mail and e-mail to clients and prospects; and add your URL address to business cards, letterhead, brochures, and ads.
• Provide an e-mail signature that explains what you do and direct people to your Web site location.
• Make sure you constantly maintain and update your Web pages.
• Your Web presence should be a reflection of your business image. What message do you wish to convey? How will you use the Web to make sure that comes across to browsers?

- Make your page professional, but be realistic. Avoid huge inline graphics. Put up a thumbnail and let users choose to download the full image (or not). Make your site simple, elegant, and brimming with content.
- As I continue cruising the Internet for interesting sites and such, there is one little pet peeve I'd like to share with you. It's audio on the Net. Right now, the reality of downloading huge audio files is horrible. The time it takes for even a small snippet or a low quality version to play usually doesn't justify the expense, and the time needed to download high quality sounds is staggering. Unfortunately, you can't cut corners when presenting your music, and you need to introduce it in the best light possible. But for slow dial-up modem connections, it's usually not worth it to include sound on your page. Until the speed and viability is changed, you are better off creating interest through text and images and then mailing a tape. I suppose a short snippet is OK, but I'm not yet convinced. Make sure you tell people how big the file is so they can decide for themselves.
- Let's face it. The Web is *not* TV. It's new media with a language all its own. I wish people would quit trying to force it to be something it's not. Stay tuned.

Here are a few sites you should visit on the WWW:
- For a good example of the techniques explained here, I humbly suggest you visit my Moneymaking Music site first: http://www.mcs.net/~fishercg/
- This comprehensive site devoted to film music is jam-packed with information and tons of links: http://www.filmmusic.com/
- The ultimate band list: http://american.recordings. com/wwwofmusic/ubl/ubl.shtml
- David Torn Home Page: http://ott-outreach.engin.umich.edu/torn/
- Creative Musician's Coalition: http://www.aimcmc.com/
- AT&T Home Business Resources: http://www.att.com/hbr/
- Fractal Music Software: http://members.aol.com/strohbeen/fmlsw.html
- Shareware Music Machine: http://www.hitsquad.com/smm/
- Aztec Camera Home Page: http://homepage. interaccess.com/~hawkfan/aztec.htm
- Transoniq Hacker: http://www.transoniq.com/~trnsoniq/
- Harmony Central: http://www.harmony-central.com/
- Mix Bookshelf: http://www.mixbookshelf.com

Once you get up and running online, participate in forums and newsgroups and invite people to visit your Web site. You will soon begin to see the fruits of your labors. You'll get inquiries and some cash soon after. Just remember that the Internet is a low-cost but high involvement medium. You'll get from it what you put into it. It will take your time and energy to maintain a cool Web site and continually monitor the newsgroups and such. But the end results—more sales!—make it worthwhile.

CHAPTER 10

Taking Care of Business

Many artists have admittedly

no aptitude for merchantry.

—*Arnold Bennett*

Here it is, the chapter most musicians hate. This is the reality-check chapter that talks about all those boring little things—you know: taxes, invoices, accountants, contracts, lawyers, etc. *Don't look at it this way!*

How to Make Money Scoring Soundtracks and Jingles wouldn't be complete without this information, and you can't be in business without it, either. Just because you make great music doesn't mean people will buy it or, more importantly, that they'll pay you. So, to help you succeed, here are the essentials you need to know to start and run your soundtrack scoring and jingle business. You must:

• Truly desire and want success and be willing to do whatever it takes to succeed.
• Be willing to balance opportunity with some risk.
• Be passionate and enthusiastic about your work.
• Have a vision and dream for both your business and your life.
• Gather complete knowledge about both the music industry and general business practices.
• Be able to adapt and wear many hats.
• Take control of your business. If something costs you a dollar, you'd better charge *at least* $1.01 for it. You must know what and how your business is doing. You can't be in the dark. You must take control of every facet—especially the financial ones—to succeed!

Maybe you're unsure about going into this business for yourself. If so, ask yourself these questions: Are you unhappy about what you currently do? Are your musical talents being used to their fullest? Is there no room for advancement and you're stalled? If you answered yes to these questions, running your own commercial music business may be a way for you to better express yourself as you find more meaningful work.

FULL-TIME OR PART-TIME?

You *can* run your business as a sideline. Following my guidelines, it is very easy to make an extra $500 or more a month for just a few day's work. Or you can jump in full-time. You can make as much (or as little) money as you want. If you're in a band or have a regular day job (music-related or otherwise), you can moonlight as a commercial music composer. However, be aware that clients expect you to be available during the day. For the typical nighttime band, this is easy. But if you're a computer programmer by day, it is very hard to juggle both your job and your music business. You *can* do it, though. Answering machines, fax, e-mail, and either many accrued sick days or an understanding boss make it possible. It's not easy, but it is possible. It's how I started.

I was director of marketing at a computer software firm for several years while I ran my business on the side. You see, clients don't care *when* you compose, but they do expect phone calls between nine and five. I used my lunch hour to respond to messages left on voice mail and fax information when necessary; and I used sick and vacation days for the occasional meeting. Also, I made a point of encouraging clients not to meet with me in person. I'd say to them, "Tell me what you want and send me a copy of the video. I'll write the music and ship it back to you in a week." And for most projects, it worked.

My advice is simple: *Never, ever quit a gainful means of employment to pursue music full-time.* Start part-time and work your way up. Be realistic about your expectations and your goals. I want you to succeed, and I'll help you any way I can. But don't make the jump until you are ready. Start out moonlighting and move steadily forward. You won't regret your caution.

When I finally decided to go full-time, I already had an established track record and a list of satisfied clients. Plus, diversification into related areas is the number one contributing factor to business success, and I run several different businesses. (I compose soundtrack music and jingles and am also a business consultant. Of course, writing about my music business was a natural extension of my talent—hence this book you now hold.) This concept is so significant that there's an entire chapter devoted to this subject.

SAGE ADVICE FOR THE BEGINNER AND PRO

In things pertaining to enthusiasm,
no man is sane who does not know how
to be insane on proper occasions.
—HENRY WARD BEECHER

- Don't make a switch to running your own business if you have other conflicts in your life. Let your current stress subside before moving forward.
- Take time to prepare for your business. You may need to continue in your current job as you study your chosen business, sharpen your skills, and save enough money.
- Don't change for change's sake. Make sure you understand that running your own business requires time and attention. It's not for the squeamish. Before undertaking this adventure, make sure the transition is right for you. While you may experience some fear, your gut should reassure you that you are on the correct path.
- Start small, perhaps part-time, and see if running your own business is right for you. Better to find out while your risk is low than to commit and be dissatisfied and disappointed.
- Be prepared for a few months of slow progress before you get your first important client. Your marketing needs time to take effect.

- Educate yourself about the technology available to you and every aspect of the craft of composing good music. Experiment, learn, and grow both as an artist and a business professional.
- Do your homework. It's better to make a $100 mistake than a $1000 mistake.
- Understand the marketplace by following trends in business, advertising, TV, films, and music. You need to know what's global and recognize local nuances.
- Be persistent and obsessive about success. This is a highly competitive industry. Work hard and demonstrate your skills effectively.
- Try to reach prospects cheaply and motivate them to hire you. Hit them repeatedly with your message and get them to buy right now.
- Stop wasting your time on the wrong prospects and clients. At first, everyone seems like a potential client, but you must ruthlessly sort through the dead wood and concentrate on those who need and can afford your expertise.
- Don't be the cheapest composer in town. This is the single biggest mistake made by fledgling businesses. It can get your foot in the door, but it can backfire as well. Strike a balance.
- Forget the quick sale. If you follow much of the advice in this book, your marketing and promotion will be a carefully constructed plan. The ultimate intention is to uncover customers, build relationships, and profit from them over many years. This *is* the secret, plain and simple.
- Make sure you keep sight of your personal goals when planning, starting, and running your business. Write down your goals for this year, next year, and five years from now. Put them on a piece of paper and keep them where you work. Every day you'll see your goals—both personal and professional—and can work toward reaching them with everything you do. While you don't need to be a paper slave, it *does* help to have a guideline to follow. Deadline pressure is often very stimulating; having somewhere to go is equally motivating.
- This is a creative business. Be innovative, stand above the crowd, and project a successful image. You will succeed.
- Stress your service. Show your clients how you will help them, and put your commitment to them in your letters and your contracts.
- Make sure you keep any promises you make. If you get in too deep, get help. There is nothing wrong with subcontracting some of your work. It's better to make a little less money than to miss a deadline or, what's worse, deliver substandard work.
- If a client complains, go out of your way to solve the problem. On the average, a person will tell almost

20 other people about their bad experiences. You can't afford to have your reputation smeared unknowingly. Go one step further and make sure your clients are very happy. If there is a problem, do what it takes to fix it.

- Watch your expenses. You must be careful not to overspend. Look carefully for the free or less expensive method and evaluate whether you really need to spend the cash at all. It's easy to get carried away with spending. Be cautious.
- Don't neglect the *real* costs of doing business. Don't forget about taxes, health care, retirement, and all the myriad business details that you must control. It can seem overwhelming at times, but your mastery of these basic areas is crucial.
- Take advantage of existing knowledge. You can and should learn from what others can teach you. This book is a first step, designed to help you get started. Don't let your schooling stop here. All that you need is out there for you to exploit. Take the vast information available and use it to your benefit.
- Enjoy your work. There is a saying that if you do what you love, the money will follow. Make sure your joy and exuberance shine through all your work and all your client contacts. Your enthusiasm gives clients confidence and reassures them that you can and will do the job right. It is the easiest and cheapest marketing tool you can use.
- Immerse yourself in your life's work and live with purpose.

A CAUTIONARY NOTE

Consult. To seek another's
approval of a course already decided on.
—AMBROSE BIERCE

- -

What I'm about to tell you is what I do; it's what has worked for me. I'm neither an accountant nor a lawyer (thankfully). The following systems, contracts, and legal stuff are what I use to run my business. I paid for professional advice to develop these systems, *and you should, too.* This material is pertinent to my particular situation (and my local laws as well). Use this *only* as a guideline or outline to follow when you sit down to talk with your accountant and lawyer. This chapter provides a thorough and solid foundation on which to build your empire. Learn from it and get help to adapt it to your life.

STARTING AND MANAGING YOUR COMMERCIAL MUSIC BUSINESS

Here is the list of essentials that you need for your business to succeed:

- Professional advisors (accountant, lawyer, and others)
- An accounting system
- Contracts
- Invoices
- Business cards and stationery
- Business telephone
- Answering machine or voice mail
- Optional: fax and copy machines
- Courier or overnight mail service
- Word processor or computer (to store letters, invoices, etc.)
- Planning calendar or scheduler
- Various office supplies

EXPERT ADVISOR ASSISTANCE

When a man comes to me for advice, I find out the
kind of advice he wants, and I give it to him.
—JOSH BILLINGS

- -

While you may choose to run your music business as a one-person shop, you'll still need the separate functions that all businesses do. You'll probably handle most of these jobs yourself, but in some areas you may need to seek professional advisors. Treat these people as an integral and crucial part of your business, almost as employees or partners. Their assistance is vital to your success, and their involvement could mean the difference between coasting along and bursting ahead.

I must stress this point again: Get professional advice to help you run your business. A few dollars spent here (accountants generally charge from $75-100 an hour; lawyers $100 and up) will save you plenty over the long haul. And since all these fees are tax deductible business expenses, this is really a smart *investment* in your future success. Go in prepared (take this chapter along), and ask every question you can think of. If your lawyer or accountant complains of a headache after you leave, you'll know you got a good deal! What advisors do you need? Here's a handy list:

- Accountant
- Lawyer
- Bank and investment advisor
- Insurance provider
- Marketing or business consultant
- Copywriter
- Publicity and advertising specialist
- Graphic designer

- Printer
- Photographer
- Travel agent
- Other musicians
- Recording studios
- Equipment rental houses
- On-call electronics engineer

You may handle many of these jobs yourself; others require retaining a professional. Contact these people and build a relationship *before* you desperately need their help. Explain how and when you will use their services, and get a commitment from them that they will help you.

You should meet with your accountant one to two times each year. Mine set up my business structure, gave and continues to give tax advice, and does my quarterly and year-end Uncle Sam stuff. He also approved an accounting system based on a few off-the-shelf resources. My lawyer reviewed the various contracts I planned to use and has consulted with me occasionally on other contracts and legal matters. I don't call often, but he knows me and my business and is ready when and if I need him.

Don't forget your outside musicians, recording studios, and equipment rental houses. If your studio is complex, you might consider adding an on-call electronics engineer who can fix your broken tape deck quickly when you're on deadline. Also, promotional opportunities can often arise quite fast. That's why you might need a graphic designer, desktop publisher, and printer as part of your advisor group. Some quick print shops offer one-stop shopping. You give them your words and layout ideas and they set it up, print it, and even mail it for you. When you need help fast, this is the ticket. Of course, you can do your own desktop publishing if you are so inclined; I often do little projects myself. But when the job is too big or when the work is critical, hire outside help. Other advisors round out your business network and fill in the gaps in your knowledge.

Another important part of your team is a dependable partner. You don't necessarily need a partner in the formal, legal sense. But what you do need is a cheerleader, someone to bounce ideas off of, someone who listens and understands your work and lifestyle. This partner can be a spouse or significant other, or it can be another business associate. When you're down, this friendship can help significantly. And when you're up, you can celebrate together.

Here's an approach to management that even the humblest business can exploit. Gather a few different people of varied backgrounds and form an informal, ad hoc executive board. You might want to call this your "kitchen cabinet." The purpose of the group is to share valuable experience. These outsiders can give you a completely different perspective on your current picture. Try meeting quarterly (at your kitchen table, of course) to discuss the various aspects of your business. While it would be nice if this cabinet included your lawyer, accountant, and others, the cost might be prohibitive. I suggest you include a few family members, some friends, fellow business peers, and perhaps some good clients. Use this time to find solutions to problems and bounce ideas around. You'd be surprised the kind of help you get from regular sessions such as these. This is information you can really use to run your business better.

CHOOSING YOUR ADVISORS

Finding the right advisor requires some time and energy. Here are five steps that will help you make the right decision.

◗ DETERMINE YOUR GOALS AND OBJECTIVES

Review your current situation and make sure you know where you've been, where you are right now, and where you wish to go. Finding the right advisor is much easier when you have a clearly defined objective. This way you can evaluate how a specific advisor's strategy can help you get where you want to go.

◗ CHOOSE THE SERVICES THAT ASSIST YOU IN ACHIEVING YOUR GOALS

When you know your objective and understand your position, selecting the appropriate advisor to match your needs is easier. Don't go to a general practitioner when a specialist may be more appropriate. However, you don't necessarily need an entertainment lawyer or accountant, because a good contract lawyer and small business accountant can do the job satisfactorily.

◗ SELECT A FEW POSSIBLE FIRMS TO INTERVIEW

Once you know the kind of professional—lawyer, accountant, recording studio, copywriter, etc.—that you need, find three or four candidates who provide these services. Try asking friends, family, and business associates for names of people who have success in your area. You may want to ask them to help with your evaluation, too. Once you get your list of possible professionals, contact each one and request information about their services, qualifications, and past performance. This information should help you narrow the field.

◢ MAKE APPOINTMENTS TO MEET WITH THE MOST PROMISING FIRMS

This is the most important aspect of the whole process. Use this meeting to assess each advisor. You need to see if their services, performance, and philosophy match your needs and goals. There are certain key questions you need to ask each candidate. These include questions about services, philosophy, other clients, fees, licenses and registrations, and references. Even if your questions are answered satisfactorily, don't forget the intangibles. Use this meeting to see whether you are comfortable with this person. Make sure you get the answers you want. Each firm should also have sufficient documentation to back up any claims they make. Ask for everything you think you'll need to make an informed decision, and scrutinize everything carefully.

◢ CHOOSE THE BEST PROFESSIONAL

If you've followed these guidelines, you should have what you need to make your decision. The key is doing your homework. Take the time to investigate possible firms, ask the right questions, and then choose the advisor with a philosophy that best matches your own. Your professional advisors are vitally important. You can't always do everything yourself. Take advantage of professional expertise in these and other areas where your knowledge may be lacking.

ZONING AND RENTING PROBLEMS

There has been a lot of talk about using a residential area for business. Although the laws about this are antiquated, they are enforceable in many areas. Be careful. If you use your home to conduct your business and do not disturb your neighbors, you should be safe. When you start renting out your studio to others, having trucks making deliveries, and allowing clients to come in at all hours, you are walking a fine line. Check with your local municipality for complete information about their zoning laws. If you are a renter, also check your lease. Your landlord may expressly prohibit you from running a business from an apartment.

WHAT'S IN A NAME?

Selecting your business name is one of the first crucial marketing strategies. This is surely one of the toughest things you'll ever do. Pick a name for your company that will stand the test of time, and pick one that says what you do. Amalgamated Inc. is not a good name by any means. Commercial Music Producers is better.

Though my company, Fisher Creative Group, has several subsidiaries, such as publishing and business consulting services, I use my own name for my music division: Jeffrey P. Fisher Music. It tells who I am and what I do. I am a hard-working, aggressive small company and not some huge music factory. So I picked a name that represented that niche.

In some states, you must file a fictitious name statement or d/b/a ("doing business as") if you run a company bearing a name other than your own. Check with your local municipality, county, or Secretary of State for more details on licenses and d/b/a information. They should provide you with all the guidelines and legal requirements for doing business in your area. And check with a lawyer, too.

Filing a d/b/a and getting proper licenses are painless experiences. The fees are quite reasonable (and are tax deductible business expenses)—they're certainly much less than penalties you would incur by doing something illegal. Ignorance is not an acceptable legal defense. Remember the Boy Scout motto: Be prepared!

YOUR BUSINESS STRUCTURE

Use my model for running your commercial music business. I work from my home in a combined studio, office, and control room. My main business functions are music composer, producer, and business consultant. Fisher Creative Group is a sole proprietorship. This means the business is owned completely by me; I therefore file my business profit as part of my personal income tax return using Schedule C.

FCG has no employees. All musicians, voice artists, and other advisors are paid on contract, therefore I pay no employment taxes. I do, however, file 1099 forms at the end of the year for those contracted personnel to whom I paid more than $600 in a year (this dollar limit is current for 1997). My income taxes get paid quarterly by filing the 1040ES (estimated tax) form for both federal and state income taxes. This payment also includes self-employment tax (my contribution to FICA, also known as social security and medicare) at the wonderfully hefty and somewhat discriminatory rate of 15.3% of my income. You see, when you are self-employed, you must pay both the employee *and* employer contributions to FICA (many people don't realize that their employer matches what's deducted from their paycheck). You do, however, get to deduct half of any self-employment tax you pay on your tax return, so it all evens out in the long run. Sort of.

All your equipment purchases can either be expensed or depreciated, but I let my accountant worry about these details. Of course, *all* business-related expenses can be deducted. This includes advertising costs, postage, office supplies, music-related supplies, equipment, etc. If you are just starting out, all the expenses you incur are deductible, but not all at once; business start-up expenses must be amortized over five years.

By definition, I don't consider myself an entrepreneur. An entrepreneur is someone who loves the *business* side of being in business. Paul and Sarah Edwards have a newer word: the *pro*preneur. A propreneur is a professional person who provides a service and is more interested in *providing the service* than in running the business itself. I consider myself part of this new breed of professional entrepreneur and you should, too. Don't sweat the business aspects, just recognize, understand, and deal with them as best you can. The business part is a necessary evil, but don't let it discourage you. Remember, you are a professional composer who just happens to be in business. Don't be surprised that others envy your position.

The excellent booklet *Starting and Managing a Business From Your Home*, published by the Small Business Administration, explains the four forms your music business can take. Below, I quote from this booklet and add some of my own comments as well.

◗ SOLE PROPRIETORSHIP
This is the least costly way to start a business. Just open your door and you are in business. You must register your business name and obtain any necessary licenses, but that is about all that is required. Some of the advantages include:
• It's easy to start.
• All authority is given to the owner (you).
• There are some income tax advantages for small firms.

Some disadvantages include:
• You have unlimited personal liability.
• Growth is limited to the owner's personal energies.
• Your personal life is easily mixed with business.

◗ PARTNERSHIP
Partnerships are very similar to being a sole-proprietor because each partner keeps track of business income along with other personal information. With a partnership, the parties involved agree to certain terms such as who does what, how much each makes, what each partner brings to the business, who owns equipment, copyrights, and much, much more. Don't even think about entering into a business partnership without some form of contract or agreement. Fees for starting a partnership are higher because an attorney should be consulted to create the agreement. Some

advantages include:
• Two heads are better than one.
• There are additional sources of capital.

Some disadvantages include:
• There is often a somewhat hazy line of authority.
• It can be difficult to end the relationship.
• Once again, you are personally liable.

◗ CORPORATION
A corporation is an entity unto itself. It pays taxes and files certain reports as if it were a taxpayer. Even the owner of the corporation is considered an employee. The corporation pays everyone involved, and whatever is left is corporate profit. The corporate form of business is the most costly to start and maintain. Attorney and registration fees can be considerable. Some advantages include:
• There are potential limits to liability.
• You can transfer shares and the business can continue after the owner's death.
• There is an easy separation of business and personal affairs.
• It's possible to split the company into different corporations that have separate business functions.

Some disadvantages:
• Owners have a somewhat false sense of security.
• There are higher taxes.
• Power is limited.
• You have many legal formalities to follow.
• It can be expensive to launch and maintain.

◗ S CORPORATION
An S corporation is a slightly different corporate form. The essential difference is that it is not subject to corporate tax and the business profits flow through to the owners, who record the profits on their personal tax returns.

One advantage of any kind of corporation is that it protects the employees from personal liability. Whereas a sole-proprietor or partnership can be sued with damages awarded from *personal* assets, a corporation protects the people who own it. However, a closely held corporation, such as one with only one principal employee, may not be so protected. Hence, the security issue—the reason many people form corporations—is somewhat blurry. This is a complicated issue and one that can't be sufficiently dealt with in this book alone. Ask your lawyer before you form your business structure.

PROTECTING YOURSELF WITH CONTRACTS

A verbal contract isn't
worth the paper it's printed on.
—LOUIS B. MAYER

- -

A contract is security for both you and your client. It gives piece of mind by reducing fear. I hate long, drawn out contracts because they scare prospects and clients. Your contract can be a promotional tool if you draft it carefully and make it easy to read and not intimidating. It is really just a letter of agreement that you can easily revise and amend to accommodate certain circumstances (within guidelines set forth by a lawyer). I've found that clients really appreciate this kind of contract. It shows them how easy it is to do business with me and that I'm very serious and firm.

Put simply, a contract states what you'll do, what the client will do, what it will cost, and how they will pay. They sign it and return it to you with an initial payment. You invoice them for the remaining payments. Call your contract a Letter of Agreement and keep it simple. The "Samples" section contains a contract you can use as a model for your own. Here are the essential elements of every contract:

- Print it on your letterhead.
- Date it.
- Include the client name and address.
- Name the project.
- List the services you will provide for this project.
- List any other specifications, including the tape format of the final music master.
- Indicate the date the agreement begins and the due date (when you will deliver the services you list above).
- Indicate the total fee for the project and the terms of how it is to be paid.
- Show how additional expenses are to be reimbursed.
- Indicate the amount of the advance the client must return with the signed agreement.
- Add any independent contractor language with special notes about ownership or work-for-hire. This is the Grant of Rights section, where you indicate if you are selling all rights or one-time rights, the territory (world, regional, local), and the duration (in perpetuity, one year, etc.).
- Leave room for both your and your client's signature and the date. Make two copies of the agreement and sign them both. Ask your client to sign both copies and keep one and return the other copy to you with a check for the amount of the advance.

You'll notice in the contract that I try to get some money up front. The reason is simple. Writing music is customized, by nature. Once you begin, the music may not be appropriate somewhere else. By getting money first, you have more leverage should the client decide not to continue. Plus, this payment usually helps weed out the serious people from those who might try to take advantage of you.

Get your lawyer to review these or any other contracts you might use. I hope by now you can see the importance of professional advisors who can help you get started in the right direction.

INVOICES MAKE SURE YOU GET PAID

Money is better than poverty,
if only for financial reasons.
—WOODY ALLEN

- -

Print invoices on your letterhead. You don't need tons of forms lying around (and you don't need to pay for forms you don't really need). I either print my invoices on letterhead or on blank stock with the word "Invoice" emblazoned across the top. Give each invoice a unique number. Preprinted forms come with numbers, but if you print your own, as I do, just start from 1001 and go up from there. If you prefer, you can number your invoices by date such as 062497. This says that the invoice is from June 24, 1997. It's best to itemize everything on your invoice. Show exactly what each item is and what it costs, then total it at the bottom. I don't leave anything to chance. This way, the client knows exactly what was delivered and what it cost. When you send the invoice, always type on the outside of the envelope: "Invoice Enclosed." This keeps the invoice from being put in the wrong mail pile! Translation: You get paid faster.

Send out all invoices promptly and insist on being paid immediately. Many companies will ignore your request and pay you in 30 to 60 days anyway. Fight for payment and help your cash flow by getting at least one-half of the total amount due before you release the final master. Never give up the master tape until you've been paid in full. You can be a little lenient with long-standing clients but for new ones, be firm! This is no joke. Most serious prospects and clients will appreciate your professionalism and attention to detail. Those who don't probably aren't worth working with anyway. When questioned about my practices—either why I need money up front or why I have a no-money-no-tape policy—I simply say:

This is how I do business. My lawyer and I
worked out this strategy for both your and my
benefit.

Keep a copy of each invoice in a folder or binder. When the check arrives, staple the stub or a copy of the check to the appropriate invoice copy. File these separately from any unpaid, overdue invoices. Call clients promptly when they are late on their payments and request an immediate check. If you use a computer, set up an Accounts Receivable file to monitor the money that's due.

TALENT RELEASES

Besides contracts between you and your clients, you may wish to use contracts between you and others you hire to provide a service, such as musicians who play on a recording. At the very least, have your contract talent sign a release. This should simply say that upon accepting payment, they release their work from further claims. In other words, their contribution is a work for hire and the one-time payment for services rendered is all they shall receive or are entitled to. (See the "Samples" section.)

STATIONERY

You definitely need a stationery set to help your professional image. You'll use it for everything: sales letters, follow-up letters, general correspondence, invoices, contracts, promotional materials, marketing kit pieces, and more. Specifically, you need:
• Letterhead
• Matching blank stock for second pages
• Envelopes
• Business cards
• Printed address labels

Your best bet is to check with printers in your area. Go to each one and get a quote. You'll be amazed at the range of prices. Find a small printing firm—usually a one-person shop—that can do a good job inexpensively.

Spend some money on design (the in-house designer should be adequate) and use good quality paper, too. To make an even better impression, use colored ink and coordinating color stock such as Wedgewood Blue ink on Wausau gray recycled paper. Have your envelope and business cards match this same scheme and design. Print about 1000. If you're going to use direct marketing heavily, print more. A mailing to 500 prospects depletes your stock by 50% instantly.

Strapped for cash? Get business cards first and work your way into stationery. Another alternative is to use a mail order printer. Usually their designs are fixed, but their prices are very reasonable. You can choose stock logos, stock type styles, and several paper and colored ink combinations. Here are a couple such printers. Ask for their latest catalog.
• B.A.P. Direct. 8500 Wyoming Avenue North, Minneapolis, Minnesota 55445-1825; (800) 328-2179. You can get 500 cards, letterhead, and matching envelopes from them for under $100!
• The Business Book. One East Eighth Ave., Oshkosh, WI 54906; (800) 558-0220. Their prices are equally competitive and they carry other business goodies.

Special Note: If you use a laser printer, you *must* get flat printing on your letterhead and envelopes or risk ruining your laser. If you type, write, or use an impact printer, you can use raised letter printing.

Make sure someone checks your stationery for accuracy. Once I would have forgotten my zip code if my wife hadn't noticed it was missing just seconds before the print run. Also, include your area code with your phone number. It's very common to forget this vital tidbit. You should consider putting both your e-mail and Web addresses on your letterhead and cards, too.

For brochures, flyers, newsletters, and other specialty printed items, you can get a professional image fast by using preprinted color papers that are readily available. Though these prices can be high (in the long run), they are cheap in the short run. You can buy in small quantities and print as needed. Plus, you don't end up throwing away 2500 remainders just because your area code changed (this happened to a client of mine).
• Beaver Prints. Main Street, Bellwood, PA 16617; (800) 923-2837
• Paper Direct. 205 Chubb Ave., Lyndhurst, New Jersey 07071; (800) 272-7377

OFFICE EQUIPMENT

You need a telephone, but not a telephone system. You could get call waiting instead of a two-line phone. The question of whether to use your personal phone for business or get a separate business line is up to you. The telephone company used to frown on using your personal phone for business, but the proliferation of home offices has cooled their contempt. If you do use your personal phone during the day, answer it with a professional tone and message:

Hello, Jeffrey Fisher. How can I help you?

You also need an answering machine. Get a good quality unit with remote message retrieve or use voice mail supplied by your local phone company. Don't put funny messages on the machine either. A simple, businesslike message is better:

Thank you for calling Jeffrey P. Fisher Music. I

can't get your call right now because I'm currently helping other clients get the music they need. Please leave a message and I'll get back to you.

I rarely photocopy, because my computer can print an extra copy for my files. For copies of check stubs and other things, make a weekly trek to your local copy shop. If you follow my advice and use a computer (see below) to handle most of your business routine, you won't need a copy machine.

You won't need a fax machine either. For sending or receiving the occasional fax, I go to the local print shop. The charges are steep, but my total fax bill one year was only $18.00. If you need to choose between a copy machine and a stand-alone fax machine, get a fax machine. You can make copies on a fax, but you can't send faxes on a copy machine. A fax modem is probably the most cost-effective tool if you have a computer system.

POSTAGE AND SHIPPING

Another expensive part of doing this business is postage. Between direct marketing, your keep-in-touch plan, and mailing marketing kits and tapes, you'll run up some substantial UPS and post office bills. Establish an account with UPS for your overnight shipping.

Use UPS for all your important deliveries. I once sent a first-class package to a client who was only ten miles away, and it took 12 days to get there! Lately though, I've had good luck with the post office priority mail. My promotional kit usually costs over $2.50 to send first class, so I pay the extra pennies and ship it priority mail. All my client prospects comment about how fast I deliver material. This little factor shows how much you care and how you want to help them, quickly and conveniently. Also, I'm fortunate that UPS has a big operation in Chicago. I can send any package UPS ground to a client in any area and they usually get it the next day. That really impresses my clients and prospects, and I save some money, too.

OTHER ODDS AND ENDS

Of course, you'll need some general business supplies, like address labels, oversized envelopes, stamps, UPS materials, staples, clips, etc. Shop at the local office supply superstore for most supplies. You can also get much of this mail order from places like The Business Book, cited earlier.

Another necessary item is a good pocket calendar like the Filofax or Day Runner system (or an electronic equivalent like those made by Sharp or Casio).

Use it to keep track of dates, sessions, meetings, and expenses, and to monitor your overall marketing plan. Keep names and addresses in there, too. List all your major ongoing projects and goals, and keep your daily and weekly "To Do" lists in it. Each day you'll know exactly what to do. Personally, I've moved away from my pocket calendar and rely mostly on my computer. Now my paper diary just keeps track of mileage for tax purposes.

Take a moment at the end of each day to plan your next day and at the end of each week to plan the next week. Don't live day-to-day. Make plans, establish goals and deadlines, and work to reach them. And when you do reach a major milestone, reward yourself for doing so. You deserve it.

YOUR COMPUTER FOR BUSINESS AND MUSIC

Though you may need some occasional professional help, such as legal, accounting, and other ancillary services, I do suggest you *take charge* of your own music career. That means handling most matters yourself, which can be a formidable task. If your resources are minuscule, you probably can't afford or don't wish to hire employees or independent outside help. By necessity you will need to manage your daily business demands alone. For that situation, the most cost-effective tool you can buy is a computer. You can't be in business without one anymore. Does the following sound familiar?

• When you get an inquiry you type a cover letter from scratch.

• You scramble to finish basic proposals for prospective clients.

• You have trouble locating client files, letters, contracts, and notes.

If you answered yes to any of these questions, you need help. That is why your computer is so important. It becomes your indispensable helper and often your memory. It helps you handle routine tasks with increasing efficiency. You should use your computer to find, reach, promote, sell, help, and maintain clients. It's the quintessential marketing tool. Your computer is vital to your success. Rely on it to perform all those diverse business functions—accounting, order entry, contact management, sales, marketing, business management, and much more. You simply can't deal efficiently with the everyday demands of running a small business without the help of a computer system. Unless you completely integrate your computer system into your business, you'll have a tough time handling all the details.

Let's avoid a lengthy discussion about computer hardware specifics. My personal philosophy is to find the software you enjoy, that mirrors the way you think and work, and then buy the hardware platform it runs on. Too many people do this the other way around. I advocate you consider my approach. The bare minimum software you should consider is:

- A good, all-purpose word processor
- A contact management system or personal information manager
- A mailing list manager or database system
- Accounting software geared toward small business
- Anything else you consider essential to your business success

◆ WORD PROCESSOR

For many people, a solid word processing program is all they'll ever need. Use it to draft and store all your marketing and promotional material. You can do mail merge, make rudimentary spreadsheets, and keep your files together in one place. Macros let you automate many tasks, such as standard salutations, closings, and more. You can also use it to keep track of clients, meetings, long-range goals, and more. Some even have rudimentary databases that you can use for both contact and mailing list management. Other than a financial and desktop publishing program, my word processor has everything I need to run my commercial music business.

◆ CONTACT OR PERSONAL INFORMATION MANAGER

You will be reaching hundreds—maybe even thousands—of people throughout your career. Keeping track of all those details in your head is impossible. This software helps you track inquiries, clients, meetings, to-do lists, and more.

◆ MAILING LIST MANAGER OR DATABASE

Let this software manage all the details of your business contacts. Some contact managers have extensive database features so you can get by with one program. If you need more intensive data management features, a dedicated database program is definitely the way to go.

◆ SMALL BUSINESS ACCOUNTING SOFTWARE

You must master managing your money. Let me tell you that a simple money management program can make your life much easier. Lest you think that the software will be the equivalent of balancing your checkbook on computer, you are in for a huge surprise. You will always know your true financial position when you meticulously track both income and expenses.

Another problem facing every growing business is the lack of funds to finance proper promotion. That's why I've relied on my computer to pioneer what I call Just-in-Time marketing. The phrase, which I borrowed from the manufacturing industry, means to manufacture products as needed. Rather than stock huge inventories of raw materials, you order them as you need them—when you need them, just in time and right before you consume them—and then you ship the finished products out the door. Need I tell you the potential savings in time and money that brings?

I've modified the principle and applied it to routine business tasks. You keep all your basic business information, everything you use to run your daily business, on your computer. This way, you can deliver what your clients and prospects need just in time. While your computer can't answer your phone or attend meetings, it can help you manage other tasks. Automating with your computer helps you save time and money, two important considerations for every burgeoning small business.

Of course, you must have a first class product or service, but if nobody knows you exist, it's all for nothing. Words and pictures are some of the promoter's tools. Composing music is a product (sort of), but you are really in the service business. Although your music is what you ultimately must sell, I believe that trust, dependability, knowledge, and your track record reduce prospect's fear factor. Therefore, you need to produce marketing materials to help position you as a leader.

- First, choose software that complements your method of working. The key is to get your work done efficiently.
- Next, put everything on your computer, especially general correspondence, promotional materials, sales letters, proposals, contracts, budgets, invoices, and thank you notes. It takes time to gather this material, but in the long run you save time. Once you develop boilerplate copy, you can use it repeatedly. You can personalize each piece through mail merge or by slipping in a customized paragraph or two. The rest of the piece is your standard marketing and sales information. Once you develop these parts, you can churn out documents in minutes. That's certainly less time consuming than typing something from scratch every time you get an inquiry.
- Finally, let your computer be an integral part of your everyday business routine. Computers excel at routine tasks, and most of your work is routine. Delegate some of your workload to that box on your

desk. All you should have to do is select a file, update it quickly, customize it to your target, and print.

Here's an example: When someone inquires about my services, I add their name to my mailing list in my word processor and then use mail merge to print a cover letter and envelope. I open additional files to print my brochure and other promotional items specific for this inquiry. I fold the pieces, stuff them in the envelope, grab a stamp, and the inquiry is filled. What could be easier? You get three advantages with this strategy:

• It helps your cash flow. You don't spend money to preprint garden variety brochures or other marketing communications.
• Your materials are always up to date. They aren't written in stone. You can change , customize, and print them on demand. Instead of drafting from scratch, you can spend your energies on more important duties.
• You can put together the material you need quickly and easily. Grab an old proposal, update the budget, slip in the prospect's name, and print. Only computer automation and Just-in-Time marketing make this possible and affordable.

My computer *is* my company—it's my accounting, shipping, marketing, manufacturing, and customer service departments. And it helps me with my music occasionally, too. As a one-man band, I couldn't handle the workload without the help of my computer system. All my forms, invoices, sales letters, general correspondence, books, newsletters, reports, articles, and more are stored on my computer and printed on my laser printer on demand. You, too, should follow this strategy. Just look at the examples in the "Samples" section and get started right now. Be prepared in advance and you'll use your time, resources, and money more effectively, so that you are ready for anything that comes your way.

My ultimate goal is to eliminate all paper files in my office and keep everything online where I can get at it easily. To date, I've been quite successful. The only items in my paper files are signed contracts and other materials sent by clients. All my business is on the computer. Of course, I have to back up the hard drive quite regularly, but it's worth it. This system has kept my physical client files to one drawer in a file cabinet. At the end of the year, I archive all the dead files and free up space for the next year.

A computer can help you in so many areas by taking care of the routine and, since most business is routine, the computer gives you more time to be productive and successful. By liberating yourself from the mundane tasks, you have more time to be creative—writing the best music you can for all your clients . . . and yourself!

CHOOSING YOUR COMPUTER SYSTEM

You must think of your computer as a system—a specific methodology for making your business better, easier to run, and more profitable. Choose software that works together well and matches *your* personal working style. Remember that besides using the software for business, you are also the system administrator. You are the one who installs new software, troubleshoots, backs up the disk regularly, etc. All this makes your task even more difficult. That's why it's important to choose a hardware and software system that you can handle both from the end-user and the system administrator's point of view.

To give you a better idea of how to integrate your computer into your business, let's take a closer look at my hardware and software package.

• Packard Bell Pentium, 16MB RAM, 1.2GB hard drive, and VGA monitor
• Lexmark 4029-010 laser printer
• Fax/data modem
• Windows 95
• Lotus Ami Pro 3.0
• Microsoft Access 2.0
• Microsoft Money 97
• Microsoft Publisher 97
• Norton Utilities 2.0
• Netscape 3.0

I've recently converted to Windows 95. Since you are the system administrator, managing folders, files, and back-ups must be easy. I appreciate the way Windows 95 lets you customize your desktop to the way *you* work. Throw in the Norton Utilities and you have a solid business computing environment.

I create folders for all my clients, then place shortcuts to every pertinent file—regardless of software application—into its corresponding folder. From there, I can launch any client document (and its associated application) and begin working immediately. When you're jumping back and forth between a bevy of clients and projects, this simple organizational tool helps tremendously.

A simple day planner reminds me of important deadlines, appointments, etc. If an event takes place while the computer is off, a message pops up when I turn the system on.

The Norton Utilities have saved me several times. (I really love the way you can recover an accidentally erased file and pick up right where you left off.)

For tracking clients and prospects, I use my

database. Between it and my word processor's mail merge, I have no complaints. I've written several different database applications that run under Microsoft Access. Each is custom-tailored to my specific demands. That's the flexibility a programmable database has over a fixed piece of software. However, unless you are a pocket protector-wearing computer geek (like me), stick with off-the-shelf stuff.

Microsoft Publisher is an ideal program for brochures, flyers, newsletters, Internet publishing, and more. No other program gets you looking good on paper faster. Add in some clip art and you get a powerful and sophisticated Desktop Publishing System.

Microsoft Money handles my personal and business finances adequately. With it, I can produce reports and charts sorted by customer to obtain any information I need.

Lotus Ami Pro is for correspondence, marketing materials, articles, invoices, mailing lists, and everything else not covered in the other programs. And the modem brings me into modern telecommunications.

If your funds are short, you can handle many tasks using only a decent word processor to store all your client files, letters, and addresses; track income and expenses; and more. Forcing your word processor to do these tasks is a compromise, but with a little perseverance, it can suffice for many years. Use it to keep track of pertinent information, such as meeting notes, follow-up details, and so forth, and create master documents for all your clients. And be sure to follow the Just-in-Time principles explained earlier.

With today's hardware prices at an all-time low (and possessing incredible power), there is no reason to put off computerizing even the humblest business. You won't regret it. You'll be more efficient, more knowledgeable about what is really happening, and ultimately more profitable.

WORK AT HOME STRATEGIES

Earlier I suggested you work from home during the initial phases of your burgeoning commercial music business. Unfortunately, the versatility of a home project studio also brings many other temptations and distractions. Friends call, relatives stop by, and many people may not think you are *really* working. It's best to stick to a regular schedule. Exercise too much flexibility and you seldom get anything done. Since most clients call between nine and five, you need to be available. Plan your day accordingly. Of course, you can use an answering machine or voice mail when you are away. But even if you pursue this business only part-time, you need to devise a routine. Procrastination can be your worst enemy.

When using your home as your base, you may discover some conflicts with other family members, too. Follow these simple guidelines and use some good common sense to reduce the possible frustrations of combining family, fun, and your important work.

- Get into a routine. You can't run your business occasionally. You must set a schedule of some kind. Though it need not be precise, it should be functional. Recognize your limitations and personal preferences and know what to do to complete each project. If you're not self-motivated, you might need some nudging to get going. Do what you must to make sure you start working toward your goals.

- Explain your situation. Spouses, significant others, and especially children need to understand what you are doing. Show them what you do, what you plan to do, and share your goals with them. Make sure you include your family in your plans. They are an integral part of your success machine. Work out a schedule so they recognize when you are working and when you are available to them.

- Set up a specific work space. A spare bedroom or basement home office will help you avoid household distractions. Plus, you can close the door when the day is over and leave your work behind. Walking past your work can be too much of a temptation when you're supposed to be relaxing. Get a separate telephone line just for your business matters and let it ring only in the office. You'll avoid embarrassments like having your two-year-old hang up on an important client.

- Child care may be a good solution. If you're choosing to work from home so that you can spend more time with your family, you may encounter difficulty. One solution may be to combine some child care with your home routine. Even a sitter for a few hours each day can free you for important, uninterrupted business tasks.

MANAGING YOUR TIME BETTER

*A well fed waste basket will
serve you better than the best computer.*

—ROY WEST

When you are a one-person shop, your single biggest enemy is time or the lack thereof. How can you handle all the details that you must attend to and still have time and energy to compose? You must manage your time effectively. Your computer system and my Just-in-Time strategy should go a long way toward making you more efficient. Meanwhile, here are a few other tips:

- Set goals and objectives. These should be personal, creative, business, and financial goals. Write them down on a piece of paper and put them where you can see them. My goals pop up on my computer screen when I start each day. It's hard to ignore that constant reminder. When you achieve one goal, set another.

- Handle your papers only once. Decide what action you must take, such as read, file, or destroy. If you are not sure what you should do with it, roll it up into a ball, toss it into the air, and score a basket! Jordan for three . . .
- Discourage time-wasting phone calls and meetings. Get to the point quickly by simply asking how you can help.
- Make an agenda for each meeting with a list of expected decisions that *must* be made. Start with a goal and use the meeting time to accomplish that goal.
- Take time each day to manage your main activities. Even just one hour of uninterrupted time each day can make running your business easier. Many people don't take calls or schedule meetings for the first half of the day and use this time to get things done. I use this time to write or compose.
- Finish one project completely before moving on to the next. Though this isn't always easy, it is a good objective. Set a quota by breaking the big projects into smaller bits and prioritizing each task. When you completely finish one part, move on to the next. This is a useful psychological tool, especially when you get terribly busy.
- Think positive thoughts. Nothing is ever prefect . . . er . . . perfect. Do your best job under the given circumstances.
- Say "no" when a project is beyond your skills or time constraints.
- Accomplish little tasks in your spare time, such as stuffing envelopes and sorting paperwork. Or you can do some light business reading while you watch TV.
- Take time to relax. A few hours (or days) away from your work will make you more efficient and creative. Take a friend to lunch or take an occasional long weekend.

DEALING WITH STRESS

Though some stress is important to your well-being, too much stress can adversely affect your mental and physical health. When you take charge of your musical career, you become responsible for so many details that the stress of handling it all can be overwhelming. What makes running your own commercial music business so exciting and challenging is the same thing that can really damage your life. I consulted with the U.S. Department of Health and Human Services for these tips to prevent or minimize the effects of stress on your daily life.

- Try physical activity. Release all that pressure through exercise. Just a brisk walk may help reduce stress levels. Or you can try a more strenuous workout to alleviate the bad vibes. Personally, I'm fond of Tai Chi. This exercise strikes a wonderful balance between a hard workout and enriching relaxation.
- Share your stress. It may help to talk through matters with a friend, family member, or fellow business colleague. Don't just unload your troubles. Make the session productive by working through your stress and arriving at possible solutions.
- Know your limits. If a problem is beyond your control, don't fight the situation. Learn to accept some things as they are. As the adage goes, don't sweat the small stuff. And by the way, it's all small stuff anyway!
- Take care of yourself. Get enough rest and eat well. Starting your day stressed out will only make matters worse down the line.
- Make time for fun. You should schedule time for your work and your recreation. Play is as important to your health as work is to your wallet. You need an occasional break from your routine to just relax and have some fun.
- Check off your tasks. Trying to take care of everything at once is often overwhelming. Before you bite off more than you can chew, break up the big chores into many tiny, bite-sized pieces. Completing each small task moves you closer to finishing the big picture, and it does so in a much less stressful manner.
- Find a quiet place and go to it. It doesn't need to be an idyllic country scene. Create a quiet place in your mind and take some time to bathe in the mental picture. I grab some headphones, a Mahler CD, close the door, crank the volume, and float away . . .

Your best attack against stress is to relax. Take time out for yourself and let matters slide. A little perspective can go a long way toward both reducing your stress and beating the causes of that stress. So loosen up, dude. Stay cool!

- *Slow Down and Get More Done*, Marshall J. Cook. F&W Publications; 1507 Dana Ave., Cincinnati, OH 45207. Here's a terrific resource for you to consult. It's not just another time management book, this is a *life* management book. Use it to be more productive, creative, and relaxed. Good stuff!

ADDITIONAL BUSINESS RESOURCES

For a listing of all the free and super cheap helpful government publications like *Starting and Managing a Business From Your Home*, write to:

- Superintendent of Documents. U.S. Government Printing Office; Washington, DC 20402; (202) 783-3238

• U.S. Small Business Administration, Office of Business Development. SBA Publications; P.O. Box 30, Denver, CO 80201-0030; (800) 827-5722; www.sba-online.sba.gov. The SBA is an informational powerhouse. Take advantage of what they have to offer.

Here are some other useful business resources for those just starting out. They are equally effective for experienced entrepreneurs, too.

• *Homemade Money: The Definitive Guide to Success in a Home-Based Business*, Barbara Brabec. F&W Publications; 1507 Dana Ave., Cincinnati, OH 45207. There is no better book on home-based success anywhere. "The A-Z Crash Course" in business basics alone is worth adding to your personal business reference library. And it was recently updated to its fifth edition.

• *The Home Office and Small Business Answer Book,* Janet Attard. Henry Holt; 115 W. 18th St., New York, NY 10011. This helpful resource is subtitled *The Solutions to the Most Frequently Asked Questions About Starting and Running Home Offices and Small Businesses.* Just starting out? Get what you need right here.

• *Working From Home* and *Making It on Your Own*, Sarah and Paul Edwards. Jeremy P. Tarcher Inc.; 5858 Wilshire Blvd., Suite 200, Los Angeles, CA 90036. The first book is a strong, basic summary to setting up a home-based business. The second is more inspirational than practical.

• SCORE, the Service Corps of Retired Executives. For *free* advice about business, management, taxes, record keeping, advertising, marketing, financial plans, and more. Most cities have local chapters. To take advantage of this helpful service, contact your local U.S. Small Business Administration office or call the SBA national answer desk at (800) 827-5722.

• Office of Women's Business Ownership. 1441 L St., N. W., Suite 414, Washington, DC 20416; (202) 653-8000. Another SBA service exclusively for women business owners.

• Office of Minority Business Enterprise. U.S. Department of Commerce; Washington, DC 20230; (202) 377-2000. A special service just for minority business owners.

• Try your area's Department of Commerce and Community Affairs. Many states have training resources to help your business succeed.

THE REWARDS OF YOUR LIFE'S WORK

If you love what you do, you'll be good at it. If you're good at it, you'll be a success at it. You may not necessarily make a huge amount of money, but we're talking about making a life, not making a fortune. You'll find a way to make a living, and that living will feed you with energy and satisfaction as well as bread, and it will not be separate from the rest of your life.

—MARSHALL COOK

How do you gauge your own success? Is it money? Recognition? Satisfaction? Don't equate your own success with someone else's measure of success. You can—and should—work on your own level. Do what *you* want to do and in the way *you* want to do it. Don't be concerned with other people's perceptions. You must be happy first!

There will always be someone who writes better lyrics, composes sweeter melodies, and uses fancier recording tricks. Forget about all that. Each of us has a unique gift to share. Stop worrying about the other guys and get on with it. Because the rewards of finding and following your life's work can be great.

• You can do it for personal reasons.
• You can do it to learn and grow.
• You can do it to do it.
• You can do it to make money or at least support your hobby or a portion of your life.
• You can do it for satisfaction and recognition.

Your reasons may be different. It might help to think of your initial music business venture as something recreational. Your investment is much like going to the movies or on vacation. Once you've spent the money, it's gone. If you make money from it, fine; but think of it as an expense first. You can pay for classes and books, but you'll learn more by actually doing it. There's no substitute for the knowledge you gain through experience.

Special caution: Be conservative. Don't go over the edge. Be realistic and practical. Write down your goals and the steps you must take to reach them. Then take small steps and learn as you proceed. Don't stifle your exuberance, but don't bleed yourself dry either. And don't spend vast amounts of money on this venture or you'll lose your shirt. Don't expect to make a fortune, but do expect success. Monitor your progress, cover your costs, and put some cash in your pocket! Do it on your own level, make some money, and grow. You'll find the work more satisfying, rewarding—and fun!

If you are concerned about the price that
life may exact from you, you should know that a
price will be paid in either case—if you choose to
pursue your dream, and also, if you don't.
Which price would you rather pay?

—DR. ROBERT ANTHONY

What's stopping you now? Here are some final thoughts that just might help. I always wanted to run my own company and not work for someone else, but there was always that nagging voice in my head:

But you gotta get a job, man.

I don't need a job. I just need *work*. And that's a significant difference, don't you think?

There's no security working on your own. How
will you live?

There's no security on the job either. One day you have a job, then—wham, bam, thank you ma'am—you're unemployed and facing reality. Now what? Stay unemployed? Look for another job? Not me. You've got to prepare. Make your own way. Live your own life.

But there's no steady paycheck. No benefits.
No . . .

No what? Know nothing; do nothing. Know something; do anything . . . and everything. If you do it right, there *will* be a steady paycheck, benefits, rewards . . . and success.

To laugh, often and much; to win the respect of
intelligent people and the affection of children; to
earn the appreciation of honest critics and endure
the betrayal of false friends; to appreciate beauty, to
find the best in others; to leave the world a bit bet-
ter, whether by a healthy child, a garden patch, or a
redeemed social condition; to know even one life has
breathed easier because you have lived. This is to
have succeeded.

—RALPH WALDO EMERSON

CHAPTER 11

The Money Stuff

The propensity to truck, barter, and exchange one thing for another
. . . is common to all men, and to be found in no other race of animals.

—Adam Smith

You need a basic bookkeeping system to keep track of your income and expenses, for tax purposes among other reasons. I developed my own accounting system with help from my accountant. This system is detailed for one very simple reason: I want to know where my money comes from and where it goes. And since Uncle Sam demands these records (yes, you must keep every receipt), I use this system diligently. At the end of each month I know what was spent, what was earned, and how much is profit (or loss!). You must track your expenses carefully because they are all deductible.

This is known in the trade as a *cash* system. You enter every transaction as it is incurred. You get a check, you deposit it, and you record the credit. You get a bill, you write a check, and record the debit. Your balance is always up to date. This is the simplest, most efficient accounting system for any business.

This system is based around a chart of accounts. All expenses are entered in a daily diary (the Filofax or Day Runner systems are a good choice) or two-column ledger. I find using a diary to be the best way to keep track of appointments, expenses, mileage, and income, especially because it's the kind of evidence you need to back up any claims made to the IRS. Next, code every receipt with the appropriate account and file it in an envelope with all other receipts that use that code (account). Record income in the diary and file check stubs or copies of checks in the appropriate envelope or three-ring binder that holds the corresponding invoice copy. At the end of each month, total the expenses and subtract it from the total income to arrive at a profit or loss figure. Here's how your diary should look:

DATE/TIME	ACTIVITY	MILES	INCOME	EXPENSE	ACCOUNT
1/2-2:00	XYZ Video meeting	26.00			
1/2-4:00	Post office: stamps	2.00		$32.00	S
1/3-12:00	ZTS invoice #121597		$863.71		MP
1/3	Phone bill #123			$46.25	O
1/4-3:00	Acme Studio: vocal session	18.00		$55.00	E

Remember this: If you are audited, the *entire* burden of proof falls to you! The IRS is required to prove nothing. You must prove every deduction and claim you make with valid receipts and a diary or log of business activities. If you use an appointment calendar to keep track of these activities, you are in a better position.

This system is somewhat detailed. You may choose to simplify your record-keeping to just a few accounts. An even easier system is to open a business checking account. Make sure to use an interest bearing account for your business funds. (Why not earn some extra cash on your money?) My bank pays interest on commercial accounts and uses the money gained to offset any banking charges. Not a bad deal. Next, pay all your expenses by either check or credit card. Keep canceled checks, bank statements, and credit card statements by date order. Record the reason for the expense in the memo section of each check. You now have a simple, no-entry bookkeeping system. Combining my method with this strategy, you will enter the account code in the memo section, file the checks by account, and compile everything into a monthly total. Your tax preparation will be a snap. Plus, you'll always know your financial position.

To make life even simpler, pick up a copy of the Form 1040, Schedule C: Profit or Loss From Business. The expenses that are deductible are listed on a single page. I doubt you'll use *every* line. Just pick the ones applicable to your particular situation. You'll need 13 copies of this form to make this method work. All you need to do is keep track of your income and expenses, total them up at the end of each month, and record them in the appropriate space on the Schedule C. At the end of the year, you just total the individual forms and put the numbers on a new, final Schedule C. There you have it: a simple, quick business accounting system.

Why all this detail? Because business income is money in your pocket, and so is every business expense. If you have a legitimate business purchase and you fail to deduct it, that's the same as throwing money out the window. It's as good as gone, bud! Yes, it *can* get a bit tiresome keeping track of all this, but just devote an hour each week to bringing everything up to date. That way, at the end of the year all your tax records are already finished. You don't have to plow through boxes of receipts to figure everything out. All that's left to do is check the math and visit the accountant.

What kinds of business expenses can you deduct? Here is my chart of accounts for income and expenses. Take this to your accountant or use it to develop your own system. Notice that I pay talent on contract that day (or within a week) after they render their service to me. This fee is an expense. I charge my clients for the talent fee and usually add a markup to the fee to cover my administrative costs. I enter this under either "SJ" or "MP" income, depending on the project.

Income
- LS Live and session performances
- SJ Composing and arranging scores and jingles
- MP Studio music production
- BC Business consultant
- WB Writing
- ES Equipment sales or rental
- LT Lessons and teaching

Expenses
- A Auto mileage
- B Business meals and entertainment
- S Postage and shipping
- V Advertising
- P Printing, copies, and fax
- M Musical equipment and supplies
- O Office expenses and supplies
- T Travel expenses
- E Equipment and studio rental
- F Fees and commissions paid to talent
- X Legal and accounting fees
- D Cost of equipment over $300

All of these expense categories are tax deductible. Many are consumable items, meaning their value is limited to one use, such as paper. You deduct the item's full cost in the year it is purchased. For an item that lasts beyond one year, you depreciate or spread its cost over several years. You can elect which items to write off and which to depreciate. For example, though a stapler has a useful life beyond one year, its low cost is better written off, meaning you expense it all at once. Some major equipment purchases are depreciated rather than written off as expenses, hence the "M" and "D" categories with an arbitrary limit of $300. If I buy tape or strings, it goes under "M," but if I buy a new synthesizer, that goes under "D."

By keeping track of both monthly and year-to-date totals of income and expenses, I can see exactly how good (or bad) business is. I heartily suggest you either follow my system or use an off-the-shelf resource like those by Dome, which you can find in office supply stores. You won't regret it. I'm no accountant, but I find it very satisfying to know my financial situation in detail. This system works very well.

Also, make sure you check with your state for special benefits. For example, Texas now gives tax exemptions on certain rented and leased film, video, and music equipment. It's hard to know all the little benefits that are available to you, but it's crucial. You need to stay informed, and that means using both casual and specific research. Read the daily paper, local papers, the trade press, and ask questions of your advisors. You'll save yourself money and aggravation.

COMPUTERIZED ACCOUNTING

*Live within your income. Always have
something saved at the end of the year. Let your
imports be more than your exports, and you'll
never go far wrong.*

— Dr. Samuel Johnson

Recently, I started using Microsoft Money, a Windows financial program, to handle my records. It's a simplified accounting system that has everything you need to keep track of both personal and business finances. I've also heard good things about Quicken. If you have a computer, check out one of these packages. You run the system just like a checkbook—entering transactions and keying them to accounts, either business or personal. You can generate a multitude of reports, including all the tax records you need. You still need your diary (for mileage and keeping track of business activities) and you still need to keep those receipts, but these systems make accounting painless. Since switching from my paper version, I've cut the time I spend each week consolidating my records down to about 15 minutes.

Many accounting software programs automatically create the appropriate tax documents I need. Here's an example of how my program takes all the information collected throughout the year and simplifies it for tax preparation. I just give this to my accountant and he does the rest.

JPFM Tax Report—Schedule C

• Gross receipts	$47,214.39
• Cost of goods sold	$6,207.84
• Commissions paid	$973.68
• Legal and professional	$475.00
• Supplies	$2,589.62
• Advertising	$841.08
• Office expense	$2,168.28
• Telephone	$453.71

THE IMPORTANCE OF YOUR CREDIT CARD

*I'm living so far beyond my
income that we may almost be living apart.*

—Saki

To be successful in business means having credit when you need it. You need to secure a good credit rating. Having a credit card helps. Many rental companies will charge you the full amount of the equipment rental and then credit your account when you return their equipment. Do you have enough credit for a $1500 deck? Or a $3000 keyboard workstation?

Have one credit card to use specifically for business purposes. Keep it clear, because you never know

what you'll need to buy. Also, the 30 to 60-day grace period allows you to float some of these out-of-pocket business costs. When I know a major purchase is coming up, I wait for my card to rollover and then buy what I need. This gives me the 30-day billing cycle plus the 25-day grace period before I have to pay. That means I have 55 days to raise the money I need to pay off the balance. I use this method more than any other financial strategy.

Credit helps the cash flow since you are not paying for expenses until *after* the client pays you. Use your credit wisely, and make sure you pay it off! Use it for convenience and to float costs that are due you from clients. Do not use your credit card to finance your business or your life. It's best used as a short term, stop gap measure.

CUT YOUR TAX BURDEN THROUGH SECTION 179

Let me further clarify expensing versus depreciation. When you expense an item, you deduct its entire cost in the year you place it in service. To depreciate an item, you deduct a portion of its cost over several years. For most electronic equipment, this is either five or seven years. Under IRS section 179, as of 1997, you can expense up to $18,000 (increasing to $25,000 by 2003) worth of equipment each year. This applies to major equipment purchases, not consumable items, such as office supplies that you can deduct as incurred. Essentially, you have a choice of writing off your major equipment purchases or carrying portions of their cost over several years. Your accountant can help you decide which is the right option for your particular situation.

However, let's look at how investing in your business can mean substantial tax savings to you. For example, you compose a score for $2000 gross income. If you are in the 28% tax bracket, pay the 15.3% self-employment tax, and have a 3% state income tax, your net income, after taxes, is $1074 (2000 x .537). You would write the government a check for $926!

If you spend $2000 for a new synthesizer, you reduce your gross income to zero. You pay no taxes because you can expense the equipment purchase (under the $18,000 limit), thus offsetting your income. In reality, you still spent the money, but instead of paying the government, you've strengthened your business through a wise equipment purchase. At the same time, you've saved 46.3% (the amount you would have paid in taxes) and therefore acquired a new synth for almost half-price!

This is just one example of the power of being in business. I am a firm believer that there is *absolutely no advantage* to running your business secretly, in the so-called underground economy, because there are so many legitimate business deductions and other advantages when you start and run a business. If you make $17,999.99 in a year, you can spend every last penny on new equipment and other items that make your business more profitable. If you don't need this income to live on, you can get a decent studio together quite quickly. Just remember that you must show a profit from your business three out of every five years, or the IRS says your little business is really a hobby. Talk to your accountant for all the details about this and other business deductions.

• IRS Publications: (800) 829-3676 or www.irs.ustreas. gov. You can get many free business tax-related publications directly from the Internal Revenue Service. Here are some of the most useful: Tax Guide for Small Business #344, Business Use of Your Home #587, Business Expenses #535, Self-Employment Tax #533, and Tax Withholding and Declaration of Estimated Tax #505.

ANOTHER TAX STRATEGY

Here's a tip that every small business can benefit from. The day after Thanksgiving, study your business financial picture. Gather up your income and expense reports and grab a copy of your business goals, specifically, your plans for the next year. Now use this information to look for ways to reduce your tax burden. There are only two legitimate methods you can employ:
• Delay your income
• Accelerate your expenses

What this really means is you should look for ways to either reduce the money you have coming in or uncover major purchases you can make *before* the end of the year. I'm not suggesting you stop working but rather that you should bill your clients later and offer liberal credit terms. This way you put off the income you would receive in December to January of the next year (worry about next year next year!). Contemplating a new computer? A direct mail campaign? I've printed and bought stamps for my catalog in late December just to get the tax break for a legitimate business expense. You can benefit from this strategy, too.

OTHER COSTS OF YOUR BUSINESS

Insurance, health care, retirement, disability, taxes, and advisor fees are other costs you must consider when starting and running your business. You need to insure your equipment; protect yourself from disability; and pay for your own health coverage, taxes, and all the expert advice you get from lawyers, accountants, and others.

If you have a full-time job and will only be composing music part-time, use your present employee benefits to cover health care and retirement. If you pursue this business full-time, try to get on a policy with a spouse, if possible. Paying for your own health insurance can be quite costly, but you can't live without it. You might need to get creative. Consider joining the Musician's Union for their health plan or weigh purchasing a stripped-down major medical policy to handle emergencies and hospitalization and pay for routine medical care yourself. Your homeowner's or renter's insurance policy should protect your equipment arsenal. Meet with your insurance agent to discuss all these options.

SAVING FOR YOUR FUTURE

There are two times in a man's life when he should not speculate: when he can't afford it, and when he can.

—MARK TWAIN

A dozen or so years ago, I didn't give a hoot about savings, pensions, IRAs, investing, etc. When you're young (and foolish), you just want the cash *now!* At 21, it's very hard to imagine retirement and even harder to start planning for it. But the reality of it is if you don't plan for your golden years, nobody will. Social Security probably won't be around, so you'd better stash some of your hard-earned cash away now.

There are some tax advantages to pension plans, too. You can start and contribute to a personal IRA that gives singles a $2000 tax deduction and couples one for $4000 each year. Plus, the interest on your nest egg grows tax-deferred until you reach age 59½. Be aware that your actual contribution level may vary depending on your particular tax situation, though.

Another option for sole proprietors and partnerships is a SEP—Simplified Employee Pension Plan. A SEP is easier to start than a 401(k) or Keogh plan because you contribute to it just like a personal IRA, but you can sock away up to 15% of your earned business income up to a total of $22,500. The actual percentage, due to funky IRS math, is 13.04% of your net business income minus one-half the self-employment taxes you pay. Anyway, the deduction for you (and your employees) is a deductible business expense, and the money earns tax-deferred interest until withdrawal. What's nice about this strategy is that, should you have a very profitable year, you can put more away. If times are tough, you can cut back. A SEP is flexible.

Talk to your accountant about pension plans.

Which would you rather do, pay taxes on your income and kiss the money good-bye forever, or defer some of your earnings through a legitimate pension savings plan and have the money when you retire? The choice is simple. You may have to wait until you're 59½, but that tidy little nest egg will be all yours. You must start thinking of investing as just another way to earn income.

Don't ignore this section. It is very important for you to understand that saving for the future is an important part of running both your music business and your life. If only someone had told me about all this when I first started my business. I learned much of this the hard way, and that is one reason why I wrote this book. I wanted to help others like you avoid the mistakes I made. Reading this book puts you at a distinct advantage above other would-be composers. Take heed: This is significant advice, and you'll thank me someday.

PLANNING FOR YOUR FUTURE MAKES DOLLARS AND SENSE

Just look at these numbers: If you're currently 34 years old (guess who is?) and invest $250 each month until you turn 65, you'll contribute a total of $93,000 to your plan. At 6% growth, your nest egg grows to $261,327. At 10% growth, it's $570,417. Contribute $500 a month for a total investment of $186,000 and it grows to $522,655 at 6% and $1,140,834 at 10%. I could retire on that. How about you?

But say you wait until you are 44 to start saving. If you invest $250 each month until you turn 65, you'll contribute a total of $63,000 to your plan. At 6% growth, your nest egg grows to only $123,242. At 10% growth, it's a measly $200,656. Contribute $500 a month for a total investment of $126,000 and it grows to $246,485 at 6% and $401,312 at 10%. Ah, what a significant difference a decade of compounding interest makes in your bottom line!

But just think of this: If you'd put $10,000 in an investment paying 8% when you turned 21, by age 65 you'd have a whopping $295,559 *without* having contributed another penny to the account. Right now my son is 64 years away from retirement. A *single investment* of $10,000 today at 8% would make him a millionaire at retirement with $1,377,591 in his account. Now, granted, this simple example doesn't account for taxes, inflation, or other circumstances that take a bite out of the nest egg, but I hope it clearly shows that starting your retirement planning *right now* pays off handsomely down the road.

What's especially nice is that any funds contributed to a SEP or other qualified pension plan earn tax-deferred interest and part, if not all, of the money you contribute is tax deductible. You not only save for your future, but you also reduce your tax burden significantly each year. Not a bad deal. And the way things are going, it's the *only* deal left to us poor American taxpayers.

YOUR ROAD TO FINANCIAL FREEDOM

The happiest time in any man's life is when he is in red-hot pursuit of a dollar with a reasonable prospect of overtaking it.
—JOSH BILLINGS

As I write and speak about my approach to music and business, one constant motif runs through my work. Running your own business is not about money. I'm talking about *building a life*, not just another job. And that is a significant difference, don't you think? One thought really helped me figure things out when I first contemplated starting Fisher Creative Group. You must uncover the work you really want to do and then take the steps necessary to create the kind of work and life that you want. There is a more spiritual side to work. To reach it, you have to put your financial worries behind you. You can work because you want to and not because you *have* to in order to survive.

If you diligently follow the methods described in this book, you will make money. This money will help you support your lifestyle. Just like a salary, these business profits bring you purchasing power. Running your commercial music business secures not just the money you need to sustain your current lifestyle, but also the money to pay for a portion—if not all—of your future lifestyle. Your money, when saved and invested, has the ability to earn more money. Your savings will pay you income—the income you use to support your chosen lifestyle.

Ultimately, the money you earn will make you financially independent. What is financial independence? It's having the money you need to live the life you wish to lead without having to work for the money. In other words, you have substantial savings that, when invested, pay for your basic living expenses. You won't be financially independent right away. First you need to get out of debt, make more money, save more money, invest your resources, and work your way toward financial independence. Despite what the pundits say, this is not some pipe dream. You *can* reach your goal by following these three steps to financial independence:

• Maximize income. You must increase your earnings substantially.
• Minimize expenses. You must decrease your expenses, first by eliminating debt and then by controlling your business and personal living expenses.

• Invest capital for savings, income, and retirement. You must learn to save and invest the proceeds that accumulate as a result of more money and less expenses. This is crucial, as you'll eventually live off the income produced by these investments.

♦ MAXIMIZE INCOME

The first step to financial independence is to develop steady sources of income. Notice I said sources, plural. Don't look at just one method. You need to explore ways of diversifying your income-producing vehicles. That's what this book is about: How to make money in the commercial music business. Later I'll explain how to parlay your experience into several other related moneymaking ventures that together will produce the income you need to reach financial independence.

Let's say it costs you $2000 each month—$24,000 a year—to support your basic living expenses. You would need $400,000 in the bank earning 6% interest to be financially independent. The $400,000 can earn $24,000 each year with very moderate return. Now that number may, at first, seem outlandish. How can I ever save that much money? Well here's an exercise that puts this in perspective.

First, you must understand how much money you are able to bring into your life. I know when I first contemplated this plan I thought there was no way I could *earn*, let alone *save* $100,000. So I ignored this step. One day, while balancing my Accounts Receivable, I accidentally clicked an option that displayed all income I received over a certain period. The figure made me gasp. Unbeknownst to me, I had brought in $99,559.83 during that time period. This wasn't *net* income, but the exercise instantly proved that I did have the ability to put a hundred grand into my hands. The next step was to control my expenses and *keep* more of that money. This becomes the capital you invest to support your financially independent lifestyle.

So, grab your tax returns for the past several years, total up the gross income and see how much money you've brought into your life during that time. Like most people, you'll be amazed at your fortitude. This initial feeling of elation is usually quickly snuffed by the realization that most of the money is gone. Where, oh where, did all the money go?

Second, you need to uncover what you have to show for all your hard work during that time. You've probably acquired some assets, such as a car, house, personal property, music gear, and such. You've spent much of your earnings on food, fun, and more. Hopefully, you've saved some, either in a savings account, investments, 401(k), or other such vehicles. And you've given some cash to Uncle Sam.

Gather up your assets and liabilities and create a net worth statement. For most assets, use the purchase price as its value. For instance, if you paid $100,000 for your house, that is the value of the asset. Do the same for your car, even though it is not worth as much as you paid for it. The number is still representative of your financial picture. Liabilities are your outstanding loans, credit card debt, and such. Grab your latest statements for these figures. Now add up your total assets and liabilities. Subtract the liabilities from your assets, and that is your net worth. Hopefully, it's a positive number. This amount is the total value of your estate, as it were. If you converted everything to cash, this is the amount of money you would have. Now, bear in mind that this is only an index—an approximation of your net worth. However, this figure is a sound representation of your current financial picture. Once you complete these two exercises, you'll realize your ability to bring in money and build a capital base.

♦ MINIMIZE EXPENSES

Next, determine your regular monthly expenses. How much does it cost you to maintain your current lifestyle? These figures may be hard to pin down. The monthly rent or mortgage is easy. So is the car payment and insurance. What about food? Clothing? Music gear? Entertainment? Doo-dads? Track your expenses for at least six months before you determine your true average monthly expenses. This way you'll account for unusual expenses that crop up occasionally, such as insurance premiums, vacations, repairs, medical costs, and other outflows. If you use a computer bookkeeping program, you may just need to click a few buttons to get the figures you need. I've been tracking income and expenses in detail since 1992 and have a very clear idea of my monthly expenditures.

Until you really know what your monthly expenses are, how can you know your income requirements? You need to keep track of every little expense. Avoid the tendency to lump expenses into larger piles. What you are looking for is waste—money you've spent without considering its consequences. Do not judge your spending patterns, just use this exercise to recognize your spending habits in a very real way. Only then can you take steps to minimize your expenses and bring them in line with your particular life goals.

♦ I SCREAM; YOU SCREAM; WE ALL SCREAM FOR ICE CREAM

Recently on a warm spring evening, my wife and I decided ice cream would top off the day nicely. Unfortunately, the freezer was empty, save for the seemingly endless supply of frozen pizzas. We were faced with a dilemma. Should we go to the local megastore and get a half gallon? Or should we stop at the Dairy Queen up the street? We chose the convenient way and spent over $5 on two sundaes. Later, we talked about the choice. We spent way too much on a completely unsatisfying and frivolous purchase. For about $3, we could have bought a half-gallon of ice cream and eaten it that night and probably three or four nights beyond that. Now, you may disagree with our choice. That's fine. My point is this. You *must* align your purchasing habits with your particular values. Did your expenditure justify what it took to acquire? If your answer is yes, then you know you've made a wise choice. For Lisa and myself, the ice cream debacle was a learning experience. We no longer trade our values for convenience unless the reward is substantial. I'm just glad that this was a $5 mistake and not a $500 mistake!

You must know where your money comes from and where it goes. Make sure your spending habits reflect your personal goals, attitudes, and values. Stop wasting your cash on things that don't contribute to your quality of life. You'll be frugal and smart, not a cheap miser. And eventually, you'll be financially independent. I'm sure you'll quickly find ways to cut your expenses. A little here or a little there can really add up to substantial savings. Now, to build your capital base, you need to save the difference between your increasing income and decreasing expenses.

▶ INVEST CAPITAL

The safest way to double your money is
to fold it over once and put it in your pocket.

—KIN HUBBARD

At this point, you are maximizing your income, reducing your expenses, and saving the difference. Remember our example: To make $2000 a month, you need $400,000 in savings earning 6% interest. Ouch! Hold on, though. Let's say you can save $10,000 each year to build your capital base. Now, using a financial calculator, the math breaks down as follows:
• Savings goal: $400,000
• Savings you have now: 0
• Annual yield on savings: 6%
• Regular contribution amount: $10,000 annually
• When you will reach your goal: 21 years

In just 21 short years, you will be earning enough from your investments to support your lifestyle at its current level. Please note: This is a simplified approach. It does *not* take into account taxes on your investment income, inflation, higher rates of return, or other factors that can both increase or reduce your earnings. Despite the simplistic formula, it's a useful financial planning tool. Twenty-one years is a long time, but it's a finite amount of time. If you're 34, you'll be financially independent by 55—a full ten years earlier than the usual retirement age. At that point, you could live off the interest of your savings and never touch your principal. You can choose to continue to work or not. Now, *that's* financial independence and real freedom. Are you convinced yet? Remember: Increase your income, reduce your expenses, save the difference, invest it to build your capital base, and eventually support your financially independent lifestyle with the income produced by your capital investments. Plug your numbers into the calculation and see what you need to do to reach your level of financial independence.

Of course, total financial independence may be beyond your reach at this time in your life. I know from experience that this very process can shock you into inactivity. But that doesn't mean you should ignore the foundation I've provided here. Don't lose heart. You can take small steps along the way. It is quite possible to reach *some form of financial independence* in your life. Even if your investments pay you just $2000 a year, that's a couple of grand you don't need to *earn*. Your capital pays you income. You can choose how to spend this money, or you can let it grow bigger.

Right now my goal is to pay my mortgage, property taxes, and house insurance using *only* income from investments. That means I never have to work to pay for my home; it's taken care of through my capital investments. Saving diligently means you too can creep up on some form of financial independence. First, you'll pay for one month's worth of expenses, then two, then three, and so on. Soon you'll have a nice nest egg of principal with interest paying for some part—if not all—of your expenses.

Here's another useful way to look at this formula. Say you have $1000 in a CD paying you 6% interest annually. That means you earn $60 a year from that investment or $5 a month. While that's a long way from paying for your mortgage or rent, it is money earned in a passive way. You did not need to work for it. Now think of what $60 buys for you. Perhaps it's four tanks of gas, two months of electricity, your phone bill, or a week's worth of groceries. Your capital investment has paid you money that you can now use to support a portion of your current lifestyle. The best part is you still have the original $1000 (and its ability to pay you another $60 next year). Now if you're really smart, you won't spend that $60. You'll leave it in your capital fund and begin earning interest on the interest. $1060 will earn $63.60 in the second year. That's the secret of compounding interest, and it's the key factor to helping you reach your goals faster. Hold that $1000 CD for 30 years, let the interest accrue, and its value will reach $5,743.

Now, imagine $10,000 in savings. That's $600 a year, $50 a month. Now we're getting somewhere. Double your principal, and you're probably earning enough cash in one year to cover one month of your expenses. Imagine that. You don't have to work for one month to cover your basic life necessities. That's financial independence. Get to $50,000 at 6% and your nest egg pays you $3000 a year or $250 each and every month.

▶ MISCELLANEOUS FINANCIAL TIPS

- Make sure you have enough money to cover six months of basic living expenses in a safe, interest bearing account. Once you determine your average monthly expenses, multiply that by six to arrive at that amount. This figure is the minimum amount of money you need in a liquid savings account. After you've saved that portion, you need to embark down the road of saving for your financial independence.
- Make sure you have another source of quick cash for an immediate, dire emergency. Perhaps this is house equity, a credit card, an IRA, or some other method of getting emergency cash. Note that I think medical emergencies and other catastrophes are real emergencies; needing a new stereo system isn't.
- If you choose to invest in mutual funds or stocks, the most important thing to remember is to invest the same amount regularly. For example, contribute $50 a week to your investment account. This lets you take advantage of dollar cost averaging and minimizes your risk during wild swings in the stock market. In essence, you buy more shares when the price is low and less when the price is higher. When you average out the costs, you come out ahead.
- Probably the safest investment, though conservative, is buying United States Treasury Securities: Treasury Bills, Treasury Notes, and Treasury Bonds. These don't promise the high returns of the stock market, but they do offer safety of capital and sure, steady income. Plus, you can buy them easily (without commissions, fees, loads, etc.) through Treasury Direct. Get a copy of *Buying Treasury Securities* from the Consumer Information Catalog at http://www. pueblo. gsa.gov/ on the Web.
- Having too much consumer credit hurts your ability to get credit when you really need it. Experts suggest you pare down to one credit card and cancel all those others. Make sure you never carry balances on your credit card. The interest rates are too high and

the temptation to spend beyond your means is too much. If you're heavily in debt now, use your initial savings to eliminate your debt before you move down the road to financial independence. Also, studies show that people spend 20% more when they use credit (even more when you count the interest charges!). I've been guilty myself. When I know I'm going to charge a purchase, I'm apt to add a few extra items because of the convenience. Fight this temptation!

- Pay down your mortgage faster. If you have a $100,000 30-year mortgage at 8.5%, paying just $70 more each month will pay off the loan in 22 years and save $55,728 in interest. If you follow the above formula, you'll be paying off your mortgage the same time you reach financial independence. You'll be able to subtract your mortgage payment from your expenses, leaving you with more money than you actually need to sustain your chosen lifestyle. Wow!
- Do you know that 70% of all people take only the standard deduction when preparing their taxes? You need to carefully consider your situation so that you minimize your tax burden. There are so many legitimate deductions that you are foolish not to take advantage of all those applicable to you. Don't pay a cent more in taxes than you need to. I hope you understand the advantage of keeping track of your deductible expenses, both business and personal.
- You shouldn't be getting large tax refunds. *This is not found money.* This is *your* money that you have given, interest free, to the state and federal governments. Pay exactly what you must pay and not a cent more.
- If you've never invested before, *start right now.* The sooner you take advantage of all the options available to you, the better off you will be. Make sure that sound financial planning and investing are a major part of your business and personal life. By familiarizing yourself with possibilities and taking advantage of professional experience and services, you will reach your objectives sooner.

Here are the questions to ask as you work these strategies: Are you living the life you want to lead? Do you have shelter, food, a few luxuries? Are you earning a living? Are you controlling your spending? Are you on your way to an independent lifestyle with no dependence on your job, the government, or any other entity? If you answer yes to these questions, you are doing fine. What more could you ask for? You are well on your way to financial independence.

I hate quotations.
—Ralph Waldo Emerson

Getting the seed money to start your new enterprise or to fund a major capital expenditure (new equipment, CD production, etc.) is a problem every small business faces at some point. Under-capitalization is a leading cause of business failure. Don't let that happen to you. How do you tap into the money stream when you're tapped out? Follow these tips and secure the money you need to strengthen your business.

◗ WHISTLE THE CONSERVATIVE TUNE
I find it very hard to overextend my money reserves. I'm quite conservative by nature (sometimes to my detriment). I usually won't spend any money unless I have it first. I recommend this approach to you. Don't spend a huge amount of money on any venture or you'll lose your shirt.

◗ FRIENDS AND RELATIVES
Often your first source of cash comes from those closest to you. Be careful about asking these people to help you out, though, as this strategy can often ruin even the hardiest relationship. You should be very clear about your intentions. Spell out precisely the amount you need, how you intend to use the money, and specifically how you plan to pay it back. Create a simple, amicable, and equitable loan agreement to protect all parties involved. This does not need to be a long-term loan. I know someone who borrowed $1000 for one week and paid back $1050. Where else could you get that return on your money for doing absolutely nothing?

A better strategy is to trade in-kind services with friends and relatives. Have an uncle with a print shop? Instead of borrowing money, ask him to donate print services to you until you get your project off the ground. Or work part-time at the print shop in trade for his services.

◗ YOUR HOME EQUITY
If you own your home, you can secure a line of credit from your bank. This credit line is based on a percentage of the equity you've built in your home. Equity is defined as the difference between what you paid for your house and what you currently owe. The bank will usually extend credit no greater than 80% of that amount. This financing option is often cheaper and easier to get than most conventional loans. The interest rate is well below credit cards and qualifying is frequently simple. The interest may even be deductible. However, there is a downside. You are guaranteeing the loan strictly from your personal assets—you are putting your house on the line!

◗ YOUR CURRENT CLIENTS
This is the easiest method to raise cash and often the most overlooked. Instead of extending credit to your clients, ask to be paid in advance for some products and services. On big projects I always insist on getting some money up front (33-50%). Before printing the previous edition of this book, I began promoting it and subsequently sold dozens of copies in advance. This way I recouped much of my investment *before* the books were finished. Pushing a little harder meant I presold enough copies to pay the entire printing bill and reached the break-even point before the press run. That's a comfortable position to be in. All bills were paid before a dime left my pocket.

◗ YOUR VENDORS
After asking your clients for money in advance of services, turn your attention to vendors. Ask for credit terms of 60 to 90 days on the products and services you buy. You might not get this at first because you may need to build up their confidence in you. So, take the time to build good relationships with your vendors and pay on time. Soon there will come a point when you can ask for extended credit. Basically, this strategy lets you defer your bills until you get funds from future business. Used wisely, this technique keeps your cash flow in the black.

Not too long ago, I faced a $5000 production bill and didn't have the cash to pay until after my client paid me. At first I considered the home equity course mentioned above, but then I decided to ask the supplier. After explaining the situation to her, she agreed to offer me 45-day credit terms. I then convinced my client to expedite payment to me. This let me pay the production tab in 25 days, and now I never have any trouble getting liberal credit terms from this vendor.

◗ CREATIVE CREDIT
Use one credit card specifically for your business purchases. Use it wisely and take advantage of special offers, such as earning frequent flyer miles, cash rebates, and other incentives. Also, look for special credit terms and other bargains. I recently bought a new computer on a six month, no-payments-no-interest plan. When you pay the purchase off on the due date, you accrue no interest and no finance charges. Most importantly, you get to use the item for a half year for free.

BANK, SBA, AND OTHER LOANS

These are by far the hardest ways to get cash. Basically, you go to a bank and apply just as you would for a mortgage or auto loan. The only difference is that you'll need a detailed business plan. Of course, building rapport with your local banker means you'll have an ally when the money crunch comes your way. What are the elements of a formal business plan?

• Cover page
• List of contents
• Introduction or executive summary
• Financial plan
• Marketing plan
• Growth plan
• Detailed cash flow projections
• Personal information including copies of tax returns

Additional items include:
• Pictures
• Example promotional material: brochures, ads, etc.
• Audiovisual presentation either on video or computer
• Testimonials or other letters of recommendation

Make sure your package answers these fundamental questions:
• Business name
• Vision or mission statement
• Product and service definitions
• Marketplace description and market research findings
• Production and distribution methods
• Business organization
• Capital and start-up costs
• Sales projections for the first five years
• Expense projections for the first five years
• Business assets
• Personal assets and liabilities
• A list of strategic goals and the action plan to achieve each one

◗ LEASING

This is always a good alternative when your cash is tight. New equipment, cars, and more can all be leased. The considerably less up-front costs make leasing very attractive. On the plus side, you get the latest and greatest equipment for your business because you can choose better, more expensive options that you otherwise couldn't afford. Make sure you carefully consider the leasing restrictions, though. Don't get into long-term leases on equipment or material that is outdated quickly.

While I have no formal leasing agreements, I do *rent* all the time. This strategy gives me access to state-of-the-art music gear without my having to pay the sometimes exorbitant prices. Instead of buying that new digital multitrack, I rent, borrow, or visit a commercial studio. You pay far less than you would if you bought the deck, and you pay it one tiny morsel at a time instead of all at once. That's sound financial advice.

◗ BRING IN MORE BUSINESS

Double your efforts, land some additional business, and increase your cash flow accordingly. What promotions can you run to get clients fast? Though it may take a little money before you can make money, it's a prudent investment. Offering a discount—a sale of some sort—is a sure-fire way to generate new business and reactivate old accounts.

◗ INCREASE YOUR FEES

How much are you charging for your music products and services? Find out what the going rate is and adjust your fees to match. A 7-10% price hike may be all you need to infuse your bank account.

◗ BARTER PRODUCTS AND SERVICES

There are many formal bartering organizations across the country. You might want to consider joining one if this is something you'll be into heavily. Basically, you offer products and services to the pool and buy products and services from the pool. You earn "money" for what you sell and can then "purchase" other goods and services. You can use a much simpler version of this technique by trading with other businesses. For example, I often trade articles for ad space in magazines and newsletters. I'll write an article on a music business topic, and the media source pays me in ad space. I then use the free ads to promote my music business. My investment is mostly time and very little money.

◗ ORGANIZE YOUR BUSINESS RECORDS

I've already spoken about this subject at length. Just remember: You can't know your true financial picture if you don't carefully scrutinize your records and make sure you are not overlooking income or expenses.

Use these strategies and in no time at all you'll manage your cash flow better and have all the money you need to start and run your music business.

CHAPTER 12

Copyright and Other Rights

Next to the right of liberty, the right of property is the most

important individual right guaranteed by the Constitution

and the one which, united with that of personal liberty, has

contributed more to the growth of civilization than any other

institution established by the human race.

—*William Howard Taft*

This is a complex issue; even more complex in the commercial music industry. Basically, you either give up all the rights to your music or you keep all rights to your music. There is rarely any middle ground.

A work-for-hire agreement means that you give up all rights to the music. Aside from what you get paid, you realize *no future money* from the ongoing use of your music. This buyout of the copyright is something you should try to avoid or, at the very least, make sure you get a substantial sum of money for! I've heard horror stories of composers giving up all rights to a composition for $100. That's ridiculous. Your music has far more value than that. Don't be foolish—charge what it's really worth.

You'll note that the sample contract discussed earlier specifically states that it is *not* a work-for-hire agreement. You must protect yourself and your music by having such language in your contracts and agreements. The contract also mentions one-time rights— it licenses the music for one single use. And although all rights are mine in this agreement, there is a clause that states I will not exercise those rights for one year. This is a neat little marketing tool that assures clients the music they buy has some exclusivity, albeit only temporary. Even so, I *never* sell the same music in the same market. I have, however, sold previously used music in another state.

WHAT ARE ONE-TIME RIGHTS?

Simply stated, one-time or first-use rights grant a license for unlimited use of the music only for the single production for which it was written. It does not grant the right to use the music for another project or in another form without seeking an additional license from and paying the appropriate fee to the composer.

With this option, all rights belong to the composer. The music can be licensed to other markets after an agreed upon amount of time has elapsed. This means that you can sell the same music repeatedly somewhere else. In other words, you are simply *renting* your music to the production for a fee. You still own it! This license does not, however, limit the *distribution* by the client of the original project. It can be shown multiple times without the need for another license as long as it exists. It is when a client wants to use the same music again for a different project or for a longer time period that they must seek a new license.

WHAT ABOUT BUYOUT RIGHTS?

Buyout or all rights means the client has purchased the entire copyright and owns the music outright. They have unlimited use of the music for any project. Since you give up the music for a single fee, the cost to the client is much higher, typically at least ten times more than one-time or first-use rights. Any music you give up is gone forever. If it goes on to make a company millions, you're out of luck. You are effectively giving the copyright to another person or company. Even though you remain the author, they now own and control the music. Avoid this situation at all costs or get as much money as you can when you sell all rights.

WHICH RIGHT IS RIGHT?

One-time rights are ideal for most corporate projects, small documentaries, and independent films. Buyouts are the norm for jingles, television and film scores, and other big budget productions.

A LITTLE RIGHTS TRICK

In addition to protecting your work with contracts, you can endorse the checks from your clients and add this line underneath:

All rights to the music belong to the composer.

Also, insist on being given attribution for your work. You never know who might see your name on the end credits of some production and call you. It's happened to me several times! Make it read something like this:

Music composed and performed by Jeffrey P. Fisher.

COPYRIGHT ESSENTIALS

Congress revised the United States Copyright Law in 1976, replacing the 67-year-old law that was adopted in 1909. Article I, Section 8 of the U.S. Constitution provides:

[That] *Congress shall have power . . . to promote the Progress of Science and useful Arts, by securing for limited Times to Authors and Inventors the exclusive right to their respective Writings and Discoveries.*

This constitutional provision mandated Congress to adopt the Copyright Law from which this section originates. The general nature of copyright protection under section 102 of the 1976 Law states:

Copyright protection subsists . . . in original works of authorship fixed in any tangible medium of expression, now known or later developed, from which they can be perceived, reproduced, or otherwise communicated, either directly or with the aid of a machine or device. Works . . . include:

(1) literary works;

(2) musical works, including . . . words;

(3) dramatic works . . . including music;

(4) pantomimes or choreographic works;

(5) pictorial, graphic, and sculptural works;

(6) motion pictures and other audiovisual works; and

(7) sound recordings.

Section 102 (b) does not extend copyright protection to:

. . . any idea, procedure, process, system, method of operation, concept, principle, or discovery, regardless of the form in which it is described . . . in such work.

When a work of original authorship is fixed in any tangible medium (tape, paper, videotape, computer code, etc.), the author gets copyright protection. This protection includes five exclusive rights, named later in this chapter. However, ideas are not protected regardless of the form the idea takes. Only the exact way the idea is conveyed, like the words on this page, is given copyright protection. A principle of operation like a copy machine is not given copyright protection, but it may be patented. The title of a book or motion picture may not be copyrighted, but can be trademarked. Trademarks also apply to some advertising copy.

The McDonald's slogan, "You deserve a break today," is not given copyright protection. For example, a character in a video might say, "Why don't you go home. You deserve a break today." If this wasn't the case, McDonald's could enforce exclusive rights to the phrase. Use of that particular phrase would be severely limited. This is a simple way to understand the difference between trademark and copyright law. McDonald's can only trademark the phrase as it pertains to their business, thereby allowing others to use the words outside of their market.

One additional trademark case involved the Strategic Defense Initiative (SDI). George Lucas tried to prevent SDI from being called the "star wars defense" because he felt it was trademark infringement. The court ruled that the use of "star wars" became a generic description of SDI and since the motion picture *Star Wars* was completely different in purpose from that of SDI, the use of the term "star wars defense" caused no harm to the *Star Wars* trademark.

The owner of the copyright is the author of the original work. The term owner is defined later. The owner has, under Section 106:

> the exclusive rights to do and to authorize any of the following:
>
> (1) to reproduce the copyrighted work in copies;
>
> (2) to prepare derivative works based upon the copyrighted work;
>
> (3) to distribute copies . . . to the public by sale or other transfer of ownership, or by rental, lease, or lending;
>
> (4) in the case of literary, musical, dramatic . . . and motion pictures and other audiovisual works, to perform the copyrighted work publicly; and
>
> (5) in the case of literary . . . pictorial, graphic, or sculptural works, including the individual images of a motion picture or other audiovisual work, to display the copyrighted work publicly.

These five rights are exclusive. They are not waived through inactivity or a failure to enforce. These rights can be enforced at the owner's discretion and at any time. The differences between (4) and (5) need further clarification. To perform a work—showing a video, for example—is to show the work in its entirety. To display a video would be to show individual frames nonsequentially. Also, a sculpture cannot be performed; it can only be displayed.

The Copyright Law is very detailed in this area of exclusive rights for owners. It is not so clear, as we shall soon see, in the limitations of those rights. This will be more apparent when I discuss Fair Use. The owner of a copyrighted work may transfer the ownership, and therefore his rights, to another party. Section 201 (a) says:

> a transfer . . . is not valid unless an instrument of conveyance . . . is in writing and signed by the owner.

HE WHO CREATES, OWNS

This clever phrase simplifies the entire copyright law. Copyright protection is automatic. Repeat that phrase ten times! One exception to this rule is "work for hire." A work that is prepared "by an employee within the scope of his or her employment" is considered a work made for hire. In this case, the copyright ownership belongs to the employer.

Work that is "commissioned for use as a contribution to a collective work" is a work made for hire *only* if the parties expressly agree in a written instru-ment signed by them. Put simply, an employee automatically forfeits copyright ownership. A freelance, independent contractor automatically retains copyright ownership. Both situations can be reversed through a signed, written agreement. There are limitations on the exclusive rights of owners. This comes under Section 107, Fair Use:

> The fair use of copyrighted work . . . for purposes such as criticism, comment, news reporting, teaching, scholarship, or research, is not an infringement of copyright. In determining whether the use . . . is a fair use, the factors to be considered include:
>
> (1) the purposes and character of the use, including whether such use is of commercial nature or is for nonprofit educational purposes;
>
> (2) the nature of the copyrighted work;
>
> (3) the amount and substantiality of the portion used in relation to the copyrighted work as a whole; and
>
> (4) the effect of the use upon the potential market for or value of the copyrighted work.

These four points show how open the Fair Use Doctrine really is. It was designed around the philosophy that society has a need to use that far outweighs the monopoly to create. Most copyright experts agree that a good lawyer could win a fair use dispute either way. Congress' intention was that only litigation could solve copyright infringement involving fair use on a case-by-case basis. There are no fixed rules; each case must be litigated on its own circumstances. The duration of a copyright is outlined in Section 302.

> Copyright in a work created on or after 1/1/78 subsists from its creation and . . . endures for . . . the life of the author and fifty years after the author's death.

Copyright terms before this change were two consecutive terms of 28 years each. Please note that to determine the copyrighted status of a work it is not accurate to subtract the 56 years from the current date. Many factors enter into the equation, so it is only safe to consider works created before 1915 to be in the public domain. Other works should be traced thoroughly.

Registration of a copyrighted work is not mandatory. A common misconception is that a work is not copyrighted until it is registered. This is wrong! The work is copyrighted *the moment it is fixed in a tangible medium.* Remember: Copyright protection is automatic. Another misconception is that by registering the work, you prove authorship. This is also quite misleading. Registration allows the author to stake a claim to the work in question. The Copyright Office does not determine the validity of submitted work. The burden of proof falls only on the author and owner.

Registration is required in two instances. First, to correct publication without notice of copyright on works published before March 1, 1989. Second, to be able to sue for infringement. Please note that statutory damages awarded for copyright infringement are awarded from the date of registration forward.

Until March 1, 1989, it was mandatory for a copyrighted work to display the copyright notice such as, "Copyright, Jeffrey P. Fisher, 1997." Failure to affix the notice to the work effectively eliminated the copyright and the work automatically entered the public domain. Following the International Berne Copyright Convention, the United States Copyright law was amended. It is no longer necessary to display the copyright notice on works, and failure to do so no longer results in loss of rights to the owner-author. However, I heartily recommend that you register your work and place the copyright notice on all copies. It should look like this:

© 1997 Jeffrey P. Fisher

The United States Copyright law is a constitutional mandate designed to protect the original works of authors. The rights are exclusive and enforceable. There are some limitations on the rights under the Fair Use Doctrine, but this is open to interpretation. It is, therefore, highly recommended to secure written permission before using copyrighted material in any circumstance.

- For information about registering your copyrights, contact the Copyright Office; Library of Congress, Washington, DC 20559; (202) 707-3000. Request forms and instructions PA and SR.

MAKE SURE YOU FILE

When you keep the music rights, make sure you register your copyright with the U.S. Copyright Office by filing form PA to register the music and form SR to register the sound recording. If you give up all rights, it's up to the buyer to register.

Remember that copyright registration does not *prove* your ownership; it only registers your *claim* to ownership. You must still prove that your music is original. Always register your work that you sell. In addition, play your music for friends, family, and business associates who can later back up your claim to originality and authorship. Please understand that infringement is rare and, unless you are a multimillionaire, the stakes are small. Let's face it: The only valid thing worth protecting is your original idea, and ideas can't be copyrighted. Just listen to all the sound-alike bands who try desperately to copy the sounds of

other successful artists. Don't worry about someone ripping you off. Take these precautions. Should you need to go to court, you'll be prepared.

Here's a nice touch for clients who buyout your copyright. Complete the form PA and send it to them. Make sure you include the mandatory two copies of the work. All they have to do is sign the form, include the $20 filing fee, and drop the package in the mail. Several weeks later, they'll receive their official registration from the Copyright Office. Please note that on the form you will still be listed as author but *not* as owner because the buyout means your contribution was a work made for hire.

Remember this: All employees give up their rights to their work to their employer. All freelancers retain their rights to their work. Either situation can be reversed through a written agreement signed by both parties. When in doubt, get it in writing!

SAMPLE COPYRIGHT ASSIGNMENT

You must use a written instrument to transfer the copyright you hold to another party. If the music you produced was a work made for hire, this is unnecessary.

For the value received, Jeffrey P. Fisher hereby sells transfer and assigns to XYZ Production, its successors, assigns, and personal representatives, all right, title, and interest in and to the following music copyright:

[Describe the nature of the copyrighted work.]

The certificate of copyright is attached. Jeffrey P. Fisher warrants good title to said copyright, that it is free of all liens, encumbrances, or any known claims against the said copyright. Signed under seal this [day] *day of* [month, year].

OTHER RIGHTS AND ROYALTIES

It gets harder the more you know. Because the more you find out the uglier everything seems.
—FRANK ZAPPA

Besides first-use and buyout rights, what if your client wishes to use already copyrighted material? Or what if you want to use an actual sound recording by a popular artist? There are two choices:

- Clear the rights to the music so you can record the song using other talent.
- Clear the rights to the original recording.

◆ MECHANICAL RIGHTS

These are the rights to reproduce copyrighted music onto tape, CD, videotape, or film. If you cover (re-record) someone else's original song (a sound-alike, sometimes called a knockoff, doesn't count), your client must pay the statutory fee for mechanical rights. The rate is 6.9¢ per song per unit. In other words, if you used one song for a video and distributed 5000 copies of the tape, you'd pay about $350 for the mechanical rights to the music. Mechanical rights are split 50-50 between the artist and publisher. While you won't discuss mechanical rights in most corporate projects, if you write a film score, you will be entitled to compensation.

▸ SYNCHRONIZATION RIGHTS

Your client must buy these rights when they use music in its *original* form on a film, TV, or video soundtrack. When paying for sync rights, you must usually pay mechanical rights, too. To use the original track, you must seek synchronization rights to the original recording and pay that fee. Sync rights are negotiated independently. There is no set rate!

The Harry Fox Agency in New York is the place to go for clearing music. They will help you get rights—both mechanical and synchronization—from the copyright holder. Remember, you buy mechanical rights when you just want the music, and you buy synchronization rights when you want to use the *actual* recording by the artist. The Fox people will negotiate on your behalf when your music hits the big time. Be aware that most of the projects you'll be doing, as described in this book, won't earn you money through these rights. When you get your first film score or record deal, though, these rights come into play.

• The Harry Fox Agency. 205 East 42nd St., New York, NY 10017; (212) 370-5330

▸ PERFORMANCE RIGHTS

These are the rights of the copyright holder to receive royalties when the music composition is performed in public. These royalties are usually split with your publisher. If you publish your own music, you keep all the money. In most cases, you don't personally collect these fees. The two performance societies, ASCAP and BMI, keep track of how many times a song is performed and collect fees through licenses to radio and television stations, clubs, bars, restaurants, and other places where music is performed publicly. They distribute the money to their composers quarterly.

Work you do for business TV and other non-broadcast clients will not be subject to these royalties. If you are fortunate enough to write a theme for broadcast TV, you will collect this money. You must join one of the groups to be eligible. I joined BMI when my score for *Street Smarts* aired on PBS. (By the way, PBS pays far less then network TV. Even after hundreds of playbacks, my royalties were minuscule.

I'm not complaining—it's nice getting a check every quarter—but I was initially quite disappointed.)

• American Society of Composers, Authors, and Publishers (ASCAP). One Lincoln Plaza, New York, NY 10023; (213) 883-1000; www.ascap.com
• Broadcast Music Inc. (BMI). 320 West 57th St., New York, NY 10019; (310) 659-9109; www.bmi.com

Here is one other item you should know. Buyout library tracks are copyrighted. Even though many users think they have bought an unrestricted license, the use of the music is limited. For instance, if you use a library track on a network TV show, it is probably subject to an additional fee. Check the contract. You might be surprised to find that if you distribute beyond 5000 people, you pay more for the so-called buyout music.

• *All You Need to Know About the Music Business*, Donald S. Passman. Simon and Schuster; 1230 Avenue of the Americas, New York, NY 10020. This is, by far, the best book I've seen about music business issues. It is concise, thorough, and easy to understand. Use it to protect yourself, your rights, and your music!

THE MUSICIAN'S UNION

I, myself, came to music late—in my late teens. I play nothing, but I discovered what real music can do for a man, and to a man. I could not live without it. It's earth, air, fire, and water to me.

—JOHN GARDNER WRITING AS
HERBIE KRUGER IN THE BOOK *MAESTRO*

Whether it's a good idea or not to join the American Federation of Musician's Union depends on a number of factors. Most of my work is nonbroadcast, so getting union scale and royalties is not really an issue. Typically, I do all the work myself and play all the parts and, when I do contract out, it's mostly nonunion, mainly because I hire my friends and other fellow musicians. But if you start doing mostly radio and TV commercials, you should join the union. The wages and royalties are terrific. For more information, contact your local chapter. Look in the telephone book under Unions. Even if you do very little commercial composing and playing, there are advantages to joining, including:

• A pension fund
• Insurance (BMI also offers insurance to its members)
• Membership directory and referral services
• Wage scales and contracts
• Seminars

CHAPTER 13

How to Set Your Fee and Get It

There is hardly anything in the world that some man cannot make a little worse and sell a little cheaper.

—John Ruskin

How much should you charge? No other question is asked more often. Unfortunately, there are an infinite number of answers. However, the *best* answer is: whatever you can get! Or more specifically, whatever clients will pay. Many will have precise budgets. Others will ask you what your fees are. This chapter shows you how to figure your rates and how to present them in proposals. It also suggests a few ideas to use when a client complains about your price and includes the latest rates for composing original music soundtracks and jingles.

One caveat, though. This information is based on my own personal experience. The figures quoted are based on my research and reflect the procedures and rates for commercial music composition in and around the Chicago area. Fees in your neck of the world may be slightly more or less depending on any number of factors. Use this information as a guideline only, and make sure to adapt this to your particular situation.

YOUR PRICING FORMULA

It is crucial that you know your expenses before you determine your price. How can you know what to charge if you don't know how much it costs you to be in business? Following the formula outlined below, you will determine your true hourly rate. Do not quote this hourly rate. While you need to determine it, you will be more successful if you follow your rate

as a guideline and bid all projects as a complete package. You should estimate the time you think it will take to do the work, add in a margin of error to cover unforeseen circumstances, and then quote the whole job as a package. For short scores and jingles, just quote this package price. For long scores, you might try pricing by the minute of finished music. Also, you really need two fees: one for one-time rights and the other for buyout rights. Let's establish your fee for one-time rights first. There are really five different main costs used to determine this basic fee:

• Composer fee
• Studio charge
• Material costs
• Talent fees
• Business expenses

▶ COMPOSER FEE

This is what you charge for composing and arranging the composition. The first step is to determine how much money you would like to make. Think in terms of a salary at a full-time job. For example, say you want to make $30,000 a year. The cost of taxes, health care insurance, vacation, holidays, and other benefits add about 30% to most salaries. To match a full-time salary, you must factor that in. This increases your goal to $39,000. About 2000 hours are available in a typical work year. Unfortunately, you will deduct time spent marketing and administering your business; time lost to vacation, holidays, and sickness; and time when you have no work to do. A conservative estimate means that only about 1000 hours a year are actually available to bill. So if you want to gross $39,000, you need to make about $39 an hour. Perhaps you only want to work part-time or run your commercial music business as part of another business and just want to gross an extra $5000. You should base your part-time fee on the same full-time hourly rate, which means you'd need to bill just over 2.5 hours a week (5000/39 = 128.21/50 = 2.56). But wait! Your salary is only one part of this equation. There are other costs to add up.

◗ STUDIO CHARGE

For some projects you'll record everything in your project studio, but others will require going to a professional studio. Often you'll rent equipment to handle specific situations. Essentially, you need to know what it costs to produce projects in-house, what it costs to produce music using outside facilities, and what the rental charges are for gear. The first figure should cover the costs, maintenance, and general operation of your in-house project studio. Call around and see what several recording studios are charging per hour for the second figure. And get the latest rates for rented gear from several local suppliers for the third figure.

Now you don't necessarily *need* a separate charge for your project studio. You can include that in your salary. The easiest way to determine this is to ask yourself these questions. Is your equipment paid for or do you have payments to make? If you answer yes to the latter, you should charge enough for studio time to pay for the equipment loan, insurance, upkeep, and depreciation. Personally, I own my equipment outright and just charge a higher hourly wage and include the free use of my studio in that charge. Therefore, I don't sell my studio time on composing projects; I sell only my creative services: my music. That's my niche. When I use a commercial facility for projects or when I rent equipment, I add those charges to the invoice along with my basic rate.

◗ MATERIAL COSTS

These are the direct expenses you incur when composing music and delivering the final master tape. You need the costs of tape, discs, paper, shipping, and other general expenses. These are charges you'll absorb at first and then charge back to clients through this formula. Go back to your financial records or get price lists from several vendors to see what you've been paying for blank media and other music-related expenses.

◗ TALENT FEES

Will you be composing and recording all the parts or will you hire out talent? When you use outside musicians and other artists, you need to know what their performance is going to cost you. These fees may change depending on the particular project and whether you choose union talent or not. Personally, I do not charge a separate fee for my playing on the tracks. This is included in my basic fee. You may do otherwise. If I hire outside talent, that fee is once again added to my charges.

◗ BUSINESS EXPENSES

You've already added benefits to your salary, so what's left? You can't neglect all the reasonable and ordinary costs of running your new business. This includes, but is in no way limited to, rent, telephone, utilities, letterhead, postage, equipment, advertising, and more. This is your overhead, or the cost of doing business, whether you have paying clients or not. You need to know or carefully estimate these basic operating costs. If you've never been in business before, you'll find this quite hard. Once you've been up and running for a few months, you'll have a better handle on your expenses. Until that time, you'll have to make your best guess. For the last several years, my overhead has remained at about 35%. That means for every dollar grossed, 35¢ went to pay expenses.

The next step is to lump these figures together into one fee. You need your hourly rate, studio charge, material charge, talent charge, and the overhead figure.

Wage	$39.00
Studio	25.00
Material	5.00
Talent	0.00
Subtotal	69.00
Overhead	1.35%
New hourly rate $93.15	

For this example, you'd need to charge just over $93 per hour to reach your salary goal, pay for basic studio time, recoup your material expenses, and meet your business overhead. I'd round the figure to the nearest even amount, or $95. Most composers strive to compose about two minutes of music in a single day. If you compose two minutes of music in eight hours, you'd charge $380 per finished minute of music. (95 x 8 = 760/2 = 380). Your basic rate would round up to something like $389. Now you've bundled everything—composing, arranging, recording, mixing, etc.—into one neat little package price. You should follow this formula to discover your working model. Plug in your numbers to get your rate. Keep in mind that the average cost for a nonbuyout electronic music score is between $400-500 per finished minute.

Now you don't need to quote that fee. You can just follow this formula, figure out your numbers, arrive at the fee, and *keep it to yourself.* But you should use that number as the basis for your client quotes. If your client requires five minutes of music, plug in your numbers to get $1945 (5 x 389). You might consider adding a margin of error in case you've underestimated your time. Clients are fickle and often add things to projects and expect you to comply with their additional requests for the same fee. You should build in a margin of error with every fee you quote to cover these unforeseen circumstances. If the request is minor, go ahead and do it because your margin of error should cover this. If the client request is unreasonable, don't be afraid to renegotiate your fee.

If the project seems relatively simple, I add only 20% to the first figure. If the project is difficult or if the client appears indecisive, I add 40% to the first figure. Your package quote for five minutes would fall somewhere between $2334 and $2723 (1945 x 1.2 and 1.4, respectively). A paragraph in your contract would look something like this:

> *This agreement grants you single-use, non-exclusive rights to the music for use only for the* [example] *project for the period of one year. You must seek an additional license and pay appropriate fees for any other or future uses of this music. The base fee for our music services is estimated between $2334 and $2723. That fee estimate is based on five minutes of original music at my standard rate for single-use, one-time rights. This fee includes time for composing, arranging, producing, recording, mixing, and one master tape.*

Unfortunately, your numbers may vary from project to project, so the price you quote will need to vary accordingly. You may need to figure separate fees based on changing circumstances. What if you go to a studio to record. How much does that cost? What if you need to hire a singer. How much do they charge? It's important for you to use different numbers in the equation to arrive at a range of fees for different projects. There will be times when you'll need to quote these costs separately, while other times you can put them together as a package. I suggest you stick with your lower per minute fee and just add these additional costs straight into the package to arrive at your sliding price scale.

For this example, you've incurred extra charges for studio time at a higher rate ($55) and two nonunion musicians for the session ($50 x 2). You probably wouldn't spend all your time at the higher rate. You may spend most of the time in your project

studio at the lower rate and only one hour at the higher rate in the recording studio. Just take your basic rate and add in the additional costs as they occur (5 x 389 = 1945 + 155 = 2100 x 1.2 and 1.4) and quote between $2520 and $2940. This example tacks on the additional costs as they occur. If you use this formula, make sure to mark up your expenses as explained below.

Figuring out your expenses lets you know if you can produce the score or jingle for the budget proposed. Most clients don't ask, "What do you charge?" They usually say they have $2000 and want to know what you can do for that fee. Now you'll be able to help them and feel confident that your expenses (and more) will be covered. At this point, I'm sure you understand the importance of knowing the real costs associated with running your commercial music business.

Whether you choose to quote a per minute or full package price, base the fee on the per minute number. This means you'll be selling on a project or fixed-fee basis. Clients prefer to buy on a fixed-fee because there are no surprises. They can budget accordingly and know exactly what to expect. This package makes it very clear what you will do and what they will get. Make sure the details are spelled out clearly in your contract. This package deal makes it very easy to do business with you. Convenience and client confidence are vital to a successful business relationship (and to making big money, too!). What's especially important about establishing these fees is that you can quickly offer accurate estimates up front.

> *I charge $389 per finished minute. You say you need ten minutes of music? Then my fee will be $3890, which includes everything: composing time, studio time, recording time, mixing, talent, and tape. No extras. If you use less music, you pay less, too.*

If you're asked how you arrived at that figure so quickly, tell the client that you worked this figure out with your accountant, taking salary, overhead, and material costs into consideration. You determined a reasonable figure that includes your profit and every other expense you need to cover.

YOUR BUYOUT FEE

Now that you have the basic per finished minute fee, simply multiply the figure by ten to arrive at your minimum buyout fee: $3890 for one minute of music. This figure doesn't slide as much when the amount of music increases. Ten minutes of music would be about $7500, with a cap at about $15,000 for a full-length electronic score.

HOW TO PRICE SHORTER PROJECTS

What if a client asks for only 30 seconds of music? Do you slice your fee in half? If the project is a buyout, just quote your minimum buyout fee ($3890 from the example). For one-time rights, you should set a *minimum fee* that equals your fee for two minutes of music. Since writing and recording a short bit often consumes as much time as a longer piece, figure you'll spend an entire day on the 30-second spot. Charging the example $778 minimum fee (perhaps discounted slightly to $769) will cover you for the shorter gigs. Here's how to present this concept to your prospective client:

> *I charge $389 per minute of music, with a two minute minimum. The fee for your 30-second jingle spot would be $769. However, I can write a 60-second spot for the same fee and create your :30 from that take. If you decide to use the :60 in the future, you'd already have it ready to go.*

ASK ABOUT THE MUSIC BUDGET

The next—and by far the easiest—way to determine your fee is to ask your client about their music budget. You'll be surprised how many people will tell you what they expect to pay for your music services. If you are unsure at any time, just ask what the budget is, and most clients will gladly tell you. They'll often be quite honest. Then it's up to you to decide if the fee proposed meets your objectives. Of course, since you figured your fees using my formula, you'll know instantly whether to accept or pass on the project. Why waste each other's time? If they want $5000 worth of music for $500, you save yourself tons of trouble by establishing that fact right away. Once you know the budget, you can deliver the best compromise for what they can afford. If not, adjust the project specifications to fit the budget, i.e., do less work for less money.

What you must understand is that most music budgets are dictated by the buyers. In the past, music houses had control, but now the ad agencies, productions houses, and ultimately the clients say what they'll pay. Clients have become more knowledgeable about the art of commercial music. They used to be in the dark and would pay virtually anything the music house requested. Now they know about technology and how it affects the music composition and recording process. They know in precise detail what it takes to get the music they need and therefore what they are willing to pay.

Here are some recent music buyer trends that you must recognize. Changes in the audiovisual and advertising industry resulted in five major shifts in clients' music buying habits. Here they are, and here's how you should combat them. Today's original music client:

- Wants to pay less and get more. They are more price savvy than in the past. The age of the "money-is-no-object" client is long gone. You should offer different packages that give them a choice. Consider giving free demos or sample music they can use for free. Also, offer incentives and special discounts and pricing to encourage them.
- Is buying less. Reaching for the cheap library tracks is no longer the exception, it's the rule. Again, you must present your value and work with them to get more bang for their buck. Perhaps you can write one original theme and fill in the gaps with library tracks.
- Has longer sales cycles. Face it, you are going to work harder for some jobs. It can sometimes take months to close sales. That's why you must keep in touch and be ready *when* they call you. Don't be discouraged by this trend. Just keep promoting and your hard work will eventually pay off.
- Is not loyal to one supplier. This point is a double-edged sword. You can use this tendency to woo them away from their current music supplier, but your clients may also leave you just to save a few pennies.
- Requires top-notch service, extra service for free, and no surprises. In other words, today's music buyer is in control. They are more knowledgeable about technology and recognize that if you won't give them what they need, they will find somebody else who will. You must meet their demands entirely. Make sure you quote solid price contracts that detail your services accurately.

PRICE YOUR MUSIC AS A PERCENTAGE OF TOTAL BUDGET

The general industry rule for you to follow is to charge between 1.5%-3% of the total production budget for your music contribution. This includes all music services: composition, arranging, recording costs, talent fees, tape, and more. For a project with a $50,000 production budget, expect between $750 and $1500 to be available for music. That's not a lot of cash, as you well know. And that's why so many smaller productions choose library music instead of original compositions.

Remember, library music is a prime competitor. Producers love that they can get 60 minutes of music for $60. It's cheap and it's convenient. You must make it just as inexpensive and convenient to get your music. Well, obviously you can't afford to sell original music for $60. You must increase your services' value to the producers of this world. Sure, you cost more than library music, but remember all the advantages original music gives to a producer. Don't be shy about reminding them.

TYPICAL RATES FOR COMMERCIAL PROJECTS

First, decide if you will retain rights or sell as a buyout and whether your license is local, regional, or national. As of March 1997, the average *creative fees* for a local commercial jingle when you keep all rights are usually between $750 and $1500. If it's a buyout (where you give up all rights), the minimum for local work would be $3000 to $10,000. If your project is a regional buyout, try between $3000 and $5000. A regional license would be the equivalent of a 50,000 watt radio with a signal protected for 750 miles. The rates for national spots fall between $7000 and $18,000 and beyond. These national spots are always a buyout.

Unlike our example with everything lumped together, jingles usually separate creative fees from other charges, regardless of the rights granted. In this case, all production costs are *additional* to this fee. You need to add the costs for studio time, material, talent, and such. This creative fee basically covers the composer fee and overhead parts of the pricing equation.

Motion picture film score packages start at about $25,000 and go up to $250,000 and beyond. Television music packages are somewhat lower (though you do get substantial performance royalties from scores played on TV, which doesn't happen with those played in movie theaters). Contrary to jingles, these rates reflect a package that includes not only the composer's fee, but *all* the recording costs including musicians. The burden to bring the score in under budget rests on your shoulders. Your income and profit are based on what is left over *after* you pay all the costs. You can plainly see why project studios are so popular. Your home studio saves recording costs and that means you make more money. So be very careful to budget accordingly. Make sure you add in that 20-40% margin of error.

MARK UP OTHER COSTS

When you add production costs to your basic fee, mark up or *increase* the price so you make a profit. Increase everything you buy on your client's behalf by *at least* 15%. If a studio costs you $100 an hour, charge your client $115. From my earlier example, you'd add $178.25 to your basic fee (155 x 1.15). You should increase tape prices significantly, by about ten times. You can buy a C-20 cassette for under 50¢; charge about $4.99 to clients. Think of it this way: If the cost of an item is small, mark up the fee you charge your clients significantly. If the item is expensive, mark it up less.

You'll make the most money from your project studio, your talent, and your composing fees—and you'll make some on the tape, too. You'll make less money when you rely on outside people to help you, such as other studios, musicians, etc. This is not entirely avoidable, nor should it be. You should mark up the costs charged to you and increase your profit margins, but realize that you won't make as much if you handled the job yourself. You can't always complete a project on your own. Sometimes you need outside help. But when you can keep the entire production in house, your check will be that much sweeter.

MISCELLANEOUS PRICING TIDBITS

*The best career advice to give to the young is,
"Find out what you like doing best and get someone
to pay you for doing it."*
— KATHARINE WHITEHORN

Even if the project isn't a buyout, make sure you grant clients an exclusive license in their market area for a limited time. This lets you charge them again should they wish to renew the license (this is the equivalent of *renting* your music to them). The advantage to this strategy is that it's less money up front for clients. They only pay more if they want to renew. Their success with your music can mean your success. If you decide to offer this, grant rights for a year and let your client renew the license on a sliding scale. Try 70% of the original fee for the second year, 50% for years two to four, 40% for years five to ten. This should be a percentage of the composer's fee only and *not* the one-time production costs (studio, material, and talent). If they don't renew, you can sell the music elsewhere.

Also, don't forget your other royalties, mechanical and performance, if they apply to your projects. And as a union musician or singer, you are entitled to residuals for the ongoing use of your performances if the proper union scale is paid (and papers filed). If you decide to do union gigs, make sure you play on the master recordings and, in the case of jingles, sing on the tracks. This is the only way you are assured some nice royalty checks throughout your career. Composers almost never get residuals for their contribution, unless they sing and play on the track as a union member.

As I said earlier, it's crucial to take time to determine your minimum fee—the absolute bottom dollar figure you'll take for composing original soundtracks or jingles. At the same time, you might consider developing a typical or standard fee. This is the amount of money you *really want to make* on a given project. For me, I don't usually handle any projects unless I can make at least $1000. That's my minimum price for my music services. Frankly, it just isn't worth my while to turn on the equipment and start working unless I can make about that much money.

For most projects, I *expect* to net about $3000-5000. That's my standard creative fee. If I can make that, I'm happy. I don't particularly care what the "going rate" is (though this fee is right on the mark, based on my research). This is the amount of money *I want to make* on a given gig. Your fee may be lower or higher based on your experience. That's fine.

Not every project will work out for you. I was once asked to score a 20-second promotion for a movie theater. The budget was a scant $150. Since it would cost me $80 to rent the mixdown deck needed, it left very little for profit. While it was tempting to grab a quick $100, I declined the job. It just wasn't worth the small gain. That's why it's useful to have a minimum fee, no matter how easy the work. Note: Never base your price on how easy a project is. Your client does not need to know how easy a production is. Music is a professional service and you deserve to be paid accordingly!

You should learn from this example and quickly move away from nickel-and-dime clients. Though you can compete with a low price, it doesn't make sense to be the cheapest composer in town. Otherwise, you may not earn the respect you so richly deserve and some people might take advantage of you. Your skill and time have value. It has taken you a long time to reach your current level, so place a price on your talent and charge the appropriate fees.

Are there regional differences? I doubt it. Many of you in smaller markets don't believe you can charge $400 for a minute of music. What is really happening is that you are not finding the right clients. This doesn't imply you should avoid smaller budgets, though. Get some library music and make those tracks available to those who can't afford your standard rates. You can still help them get music while making some money: 10% of something is better than 100% of nothing! You'll find more on this subject later.

When you retain rights to your music, you should control its distribution. If you write music for a radio spot and the client wants to use it for TV, you may ask them to pay again. Of course, if the track is a buyout, they can do whatever they want with the music.

Tell your clients there are no add-ons. They hate paying for this, that, and the other thing. This is why library tracks win: They pay for it once and can use it anytime they need to. You must do the same: They pay X, they get Y music. Period.

When a client has the funds for original music, quote your usual rate and don't be shy about it! **Don't**

cut your price!** Change the project guidelines instead. Listen to what the clients says and then counter with something like this: "My usual fee for what you describe would be $1000, but you've only budgeted $850. If we cut the music under the second segment, I can deliver your finished score on budget." This way you didn't lower your price, you *changed the project specifications.*

Stand firm, quote your fee, and wait for a reaction. He who opens his mouth next usually loses the negotiation. Don't let that be you. Don't apologize or give up. You provide a unique and valuable service and should be paid accordingly. Not everyone can afford your original music, so work hard to get those who can. And work hard through rights, leases, or library music to help those with smaller budgets. You're foolish if you don't structure your services to meet the needs of the maximum number of clients at various monetary levels.

TACTICS FOR OVERCOMING PRICE OBJECTIONS

When faced with a price objection, make sure you focus on the benefits your client receives from original music as you state your price and answer their objections. Here are a few other strategies you should use to overcome objections to your quoted fee:

- Divide your fee into smaller units. For example, $4000 is a lot of money, but $400 a minute for ten minutes of music sounds much less. Of course, demonstrating how your fee is a small percentage of the overall production budget is another advantage. Don't forget to stress how important music is to completing the soundtrack. **Music = Impact!**

- Make sure the specifications are equal. If your client is comparing your fee to library tracks, you need to differentiate your services from the nonexclusive music track. Don't let them compare apples and oranges.

- Remind them that a cheaper price often means inferior goods. You can justify your price with the value you deliver. Demonstrate all the benefits you offer. Follow this book's suggestions and answer these questions for your prospect.

- Create payment terms that lessen the impact of your price.

If after trying these many tactics you still don't get the gig, don't give up. Try something along these lines and keep the process moving:

I was sorry to hear that our bid was declined. Thank you for taking a minute from your day to leave a message for me. Please understand that I still hope we can do business together soon. I've had many successful relationships with other production companies in the past. I hope that soon we can work together as well. Until then, I will keep you up to date with my activities by calling periodically to see how I might help you. And I would be grateful if you would keep me informed about all the activities and successes of your company.

Follow all these strategies and in no time at all you'll set the right fee for your original music compositions *and* get the fee you deserve.

CHAPTER 14

Diversify and Thrive

Put all your eggs in one

basket and—watch that basket.

—*Mark Twain*

Let me give you this final, crucial piece of advice. If you've put together a basic project studio for your commercial music business, you have a moneymaking machine. Now you need to start thinking about all the different ways to package and sell your talent. Here's why: Earning $1000 each month from several small enterprises is far easier than trying to make $10,000 from one big business. It's far more practical to run a few micro businesses than to launch and maintain one huge business. That's why you need to diversify into related profit centers. All successful business people do it, and so should you. I'm not saying to just pick a bunch of unrelated activities. On the contrary—music is your main business. You simply need to diversify a little and offer a wider range of music related services. That is the *key* to making it in today's commercial music industry. First, evaluate your talents, and then determine the many business opportunities available to you. As long as your work shares a common music theme, you will be more successful.

Special Note: *Never* give up other successful parts of your music business. If your commercial music business is paying the bills—*don't stop*. Let these other ventures be add-on businesses—extra services that you offer. That way you can use your current resources to help you launch new services, and you'll still reap the benefits of your established work. For example, I have my original music business, plus studio services, a publishing division, business con-

sulting, and I occasionally teach lessons and play solo gigs. Learn from this example and apply its principle to your own particular situation. Diversity really is critical. Make sure you profit from *all* your musical skills.

WRITE, PUBLISH, LECTURE, TEACH

THINK!

—JOHN LENNON

- -

It is important that all your business activities be related, interactive profit centers that reinforce each other. Make sure you diversify into a series of music-based areas. Here are just some of the options available to you.

▶ PLAY IN A BAND (OR TWO)

I've never understood why more bands don't have multiple personalities. If you are dedicated to only original music, you may find your prospects severely limited. My suggestion is to go ahead and try to be the next big thing. But you should also have another band with a different personality—even if it's the same people—who play as a cover or wedding band. That's where the money is. And when you do both, you multiply your chances for success.

◗ PLAY SOLO

If you have decent keyboard or guitar chops, don't forget you can play solo at weddings, small clubs, lounges, coffeehouses, and such. There are plenty of people out there who are starving for live entertainment. You may not get paid a bunch, but hey . . . how many people get paid to practice?

◗ PLAY SESSIONS

Join the Musician's Union and get out there and land those lucrative jingle, album, and other project gigs. The competition can be fierce, but good skills and a willingness to promote yourself relentlessly can pay off handsomely.

◗ WRITE AND SELL SONGS

There is money to be made writing and pitching your original songs for others to record and play. And don't think you have to go after national acts. There are regional bands, small labels, and others looking for material for their artists. You also might consider managing and promoting other bands and artists.

◗ CREATE AND SELL PATCHES AND SAMPLES

If you can design sounds for a variety of synths and make samples available for various formats, you can run a decent and profitable sideline business.

◗ CREATE AND SELL SEQUENCES

Make sequences available for a variety of MIDI formats. Don't forget that you can offer your sequences on cassette or CD for the karaoke crowd or as accompaniment tapes for weddings, churches, schools, and more.

For those of you who create and sell patches and/or sequences, providing samples is the best way to increase your business. You should send prospects some of your best work along with your standard promotional literature. If I was selling SD-1 patches, I'd send two banks (12 patches) to prospects; if I sold sequences, I'd send five of my best songs in different styles. If you choose the latter, you're out the cost of the disk and mechanical rights and you pay slightly higher postage, but the goodwill you build is well worth the extra effort and cost. If your prospects like what you have to offer, chances are they'll want more. Of course, there will always be a few freebie seekers who will waste your time and money, but the majority of those requesting your sample will go on to buy your offering. Are you willing to risk missing them?

To promote a patch/sequence business, you could take out ads, use direct mail, send press releases, or write articles. I highly recommend that you share your expert knowledge through articles published in various industry magazines and user-group publications. What should you write about? Patch designers could offer a sample patch or write a short article about how the patch was put together. Sequence sellers can do the same thing, explaining how they dissect a popular song and turn it into a sequence. Many readers would love to know the creative process behind creating quality sequences. Or you could write an article about the business side of sequence selling—clearing rights, packaging, promotion, etc.

◗ SELL RELATED PRODUCTS THROUGH A CATALOG

If you decide to diversify into several areas, it's a good idea to create a small catalog of your products and services. You might consider offering other related items that fit with your theme. The Mix Bookshelf catalog is a wonderful example. From humble beginnings, this invaluable resource has grown to an industry leader. You are on their mailing list, aren't you? You can learn much from this success story.

• Mix Bookshelf. 6400 Hollis St., Emeryville, CA 94608; (800) 233-9604

◗ SELL YOUR EXPERTISE AS A HACKER OR MIDI SPECIALIST

If you can develop custom solutions for bands and recording studios, you can parlay that into a lucrative business. Do you write software? Can you install and troubleshoot MIDI and recording equipment? If so, quit giving away your advice and expertise and start charging for your services!

◗ ENGINEER LIVE AND STUDIO SESSIONS

Maybe you're more of a behind-the-scenes person. There's lots of work out there for those who can push the right buttons. A good live mixer is a much sought after commodity. I know many bands that would kill for someone to run their house mixer. And recording studios always need help. You might consider offering to work the overnight shift. You gain valuable skills, contacts, and make some money as well.

◗ RECORD SONGWRITERS, BAND DEMOS, AND MORE

Got a decent recording setup? Why aren't you renting time to help pay for it all? A well-equipped home project studio can quickly grow into a viable commercial or remote recording studio where you sell studio and production time. Or you can sell other audio services from your project studio such as audio-for-video sound design. You don't need to go overboard, but even a few hours or days a month can put some extra cash in your pocket.

◆ TEACH LESSONS AND SEMINARS

Hey, you worked hard to get where you are, so why not make some money telling and showing others how to play? Don't ignore the older folks out there; kids aren't the only ones learning how to play.

◆ WRITE ARTICLES, BOOKLETS, BOOKS, OR NEWSLETTERS ABOUT MUSIC

This is a good promotional tool, but you can use it to make money, too. Got all that knowledge up in your head? Get it down on paper and share it with the rest of us. For me, *How to Make Money Scoring Soundtracks and Jingles* has been a very rewarding experience. I wrote this resource for several reasons:

- To learn about the book publishing industry
- To help others achieve success through my experiences
- For the satisfaction of the completed work
- To make some money for my music business in a different, yet related way

◆ SOUND DESIGNER AND PROGRAMMER FOR STUDIOS, RADIO, TV, AND FILM

This area is somewhat similar to patch selling, but it's targeted at a different market. Here you design the sound effects and such used by various audiovisual producers. Occasionally, another composer might need your skills to develop sounds for their synths. I recently handled all the audio production for a multimedia project. This included recording the narration, sound effects, and music and mixing the different elements together for the final computer-based production.

◆ RELEASE YOUR OWN INDEPENDENT RECORD

Unfortunately, too many musicians are worried about *breaking into* the music business. They believe the only path to fame and fortune is through a record contract. Well, the truth is you have a better chance of starting your *own* music business—and succeeding with it—than pursuing the conventional path.

You see, the world doesn't begin or end with a major label. Who believes in your own music more than you (OK, but your mother doesn't count)? Who can sell your music better than you? Who deserves the admiration and sense of accomplishment—and yes, the money—more than you?

That's what releasing an independent record is all about. First, don't think that your independent release has to follow the traditional rules. What I'm talking about and recommending to you has many different levels. Your release can be just for friends and family—maybe just one copy for someone you love. Or it can be something you sell at gigs. Perhaps you want to market your music via an independent

catalog. Maybe you want to throw your hat into the ring; start your own label; and sell your music regionally, nationally, or even internationally. That's the beauty of self-releasing your material. You can start small and do it for personal satisfaction, you can build your audience slowly and steadily, or you can go full tilt. It's entirely up to you!

Hey, a record contract is *not* the summit of the music industry. You can have a lot of fun and make some decent cash with your own record. How about it? You can package your music and sell it as an independent tape or CD. This serves two purposes: You have an impressive demo and an independent, related profit center. If you don't want to pursue a record contract, there are alternative outlets for your music. The best opportunity to market your self-released music is through Ron Wallace's *Aftertouch.* This magazine devotes itself to showcasing and selling independent releases. If this is something you'd like to do, drop Ron a line and tell him I sent you.

- Creative Musician's Coalition. 1024 W. Willcox Ave., Peoria, IL 61604; (309) 685-4843; www.aimcmc.com.

◆ SPECIAL AUDIO PRODUCTION FOR BUSINESS

There are some untapped markets out there that can put some extra cash in your pocket, full- or part-time. What I'm talking about here is handling special recording and duplicating projects for a few niche markets.

Businesses are always looking for better ways to deliver their message. There is staff to train, new products and services to announce, news to dispatch, and other general marketing. Many hold seminars and conferences for members, clients, and prospects. How can you help them get their information out? You have two choices:

- On-hold telephone messages
- Audiocassettes

◆ ON-HOLD MESSAGES FOR BUSINESS

If a company places one call on hold every five minutes for only 30 seconds during a 10-hour business day, this translates to over 250 hours a year with people on hold. This time could—and should—be used to bring information to prospects and clients while they wait.

There's money to be made selling phone hold production services. It's a simple and effective marketing tool that a lot of clients adore. First, prepare about 30 short promotional scripts lasting between 10-15 seconds each. Record the scripts using voice-over talent. Then throw on some old tracks of music and mix the whole thing to mono on a C-60. Put the tape into an auto-reversing tape deck (or digital on-hold system), plug it into your client's phone hold system, and you have phone hold marketing. Anyone put on hold during the day automatically hears the promotional messages with the same script repeating. I've put packages together with a few hours studio time, talent fees, tape, and a flat rate for ten minutes of music, and the total fee was just under $500. It's a welcome change from scoring and quite lucrative, too.

- *Word of Mouth: A Guide to Commercial Voice-Over Excellence*, Susan Blu and Molly Ann Mullin. Pomegranate Press Ltd.; P.O. Box 8261, Universal City, CA 91608-0261. Want to branch out into this field? This is what you need.
- *NBC Handbook of Pronunciation*, Eugene Ehrlich and Raymond Hand Jr. Harper and Row; 10 E. 53rd St.; New York, NY 10022. If you record voice-over work, you need a copy of this book . . . just in case.

◗ AUDIOCASSETTES FOR BUSINESS

More and more people use cassettes as their main information source. Cassettes are easy, convenient, and for many people who don't have the time to read, surpass print as a way to learn. A business can deliver its primary message to prospects and clients via cassettes, or they can provide an audio version of seminars and meetings for those who could not attend. Cassette production is relatively inexpensive, especially when the majority of work you do will be recorded live and duplicated quickly. Most projects are of the simple spoken-word variety, with little need for fancy production or wall-to-wall music. In essence, you'll produce a company's cassettes for them and either charge them a fixed, flat rate for your services or work out a royalty agreement if they are going to sell the tapes. The ideal businesses are those that conduct seminars or training. Recording these meetings is the most lucrative service you can offer. Contact businesses, professionals, and associations and pitch this idea to them. Don't forget to ask your current and past clients if they are interested in these ancillary services. Let local advertising agencies know about what you do and how you can help their clients sell more of their products and services.

◗ AUDIOCASSETTES AS CHARITY FUND-RAISER

Here's a terrific fund-raiser for schools, churches, etc. For example, record a school band holiday album (direct to stereo DAT) and pay for the duplication. The school agrees to sell the tapes at their concerts, keep a royalty, and pay you the remainder. Let's look at the numbers: Say you agree to give the school a good royalty of 20% on what they sell. On a $10 tape, they'd get $2 for each unit sold. Let's say it costs you $2 to record, duplicate, and package the holiday concert release. $10 - 2 - 2 = $6 profit per unit. Even after giving the school a big royalty of 20%, you still *net*

three times your production costs. If they sell 100 tapes, you clear $600 and the school clears $200—a lot more than they'd make selling candy bars!

You can see the key is to keep your recording, duplicating, and packaging costs down, thereby increasing your profit margin. For bands, schools, churches, and such, there is already a built-in market. This kind of fund-raiser makes perfect financial sense. By carefully controlling the production costs and duplicating only what you need, you make enough from initial sales to fully fund your production costs. All other sales put cash in your pocket. It's a win-win situation for everybody!

If there are 50 people in the band, each must sell only two tapes to reach a modest goal of 100 tapes. Since probably all 50 will buy one tape for themselves, they only need to sell 50 more to make money. It helps to produce the tape *before* the holiday concert, so the tapes can be sold *at* the concert while the audience is eager to hear more. This situation is perfect for school bands, choirs, and theater groups. You could record cast albums for the school's musical and sell them before, during, and after the shows. It's hard to beat this as a fund-raiser. Don't forget, if you record copyrighted material, you must pay mechanical royalties to the music publisher. This reduces your profits a tad, but not much, and it's a variable cost. If you sell more tapes, you pay more royalties. Stick with a medley of holiday classics ("Silent Night," "Joy to the World," Handel's *Messiah*, etc.) and you avoid that issue entirely!

◗ SELLING THESE ANCILLARY SERVICES

Before spending another dime to promote your new services, try these simple ways to get business. These and more are all targets for your services.

- If you currently work full-time, ask your employer about their using tapes for marketing, training, and related areas and about using on-hold messages.
- Ask friends, family, and business associates if they or anyone they know could benefit from your services.
- Call your old music school and choir teachers, drop a note to the local theater groups, check into barbershop quartets, leave flyers at local music stores, and contact the churches or other community organizations in your area who could benefit from the fund-raising concept.

Next, create a basic promotional package. Once again, a sales letter accompanied by a standard brochure and a demo tape makes the ideal package. Your letter must talk about the benefits of using cassettes for marketing, training, on-hold, and fundraising. The brochure should provide the details of your services, and the demo tape should highlight several examples of the projects you can do—such as example on-hold scripts, live speeches, meetings, band and choral concerts, etc. Keep it short and simple, under five minutes. You might want to add a voice-over to describe your services. That way the cassette tape serves as your main marketing piece.

These markets are ready for you to show them the way. I particularly like the fund-raising concept. It's a good fit for school and church choirs, bands, and theater groups. And on-hold messages are a potentially lucrative ancillary service, too.

I hope you see the advantage of diversifying your service line and pricing options to attract the greatest number of clients. Brainstorm all the possibilities that you, with your talents and experiences, can turn into business ventures. There are many different ways you can make money from your music. While you can't do everything, you can experiment and find the work you like best—and you can find the work that is the most profitable! Are you thinking about more ways to turn your talent into cash? I hope so.

YOUR OWN MUSIC LIBRARY MAKES DOLLARS AND SENSE

The most obvious adjunct to your custom music services is a music library. Start a music library? I know, I hate them. But if you can't beat them, join them. There are people who can only afford to buy library tracks—why not be the one supplying them? This is so important that I've separated this section from the other moneymaking ideas.

What about all your unused tracks? If you're like me, you probably have many songs, sketches, mini-scores, and more sitting on tape or disk somewhere. There is no sense letting all that music gather dust when it could put money in your pocket. You have four choices:
• Sell single music tracks or your specialized collection for a single price to certain prospects and clients
• Sell other music libraries
• Sell music search services
• Sell your own music library

I make the distinction between a music collection and a library in this way. A collection is an informal way to sell old music. Make it available only to your select group of clients. This way they are assured of some exclusivity. A music library implies that you will mass produce the music (usually on CD) and sell it to anyone who plops down $50-100.

▶ TURN YOUR OLD TRACKS INTO CASH
Not too long ago, a prospect called and asked if I had music for a drama he was doing. He didn't want a track written from scratch because the work was speculative, and he could only afford to pay a small fee. He asked if I had any appropriate music lying around that he could buy at a lower price than a customized track. That started me thinking . . .

After viewing his footage, I suggested a few tracks and made a quick tape. He then decided to use two different tracks for his project. I spent an hour remixing the music, and he picked up the master tape the very next day. The charge was $150 for the music. My time invested was less than two hours—not bad for some music I'd written 18 months earlier. So, by simply recycling old music tracks, you can keep money coming in.

Since you can't rely on prospects and clients asking you for this service, you need to develop a formal system. This is a four-step process:
• Select appropriate music from your past work.
• Create a demo tape of the best tracks.
• Develop a flyer or brochure offering this service.
• Sell the music for a flat rate offering nonexclusive rights to your clients.

▶ SELECT APPROPRIATE MUSIC FROM YOUR PAST WORK
There are two approaches you can use as you search for old music tracks. You can offer a mix of styles, such as rock, jazz, orchestral, unusual, new age, world—in other words, the most popular music styles. This is probably the best approach because you give your clients a wider choice and most people look for versatility in a library volume. Cover a variety of styles and you'll be more successful. That usually translates into more sales.

You could also choose to offer only music of a specific niche. Perhaps you specialize in orchestral music and want to sell just that music style. Or maybe you play outstanding solo piano and want to offer just those tracks. While you limit your potential market this way, you can also benefit by being the only person who offers this choice. That's not a bad situation to be in.

▶ CREATE A DEMO TAPE OF THE BEST TRACKS
To sell this music service, you should prepare a demo tape of your best tracks. I suggest selecting about 20-30 pieces and preparing a montage of short snippets lasting about 8-15 seconds each. You might consider grouping your music by style, such as rock, jazz, etc. and include *only* the best parts of each track. Refer back to the demo chapter for complete details.

DEVELOP A FLYER OR BROCHURE OFFERING THIS SERVICE

The choice to include information about this service with your standard promotional brochure or to prepare a separate flyer is up to you. I suggest making it an integral part of your services, especially if you offer several music options, as I do.

SELL THE MUSIC FOR A FLAT RATE, OFFERING NONEXCLUSIVE RIGHTS TO YOUR CLIENTS

You need a sliding scale and a blanket agreement for your music collection. You should charge different amounts for different projects. Base your charges on where the music will be heard. If it is destined for a corporate video with a limited audience, something around $95-150 per track is good. If the track is for regional radio or TV, charge $150-300. For national radio or TV, double—or even triple—that. Remember, you own full rights to the music, so you can sell the same pieces repeatedly.

Make sure you develop a simple agreement that your clients sign that grants them nonexclusive rights to the music. They may use the music only for the production you license it for and must pay for additional uses. They need to understand that the music is nonexclusive and that you can sell it again and again to other people. This need only be a letter that you include when you send your client the music they buy. Or have them sign the letter and return a copy to you with their check.

THE MASTER CUE MUSIC COLLECTION

One of the services I offer with my music collection is customization. Essentially, once they select a track from my collection, they can have the track customized to their specific needs. This includes changing the tempo, instrumentation, length, etc. Each track exists as something I call the master cue (explained earlier). The work of *Miami Vice* composer Jan Hammer best exemplifies this idea. Hammer would write one full piece with many parts. Next, he'd mix several other cues based on and part of one main theme. The book *On the Track* sums up Jan Hammer's approach to contemporary scoring:

> [Hammer] *normally created one basic theme and setting of that theme per episode, and then created variations on that theme throughout the show . . . emphasizing the overall emotional content.*

Here's an example from one of my recent scoring projects. The producers of a local television program approached me to write the theme for their show. Since it was only a short piece, we settled on my minimum price, bundling the composition and pro-

duction costs into one fee. I retained all rights to the music and received a big screen credit and a favorable testimonial letter for my marketing kit.

The theme I wrote was a jazzy, up-tempo piece using drums, piano, bass, and saxophone. Since the show would sometimes deal with rather serious subjects, I decided to record a slower, darker version using lighter drums, a mellow electric piano, deep acoustic bass, and no burning sax solo. On still another version, I slowed the tempo down and added a new flute line. This gave them a version for their end credits. Next, I took all three versions and chopped them up to create bumpers to use when going to and coming from commercial breaks.

All the music used my electro-acoustic ensemble. The takes came from one master recording. I just arranged and orchestrated the versions differently. It's relatively easy when you have the right composition and technical skills. The point is this: I spent most of my time writing the main theme and then took a few extra hours to adapt the music to a variety of contexts and situations. The show producers ended up with a bouncy opening *and* two separate and completely different arrangements based around the same theme. Add the bumpers and it was a real bargain; much more music than they ever expected. That's the essence of the master cue method of writing original music. Your clients pay only for the single main take and get the alternate mixes as a bonus!

If your prospect's budget is really tight and using master cues still doesn't come in under budget, consider combining library cuts with original music. Tell them you'll write a single theme to open and close the production (and to use during certain transitional scenes), but suggest that they choose library tracks as filler to hold under dialogue and narration. Here, using a library track is suitable and less costly, and your client still maintains an original thematic element! They benefit by getting the impact of custom original music when—and where—they need it, with the added savings of library cuts. Of course, you'll make a few bucks on the original music you compose and a few dollars selling the library tracks.

MAKE MONEY SELLING OTHER LIBRARY MUSIC

Library music is very cheap. Some companies sell 60 minutes of music on CD for under $60. You might consider buying a commercial music library and selling *that* to clients. Contact a few companies and ask them about becoming a dealer. You sell their library to your clients in return for a commission, usually 15-20% and sometimes higher.

Another idea is to buy a library or two and sell music search services. For clients with tiny budgets, you can offer to find them the music they need and deliver it for one small price. All you need to do is go through the library music and find the appropriate music. This finder's fee can't be too high, but a few bucks for a few minutes work helps pay the bills. You then turn around and sell them the library music and pocket your commission on the sale.

Between your original music compositions, your personal library of music, your music-finding consultations, and other music and recording related services that you offer, you can become the one-stop shop for music in your area. That is what you must strive for!

◆ PROFIT FROM YOUR OWN MUSIC LIBRARY

If you are really serious about getting every last penny from your music, you might consider gathering up all your best music and producing your own music library. Let's face it, some producers will never buy an original composition from you even if it makes their program better. They may buy a collection of your work, though. Offer your library to all those prospects who never became clients. Show them how they can afford to get original, unique music that fits their budget. Offer your library nationwide and earn even more.

All unused music tracks and tracks where you retain the rights can put some extra cash in your pocket. You need about 20 tracks or 60 minutes of music to make an ideal music library volume. While diversity may seem a better deal, a collection of music in one particular style can be very attractive, too.

For diversity, you need slow and up-tempo music in rock, jazz, industrial, dance, etc. It can be expensive to produce a CD album, so don't jump in unless you realistically believe you can sell 1000 copies of your music library. Of course, your music library can be the demo of your original music composition services, too. Having a 60-minute CD demo is not a bad idea. Contact some of the music libraries listed earlier to get an idea of what your library should contain. Don't copy them—*learn* from them.

The steps you should use to put together your music library should parallel the steps explained above with the only difference being wider distribution. Create a promotional flyer and send it along with your regular advertising material. This way you can offer original composition services to those with bigger budgets and a music library to those who can't afford your fee. Either situation lets you get maximum advantage and profits from your musical skill.

◆ CD OR NOT CD?

Having your music library available on cassette and CD is the ideal situation. Lest you think you need to lay out $2000+ to produce your CD, there is an alternative way. You don't make as much money, but your risk is minimal.

For example, let's say you have 60 minutes of music in a variety of styles that you want to offer as a library volume. You should sell this on a buyout basis for $99. This means your clients pay the one-time fee and can use the music as much as they want for unlimited projects. You realize no future revenue, but you sell the same music over and over again. Just think: Only 100 sales at $99 each is a gross profit of $9900. You could get 500 CDs for about $2000, or $4 each. Sell them at $99 each and you pocket about $90 each after postage and advertising costs are factored in. Not bad. But of course, you do need to lay out the 2000 bucks in advance. That ties up your money.

- Disc Makers. 7905 N. Route 130, Pennsauken, NJ 08110; (800) 468-9353. Here is a company that specializes in CD manufacturing. You can get 500 CDs for around $1800. Contact them and ask for both their catalog and their free booklet, *Guide to Master Tape Preparation*.

Here's an alternative method. Why not print a few copies at a time? You can get a single CD made for about $25; ten for $200, or $20 each. You sell them for $99 and pocket about $75 after costs, postage, and promotional expenses. That's still a good profit, but more importantly, your risk is very small. As orders roll in, you can make more CDs. You minimize your out of pocket expenses and inventory and maximize your profits. Should your library prove very popular, you can then consider making more copies, reducing your per unit costs, and profit accordingly. That's not a bad situation to be in at all.

- If you want to pursue this strategy—or if you just want to put your music on CD for archival purposes or to give as a gift—many companies offer single CDs for under $30. The short run *only* makes sense for one or two CDs, though. If you want 30, you're better off getting 500 or 1000. You can use the remaining as demos, sell them as your music library, market them through *Aftertouch*, or wallpaper your studio.

Alternately, you might consider pressing your own music CDs on demand. With a decent computer system, you can add a writeable CD-ROM drive. For about $600 you can be pressing your own CDs in minutes. Blank media is under $12. At $100 each CD sale, you'd break even with 7 CDs and make a big profit on all future sales. Of course, your investment is higher, so this only makes sense if you can justify the computer hardware expense for your music business.

I hope you see how having your own music library makes complete (dollars and) sense. I suggest you take advantage of all the possibilities. My best advice is to start right now. Gather up a few tracks, create a montage demo, mention your services in your sales material, and get some sales. Start with a collection, contact a few libraries for information (including dealer commissions), and consider a full-blown library of your own. You want to get the maximum benefit from your musical talent, don't you?

Use your music library both as a profit center of its own and as leverage for more lucrative original music gigs. It makes a great demo that clients can buy, keep, and use while you make a little money on the sales. Also, work hard to land some original music work from the contacts you make selling your library tracks. Another *How to Make Money Scoring Soundtracks and Jingles* alumnus, Devin Kirschner, followed this exact advice to create his own music library. He's making both direct sales and landing original music projects at the same time. If you're considering pursuing this, get a copy of his CD.

• Entropy Music Solutions. P.O. Box 382, Unionville, NY 10988; www.intercall.com/~devin/

Also, please note that it's important to offer a wide range of music products and services and at a variety of prices. This is how you'll make the most money from your music. Here are some offers you might consider:

• A free sample music tape clients can use for their productions
• A single track fee of $99 for existing tracks
• A standard $389 per minute as your original music composition rate
• A music buyout rate of $3895 per finished minute
• A royalty-free music library to fall between $99 and $159 per volume

There are substantial advantages to diversifying both your service line and pricing options to attract the greatest number of clients.

Samples

Here's an example from one of my very successful campaigns. It always brings in an 8% response. When I need eight new client prospects, I send out 100 letters. Print this on your letterhead and mail it along with a short brochure about your services.

STOP PAYING TOO MUCH FOR
ORIGINAL MUSIC . . .

. . . by saving up to *xx*% off the national average for the next six months!

You know that using the right music makes your production more effective. And original music:

- Adds a unique and exciting musical identity to your production.
- Is flexible, versatile, and conforms exactly to your needs.
- Precisely matches your screen action and drama.
- Enhances and supports your visual imagery.
- Increases the impact of your production.
- Makes your message more memorable.

Original music makes a difference in how your audience responds and that means a better, more effective production. Put simply: *only* original music —scored specifically for your production—can do all this. So, why leave that power to a bland, unimaginative buyout library track? Because the major disadvantage of original music is the cost, right?

Not anymore.

I'll score your commercial or corporate project—exactly to your specifications—starting at just $*xxx.xx* per finished minute. This special offer includes composing, arranging, recording, tape, and talent. How's that sound?

That's over *xx*% off the national average (cur-

rently between $*xxx* to $*xxx* a minute). However, this is a limited offer. After *[date]*, my fee returns to $*xxx.xx* per finished minute (still the best deal in town).

Don't need music right away? You still need to call (or send in the order coupon below) and reserve that price. By choosing me to compose the music you need to make future productions better, I'll hold that price for *up to six months.* ANYTIME you need original music during that time, it's only $*xxx.xx* per finished minute.

So even if you don't have an immediate need for original music, you must place your order to get this special offer. HURRY, my offer expires on *[date, year]*. Don't put it off. Send me the enclosed coupon or call me today!

P.S. Even though you can get 60 minutes of library junk for 60 bucks, you'll think twice in the future the first time you hear the theme for your latest project on some 900-number commercial. Get the exact original music you want and need AND save money, too! Call me and get one step closer to original music for less.

This offer encourages prospects to get my promotional booklet.

So, you want to save money on original music?
Here's how:

You know that using the right music for your project is crucial to its success. And you know how expensive an original score can be. But you shouldn't have to settle for less just to save some money. I've reserved a copy of my groundbreaking booklet, *HOW TO GET LOW-COST ORIGINAL MUSIC FOR ALL YOUR PRO-*

DUCTIONS, in your name.

When you follow its guidelines, you stop paying too much for original music. You get the maximum music for the minimum investment—original music that fits your project exactly. Original music that enhances your images. Original music that delivers your message more effectively.

That's what you want, isn't it?

Every day I use the techniques explained in my booklet to compose music that works, sounds great, and is affordable. I can do the same for you.

When you're ready to get the music your production needs and deserves—and save money, too—call me and request your copy of my book (a $12.95 value, yours free for the asking). Also, make sure you request your information kit about my services when you call. This material shows you *exactly* how I can help you. If you let me.

Use this stimulating and useful booklet, then let me know about how its advice helped you achieve the results you wanted for your productions. Let's get started right now.

SALES LETTER THREE

Use this as a more general letter to describe your services.

Why would you want to reach for cheap library music when you can get original music that works, sounds great, and is affordable? You shouldn't have to settle for less just to save some cash! Here are the benefits you get when choosing my company:

• Personal Service. No two people are alike, and no two people expect (or want) the same music. That's the real problem with library tracks. You get the same music as everyone else. Doesn't your production deserve the unique identity that only original music provides?

• Reasonable Fees. The basic price of $3950 per finished minute is for a buyout license. That price includes composing, arranging, recording, talent, and tape. Complete. And you get full ownership and exclusivity to the music.

• Can't afford that rate? The basic price of $399 per finished minute is for a single-use license. Again, that price includes composing, arranging, recording, talent, and tape. The catch is that I own the copyright and you have limited rights to the music.

• Fast, Quality Service. Need music fast? Most tracks can be completed within a week.

• Convenient. I'm a one-man band, so to speak, which means you get my full attention. Tell me what you need, and I'll work hard to meet and exceed your expectations.

Now get professional, effective, and unique orig-

inal music at a reasonable fee. Pay just one low price per minute of music with NO hidden charges. As an experienced composer, I can save you some *real* money! My approach to composing and recording original music saves you thousands on a buyout score and hundreds on a limited use musical package. Those are both terrific deals.

I would like you as one of my satisfied customers. Call right now and let's talk about your latest music needs. Perhaps I can help you get the original music your projects deserve.

P.S. Don't need music right now? Keep this letter with your budget files and when you put together a quotation for one of your clients, make sure you give me a call. I'm ready to help you help them.

SALES LETTER FOUR

If you try the sample music tape idea, select 30-50 names and send them this letter. Wait for the response or follow up by phone in ten days. You need to insert your prices into the letter, but other than that, I suggest you make no other changes. This will generate some leads and, because these people requested your tape—and more importantly can use your music free of charge, they'll listen to your demo. This is exactly how you solve one of the main problems we commercial music composers face. This works, so be prepared for the response.

ARE YOU PAYING TOO
MUCH FOR ORIGINAL MUSIC?

Today, original music costs between $400-500 per finished minute. That kind of money puts it out of reach for many producers. So, you're forced to use library tracks. Bland, unimaginative library tracks.

But you know that original music makes a difference. Why settle for something that almost fits? Don't compromise your creativity. Get music with impact. Get music that works. Get original music.

I'll score your commercial or corporate project —exactly to your specifications—starting at just *$299 per finished minute*. Complete. This limited discount offer *includes* composing, arranging, recording, tape, and talent.

You get the best of both worlds. Exactly the right music, right now. And you get it at a price that makes sense—*over 40% off* the national average. This is your chance to get original music for small productions, test spots, or anytime you need to lower your budget, *not* your expectations.

• Original music gives you flexibility and versatility— any length and style (rock, jazz, orchestral, or exotic).

• Original music gives you precisely what you need to

match your visuals, create a mood, underscore the action, and enhance your message.

• Original music emphasizes the drama in a situation and creates a more convincing experience for your audience.

No library track can do all that.

You want to deliver your message more effectively, don't you? Using the right music is the key! And at this price, you have no excuse not to get the exact original music you want, need, and deserve.

I want us to work together making music that works for you. If ever you're not happy with the music I compose for you, I'll refund your money. NO QUESTIONS ASKED! Quality, value, and no risk. I guarantee it.

How can I make this offer? By taking full advantage of today's modern technology. I keep production costs down and pass the savings on to you. You pay for the music, *not* high-priced studio overhead. You get the music you want, the way you want it, when you want it, and at prices you can afford.

Just think of it. Original soundtrack music from only *$299* per finished minute. COMPLETE and GUARANTEED. This offer saves you OVER 40% OFF the national average. Can you get that price at another music house? No way!

Because I want to meet your music needs exactly, here's another offer. If you call me right now, I'll send you five music tracks on cassette. You can *KEEP* and *USE* this sample music to enhance any of your latest projects. The tape is FREE (a $99 value) and you're under no obligation.

It won't have the same impact as music scored *specifically* for your production, but it just might help you out of a jam when you need some good music fast. Plus, this offer gives you an idea of the music I can write for you. Other composers send a demo of their past work. I'll send you a sample of my music you can start using TODAY!

Your creative work demands the best of everything. Won't using original music make it that much better? So, stop using library tracks. Get the impact of original music with the same convenience and cost. And get it now.

But hurry, both offers expire on *[date, year]*. Call me today. I look forward to talking with you.

P.S. Why settle for anything less? Get custom soundtrack music that works, sounds great, and is affordable (not some library garbage). Let my *original* music make the difference in your productions. I'll meet your needs exactly. Don't put it off. Call me right now and take advantage of these offers.

Introducing new custom music composition services.

SPECIAL OFFER

Get original music for your next commercial or corporate project starting at just $299 per finished minute COMPLETE.

Or lease an original jingle for only $149 a month. You pay only for as long as you continue to use it. This offer is ideal for small advertisers who can't afford the big bucks charged by other music houses.

Original music makes a difference in how your audience responds. Why let your creative work be anything less? At these prices, you have no excuse for not getting the original music you need and deserve. Hurry, this offer expires in ten days. Call Jeffrey P. Fisher Music today and let's get started on your next project.

P.S. How can I afford this? Frankly, I can't. Once you sample our skill, I'm confident you'll come back for more. Let me help you be more successful . . . and make getting there far more affordable. Call me right now!

I've been impressed with the quality of your advertising on W*XXX*-FM, specifically your "Hometown Report." Your commitment to community service and general goodwill is refreshing.

However, I am surprised that you haven't included a jingle with your radio spots. The right jingle can go a long way toward enhancing your image. Jingles have the power that keeps your name alive in listener's minds.

It would be a privilege for me to present a custom music package that would give you a new musical identity—and a competitive edge. I feel strongly that using a jingle would improve your already successful campaign.

In fact, I already have an idea in mind. Could you spare just five minutes of your time to hear the new jingle composed *specifically* for you? That's right, I can play a finished jingle starring YOUR COMPANY. You'll hear exactly how your custom music package will sound on the radio. And this jingle will separate you from the advertising crowd, especially on W*XXX* where very few advertisers use jingles.

Of course, I will make this presentation without cost or obligation to you. I'll call Thursday morning to set up a time for us to meet. You need do nothing, just bring your ears and open your mind to how the right musical identity can help you improve your ads, your business, and your profits!

P.S. Get more from your radio advertising dollars. Jingles make radio ads more effective. Music influences listeners by stimulating their imagination and memory. They remember the melody . . . remember the tune . . . and remember your product. In other words: Jingles sell. And they work for both advertisers big and small. That's why you must make a jingle part of your advertising campaign!

JINGLE SALES LETTER TWO

MAKE MORE MONEY FROM
YOUR BROADCAST ADS . . .
. . . AND SAVE OVER $2100 DOING IT.

Big advertisers know the value of music in their TV and radio campaigns. Music influences the way people think. And buy.

The average jingle costs an outrageous $7500. With this special discount offer, you can get your very own jingle—one that will help sell your products and services better—for *only* $149 a month. By leasing your jingle for three years, you save $2136. That's a whopping 28% off the national average. And easier to pay for, too!

More importantly, you get a jingle that grabs attention, instantly identifies you and your message, makes a lasting impression, and actually excites viewers and listeners about your business.

Put very simply: JINGLES SELL!

The big, impersonal music factories don't think it's worth their time to put this powerful tool in the hands of smaller advertisers . . . like you. So, they make advertising music too expensive for most budgets to afford. That's wrong! You should be using the very best music—the kind I can write for you—to motivate people to buy YOUR products and services.

You need every possible tool available for your advertising arsenal. And your jingle delivers your message in its most memorable form: music and lyrics. I'm offering you this power at prices that are fair.

Our leasing packages start at only $149 per month for 36 months for a buyout license. After that time, the jingle is yours. Leasing your new jingle lets you improve your bottom line first WITHOUT hurting your cash flow. As a bonus, your new custom music package can be written, recorded, on the air, and working for you in a week.

I'll even compose a FREE demonstration of how your jingle will sound before we spend any money. You get exactly what you want and need with NO risk.

Still not convinced that a jingle can increase the drawing power of your ads and increase your profits? Call me right now and let's talk. If I don't think a jingle will help your situation, I'll say no. I won't sell you something that won't work for you. Advertising music is not for everyone.

Perhaps a simple musical background score might make your message more effective and your ads sell better. You can get a custom score for under $799 complete.

Experts agree that the right music can increase listener response by 30%. Whether you choose a jingle with lyrics or an appropriate background score, having as unique musical identity is vital to your business success!

Remember, you get a free demo and consultation, simple leasing terms from only $149 a month COMPLETE, and ongoing support and professional service. I'll work hard to make sure you music works, sound great, and is affordable.

But you must hurry. This special offer expires on *[date, year]*. It's time to get more from your advertising dollars. Call me today and let's get started.

P.S. The right advertising music (jingle or score) will make your TV and radio advertising more effective. Music stimulates customers to buy and that increases your profits. Isn't this what you want from your advertising? Call me right now!

POSTCARDS

YOU FOUND IT!

Your one stop source for original music that works, sounds great, and is affordable. Stop paying too much for original music and start saving today! Options to fit any budget. Call right now.

$AVE MONEY ON ALL YOUR ORIGINAL MUSIC

Get an original soundtrack score for only $399 per finished minute. COMPLETE! Deliver your message more effectively by getting the exact music you need and deserve. For less. Don't put it off. Call right now for music that works, sounds great, and is affordable.

PAYING TOO MUCH FOR ORIGINAL MUSIC?

Your creative work deserves original music that works, sound great, and is affordable. Why lower your expectations just to lower your budget? Let us score your next commercial or corporate project—exactly to your needs—starting at only $399 per finished minute. COMPLETE! Act now. This special offer expires on *[date, year]*. No fooling!

RADIO AND TV ADS NOT WORKING?
Jingles sell! And your advertising needs that edge. Let us compose an original jingle that you can lease for only $149 a month. Free demo, too. Call today.

YOU CAN AFFORD ORIGINAL MUSIC

Today's technology makes original music affordable. Now get the best of both worlds—exactly the right music and at a price that makes sense. Let Jeffrey P. Fisher Music score your commercial or corporate project—to your specifications—starting at only $399 per finished minute. COMPLETE! You get music that works, sound great, and is affordable. And you get it right now.

CLASSIFIED ADS

Here are some sample ads you might consider using.

• Paying too much for original music? Save money without compromising your creativity. Scores from $399 a minute. Lease jingles from only $149 a month. Contact . . .
• Radio and TV ads not working? Get a jingle and make your commercials more effective AND profitable. Leases start from only $149 a month. Call . . .
• Original music not in your budget? Let us help you get music that works, sounds great, and is affordable. Call . . .

COVER LETTER

So, you want to save money on original music? Thanks for your interest in my composition services —your one-stop source for affordable original music. You'll find the following in this music information and planning kit:
• A flyer detailing my special offer of composing your original music starting at only $399 per finished minute. COMPLETE.
• The sample cassette tape you requested that features five music cuts you can use free for any of your productions.
• More specific information about the music on the tape.
• A listing describing all my services and what I can do for you.
• Some comments from satisfied clients.
• My sample contract to show how easy and inexpensive it is to get the original music you want.
• A brief biographical sketch about my work.
• Reprints of several *SCREEN* magazine articles.
• A copy of my latest *FOR SCORE* newsletter. I'll be adding you to my mailing list and making sure you get the latest edition each quarter.

• An order form so you can purchase my booklet *HOW TO GET LOW-COST ORIGINAL MUSIC FOR ALL YOUR PRODUCTIONS*. It's only $12.95 postage paid. [*Note: Sometimes I omit this last bullet and bring a free copy to the first meeting.*]

This information and music sample should give you a better idea of how I can help you. You know the right music enhances your creative project. And you shouldn't have to settle for less just to save some money!

Get the music your production needs and deserves. I'll make sure to meet your needs exactly and give you music that works, sounds great, and is affordable.

Enjoy the tape. I'll call soon to answer any of your questions. I can't wait to hear about your latest project and talk about your music needs.

JINGLES FLYER ONE

ORIGINAL SCORES

Here's what you get with your custom soundtrack package:

Fully produced, professional compositions. The production includes the standard rhythm section of drums and percussion, bass, electric and acoustic guitar, and synthesizer orchestra (ready to produce any sound, real or imagined). Additional instrumentation changes the cost per minute depending on the specific project. Please contact me to discuss your production in detail and to get an accurate price quote. Use this as a guideline only when planning your next music budget.

—YOUR COSTS

$399 for each finished minute of music with a two-minute minimum ($798). Fractions are rounded to the nearest half-minute. This price includes composing, arranging, production (in my studio), talent, and one master tape (on either ¼-inch half-track or DAT).

—YOUR RIGHTS

This offer gives you one-time (first-use) rights to the music *only*. The copyright and all other rights belong to the composer. Exclusive (buyout) rights and work-for-hire agreements are negotiable but are *not* eligible for this special offer. Contact me for more information.

—MY GUARANTEE

Quality, value, and no risk. If ever you're not happy with the music I compose for you, I'll refund your money. No questions asked.

Get original music that works, sounds great, and is affordable. *Call today and let's get started!*

You might also consider leasing your jingles. Many advertisers can't afford the buyout rights you'd normally charge, but don't want a nonexclusive jingle (syndicated music) either. Here's how to pitch an alternative.

ORIGINAL JINGLES

Instead of buying your jingle, why not lease it? Your financial burden is lessened while you work toward complete ownership to your jingle. The following lease grants you buyout rights—full ownership to the jingle. Your costs are:

• $399 deposit to cover the initial productions costs, talent, and tape. This includes the first month of the lease.

• $149 is billed the first of each month thereafter for the next 35 months. After that, the jingle is yours.

Your total cost for this lease is $5614. If you prefer not to lease the jingle, this buyout license is $4599. We also have options for nonexclusive jingle packages that start at $1499. Here's what you get with your complete jingle package:

• Full instrumental with no words, just the melody so an announcer can easily be added

• Full vocal version with complete, sung lyrics

• Donut version has some lyrics, but generally has a hole in the middle for inserting an announcer

• Tag usually just sings the key message, slogan, or product/company name

Let me show you how easy and inexpensive it is to produce a custom music package for your broadcast advertising campaign. Call today.

YOUR ONE-STOP SOURCE
FOR MUSIC AND SOUND . . .

—CUSTOM MUSIC COMPOSITION
Scores, Jingles, and Sound Design—Options to fit any budget so you get music that works, sounds great, and is affordable.

—COMPLETE AUDIO PRODUCTION SERVICES
For radio, TV, training, sales promotion, and corporate communications, you get production, recording, mixing, and duplication for audio projects (from spoken word to full-blown cassette albums). Also, ask us about our on-hold message service.

—MULTITRACK RECORDING AND MIXING
For most productions, my in-house project studio saves you time and money while delivering the highest quality recording.

—AUDIO SWEETENING FOR VIDEO
When your soundtrack needs creative reality—music, sound effects, voice-overs, ambience, and more—get the results you want.

—AUDIO SYSTEM DESIGN AND CONSTRUCTION
From a small system to a recording environment, let my experience with electronics, acoustics, and ergonomics get you the sound system that best suits your needs and budget.

—MIDI AND MUSIC CONSULTING
Want to integrate MIDI and digital recording with your video editing system? Use technology more effectively so that your soundtracks have impact and are effective . . . all the time!

HERE'S THE MUSIC YOU REQUESTED . . .
This is *not* a demo. The five music cuts on this free tape are yours to keep and use on a nonexclusive basis. Go ahead and add this music to enhance any of your productions. All I ask is that you drop me a line to let me know how and where you used any of these tracks.

Of course, this music won't have the same impact as *original music*—the kind I can compose *specifically* for your productions—but it just might help you out of a jam when you need some good music fast. Enjoy these selections. And please *use* them!

—ABOUT THE PRODUCTION
This recording gives you an idea of the quality of today's technology. It's the equipment I'll use to make your music sound even better. All the music was composed, performed, and produced entirely at Jeffrey P. Fisher Music. Each track—from my exclusive library—was mastered to Digital Audio Tape (DAT) and duplicated to cassettes in real-time directly from the DAT master. The cassettes themselves use premium quality chrome tape with Dolby "B" noise reduction. You'll get the best results if you play the tape on NORMAL (not chrome) with the Dolby on.

—ABOUT THE MUSIC
• CLOSER LOOK (1:00)—This is a fast, jazzy track with a hot sax solo. It makes a great opening for a TV show.

• STAND PAT (3:22)—This slow, new age ambient piece is full of crazy percussion and dark sounds. Use it for a long montage or under serious narration.

• CHANNEL NEWS (:45)—Here's a powerful rock

track. It was once the opening for a cable news program.

• UPBEAT 101 (1:01)—This rhythmic basic track keeps moving to a big climax. Use it to end a motivating corporate video or under light narration.

• HIP N HOP (2:00)—It's a modern dance number perfect for any high energy production.

• BONUS—On the other side of this sample tape is a demo of music tracks from *Street Smarts* and other recent projects. This gives you a good idea of the music I can write for your latest project.

MUSIC PLANNING WORKSHEET

Here's a handy checklist to help your clients and you work together on an original music project. Omit the first section accordingly.

SELECTING YOUR COMPOSER
• Collect demo tapes from three to five composers.
• Listen and evaluate tapes.
• Narrow choice to one or two candidates.
• Interview each about style, fees, deadlines, and project ideas.
• Choose your composer.

USING MUSIC EFFECTIVELY
• Determine who your audience is.
• Choose appropriate style to complement message.
• Discuss how you are going to use music.
• Determine both where and where not to place music.
• Discuss why you use music and emotional response desired.

TAKING CARE OF BUSINESS
• Determine your budget for music, recording, talent, rights, etc.
• Determine necessary union and ASCAP/BMI affiliations.
• Develop project contract with your composer.

SPOTTING SESSION
• Meet with your composer and discuss basics.
• Screen rough cut together.
• Determine cues, length, styles, and other specifics.
• Give your composer time to develop themes.

REVIEWING THE WORK-IN-PROGRESS
• Listen and critique the proposed music. Test it with rough cut.
• Make suggestions and finalize all cues.

FINAL MASTER
• Work with composer to deliver quality music master.

• Make sure your master tape is compatible with editing suite.
• File appropriate union, copyright, and ASCAP/BMI forms.
• Add music to final project.

SAMPLE MUSIC CONTRACT

Thanks for choosing me to compose the music for your production, *ABOVE AND BEYOND*.

THESE ARE THE SERVICES I WILL PROVIDE:
• Compose, arrange, and produce approximately eight to ten minutes of original music conforming to your specifications.
• Attend a spotting session with the director to determine the musical style, number and length of cues, etc.
• Create a demonstration cassette of the music work-in-process subsequent to the spotting session, but just before the final recording session.
• Produce the final master recording on Digital Audio Tape (DAT).

YOU WILL:
• Provide a VHS copy of the production in its final edited form.
• Review and approve the work-in-process before the final recording session. Revisions will only be accepted at that time.
• Provide attribution, when possible, on the production's end credits to read: *Original Music Composed and Performed by Jeffrey P. Fisher.*

PLEASE NOTE: This is *NOT* a work-for-hire agreement. I retain ALL copyrights, phonorights, and publishing rights to the music. With respect to any and all areas outside your market area, I have the unrestricted right to sell, use, or grant licenses to the music beginning one year from the date of this agreement and continuing forever.

This agreement grants you single-use, nonexclusive rights to the music for use *only* for the *ABOVE AND BEYOND* project. You must seek an additional license and pay appropriate fees for any other or future uses of this music.

My base fee for the services I described above is estimated between $*xxxx.xx* and $*xxxx.xx*. That fee estimate is based on eight to ten minutes of original music at my standard rate for single-use, one-time rights of $*xxx.xx* per finished minute. This fee includes composing, arranging, producing, recording, mixing, and one master tape on the format listed above. Any out-of-pocket expenses incurred on your behalf and additional tape or other material requests will be billed to you in an itemized fashion.

Payment of the base fee will be made as follows: ONE-THIRD ($xxx.xx) of the above fee is due upon my starting the work; ONE-THIRD ($xxx.xx) is due upon approval of the demonstration work-in-process; ONE-THIRD ($xxx.xx-$xxx.xx) upon completion and delivery of your final master tape. If more (or less) music is composed than initially estimated, the increase (or decrease) in the fee will be reflected in your final payment.

Please sign both copies of the agreement below, date it, and return one *original* to me with your check for the first payment ($xxx.xx). Keep the other copy of the agreement for your records. I will invoice you for the remaining payments when they become due.

Again, thank you for choosing me to work on your production. I'm very excited about it and when you sign this agreement and return it to me with your check, I'll start composing.

(Please sign here)
ACCEPTED AND AGREED BY: *Mr. Joe Sample*
XYZ FILMS, *[date]*

INDEPENDENT CONTRACTOR STATUS

Recently, the IRS started scrutinizing companies that were consistently using independent contractors instead of hiring employees for the same work. As an independent contractor, you want to be careful not to appear to be an employee according to the IRS definition. To protect yourself, you may want to add independent contractor language both to your contracts and to contracts with musicians and other outside contractors you employ. Have your lawyer review this sample language before including it in your contracts.

Jeffrey P. Fisher shall be deemed an independent contractor and is not an employee of *XYZ Productions*. As such, *XYZ* shall not deduct withholding taxes, FICA, or any other required deductions. These taxes are the sole responsibility of Jeffrey P. Fisher. Also, Jeffrey P. Fisher further acknowledges that he is not entitled to any fringe benefits, pension, profit sharing, or any other benefits accruing to employees.

TALENT RELEASE

Here's a sample talent release to use when contracting musicians or other talent.

For value received in the sum of $xxx.xx, I, the undersigned, give and grant Jeffrey P. Fisher Music, its affiliates, successors, and assigns the unqualified right, privilege, and permission to reproduce in every manner or form, publish and circulate videotapes, audiocassettes, or films of recordings of my voice and/or my musical contribution arising from the production titled *ABOVE AND BEYOND* and I hereby grant, assign, and transfer all my rights and interest therein.

I specifically authorize and empower Jeffrey P. Fisher Music to cause any such videotapes, films, audiocassettes, and recordings of my voice and/or musical performance, to be copyrighted or in any other manner to be legally registered in the name of Jeffrey P. Fisher.

My contribution to this work shall be considered a work made for hire, and as such, I, my heirs, executors, administrators, and assigns, hereby remise, release and discharge Jeffrey P. Fisher Music for and from any and all claims of any kind whatsoever on account of the use of such recordings, including, but not limited to any and all claims for damages for libel, slander, and invasion of the right of privacy.

I am of lawful age and sound mind and have read and understand this Authorization of Release.

Signed this *[day]* of *[month, year]*.

BIOGRAPHICAL SKETCH

Use a biography to help personalize you and your company. You can also use it when approaching media sources to feature you in newspapers, magazines, and on radio and TV. This article helps you create an image—a real person—that clients can relate to.

Notice that my own biography promises many benefits to clients and helps explain my method of working. It also serves to position me as somewhat of a rogue, outside the normal music scene. All this is intentional and a very effective promotion.

THE ONE-MAN BAND COMES OF AGE . . .

The image evoked by the vaudevillian entertainer of yesteryear is very different from what you see at Jeffrey Fisher's electronic music studio. One of a new breed of composers and producers, he directs his musical acrobatics using a full complement of hi-tech audio and computer gear.

His particular specialty is scoring soundtrack music for film, video, and other audiovisual presentations, and he also composes the occasional jingle. "I don't subscribe to traditional methods of composing and recording music. I'm a musician first. I can't just write the parts and give them to someone else to play."

That Jeffrey—an accomplished guitarist and keyboardist—often writes and plays everything himself is unique. "I'm definitely hands-on. I see each project through, start to finish." And when his own expertise can't fill the spot, he contracts out to other musicians to play on his score.

The 34-year-old composer says he uses technology to help him better realize his musical ideas. But Jeffrey strongly insists that he doesn't write electronic scores. He calls his unique blend of acoustic instruments and electronics an electro-acoustic hybrid. He weaves melodies through a solid rhythmic foundation of guitar, bass, and percussion, then sweetens the music with synthesizers.

Sitting in the center of his combined project studio and office, Fisher comments on the musical instruments that literally surround him. "My equipment offers an astounding range of sounds, colors, and textures. It lets me mix realism with impressionism." And with characteristic humor, he adds, "If this stuff was around during the late nineteenth century, those Impressionist painters would have been musicians."

Besides writing and playing all the parts in his electro-acoustic ensemble, Jeffrey handles the recording, too. His complete MIDI and tape-based studio produces broadcast quality masters ready to roll. "I feel composing and recording are integrated, not mutually exclusive. I can't write without hearing how the final version will sound." This special working method creates a complete package characterized by strong, effective music and first-rate production values.

Jeffrey knows the real benefit of modern technology is how it makes an original soundtrack more affordable. He offers several service options, from full scores to his own buyout music resource, to help audiovisual producers get music for their projects, no matter what the budget. Jeffrey's booklet, *HOW TO GET LOW-COST ORIGINAL MUSIC FOR ALL YOUR PRODUCTIONS*, is a necessity for anyone seeking specific strategies on how to get affordable scores. "I wrote it to help my clients. It shows them how to get more music for less, IF they follow my advice." Contact Jeffrey to get your copy of the booklet.

Having studied film and video at Columbia College in Chicago, Jeffrey understands how sound and image work together. He says he learned the production process through making his own films and videos and that experience helps him compose better music. "Sometimes I either read the script or screen a rough cut of a project. Usually, I talk with the producer and director to find out what is the most appropriate music for the project, always with an eye on the bottom line!

"I think too many producers opt for overpowering music. I'm definitely from the less-is-more school of music composition. The ideal score is usually quite simple. Almost elegantly so. It is often supple and sometimes bold; organic, yet intricate; atmospheric, but vivid. I try to strike a balance between simplicity and depth. Sometimes it's in the writing; other times it's the choice of instruments and sounds and how they're orchestrated." His propensity for the offbeat, ambient piece doesn't cloud his judgment, though. "I write exactly what the producer and director want to deliver their message effectively."

The burden of the one-man band extends into Jeffrey's business routine. "Many days I spend far more time at my computer taking care of business when I should be composing." When you must handle marketing, accounting, licking the stamps, and of course, writing and recording all the music, you take the good with the bad. "It's a challenge really, but very rewarding."

The flexibility to work when he wants and as ideas strike is very important to Jeffrey. "My three-second commute from my kitchen to my office is a terrific way to work. I wouldn't have it any other way. Because if the muse strikes at 3:00 AM, I can complete a composition, production and all, and have it on my client's desk by 8:00 AM. You can't do *that* in the traditional music production world."

Jeffrey Fisher is content taming this new frontier. "I'm fortunate that I can draw upon all the past, great musical traditions while exploring progressive instrumental music composition."

You can reach Jeffrey at his office: Fisher Creative Group; 323 Inner Circle Drive, Bolingbrook, IL 60490; or call (630) 378-4109.

A Q&A BIO

Here's another biography that follows a format inspired by a magazine. It provides more facts, as opposed to the philosophical insight stressed in the previous example. Media people will love this format because it will help them better prepare their stories.

- *Jeffrey P. Fisher:* Owner of Fisher Creative Group.
- *Birthdate and place:* January 22, 1963; Hinsdale, Illinois.
- *Family status:* Married, wife Lisa; one child, Adam Jeffrey.
- *Services provided:* Composer and producer of music scores and jingles for business TV, corporate audio-visual presentations, commercials, and film.
- *My first job was:* Working for my dad's construction company. I used a 12-ounce hammer, which means it took about 30 hits to drive a 16-penny nail.
- *My background is:* I studied film and video at Columbia College in Chicago. After a stint in cable television, I moved into the corporate world as director of marketing for a software firm. All the while I ran my music business part-time. In 1991, I decided to go

full-time and haven't looked back since. Technology has changed the commercial music industry dramatically. The advent of electronics and digital-quality recording has pushed prices down. Many audiovisual producers know how the right music enhances their productions and helps them deliver their message more effectively, but until now, original music was just too expensive. The lower overhead from working at home really gives me a competitive advantage and my clients benefit by getting the original music they need and at a price they can afford.

- *Why I work from home:* It's the flexibility. I'm not always my most creative between nine and five. If an idea strikes me in the middle of the night, I can sit down in my office and complete a composition. My clients expect me to be available during the day, but they don't really care when I write. Just that I compose my best for them. This environment is very conducive to the work I do.
- *My home office setup:* I'm a kind of modern day one-man band. I use an IBM clone and laser printer to handle business writing, accounting, marketing, and so forth. And I have my arsenal of electronic music instruments and recording gear, too. I'm always at the keyboard, whether it be ivory or QWERTY.
- *The book I'm recommending these days is: How to Make Money Scoring Soundtracks and Jingles* by Jeffrey P. Fisher.
- *My favorite writers are:* William F. Buckley Jr. when he writes Blackford Oakes spy novels and John Gardner as he explores Herbie Kruger's complex life.
- *The person I admire most is:* George Martin, Beatles producer and recording industry pioneer.
- *If I could do things over, I would:* Learn to read music fluently and at an earlier age.
- *If I could live in another time in history, it would be:* The Cretaceous. I think dinosaurs are fascinating.
- *If I won a million-dollar lottery, I would:* Build a state-of-the-art recording complex in some picturesque, remote area as a kind of music and sound resort.
- *Most people are surprised when I tell them:* I don't particularly care for Bach, Mozart, Beethoven, or any music written before the 1870s.
- *It never surprises me when:* Either Ensoniq or Microsoft has another upgrade for either my keyboard or computer software.
- *If I've learned one thing from life it is:* Just do it (with all deference to gym shoes). Talk is cheap. Swallow hard, have faith in your abilities, and charge ahead!
- *My favorite pastimes are:* Reading, writing, and eating pizza.
- *My favorite restaurant is:* Porta Bella in Madison, Wisconsin.
- *My all-time favorite movies are: Bonnie and Clyde, North by Northwest, Young Frankenstein* (it's pronounced "Fronkinsteen"), and *Local Hero.*
- *My favorite music scores are:* Anything by Bernard Herrmann and Maurice Jarre's wonderful music for *Witness.*
- *My favorite saying is:* "When love and skill work together, expect a masterpiece," by John Ruskin.
- *Working at home has kept me happy because:* Being at home is more relaxing. I have more time for work, less pressure, and that frees my creativity. I'm more efficient and productive. And I think my music composition skills have improved dramatically. I owe much of that to being at home.

MISSION STATEMENT

You might want to add a mission statement or position paper to your promotional arsenal. This helps clarify your business philosophy.

Jeffrey P. Fisher Music works with small advertisers and local accounts. We don't really try to compete for the national accounts or compete with the big music houses. Our niche is small, aggressive companies who market like guerrilla warfare. They can't afford the big bucks, so we save them money in a variety of ways: rights, area restrictions, and some very innovative pricing strategies that include leasing music packages. We're better on their budgets. They don't get saddled with a huge bill because we make their payments easy. They can test the waters.

And we're a small, smart, aggressive company, too. We give top service and ongoing support. Our in-house studio saves us money and we pass those savings on to our clients. We keep our overhead low and rely on creativity, NOT equipment. And we work extra hard to do good, quality work AND make it affordable.

Most important, we always give something extra to every client. If they want a :60 jingle, we take a few minutes to cut a :30 or :15 and add it to their reel. In a month the client will call and ask us for the shorter version. We can tell them it's already done—and you can hear the smile on the other end of the phone.

Do good work, price it fairly, and give more than anyone expects. We are a firm believer that what goes around, comes around. Help yourself by helping others. We are willing to go the extra mile for every client. That pays off for everyone involved.

LETTER TO UNRESPONSIVE PROSPECT

Here's another useful letter you may need to use.

PLEASE DO ME A FAVOR!

Can you take a moment and let me know whether you received and reviewed my original music demo and services material?
- Did you get all the information you needed?
- Are you still interested in getting original music for your audiovisual productions?
- Do you have any problems with or questions about the material sent to you?

If so, please either write or call. I'd be happy to talk with you further about your music needs. I'm sure that I can help you. If you have changed your plans or made other arrangements, I will be happy to remove your name from my list and no longer send you further letters, newsletters, and literature.

Feel free to use the back of this letter for your reply. Or if you prefer, just give me a call. I hope to hear from you soon.

THANK YOU NOTE

Thank you for your kind words about my *FOR SCORE* newsletter and especially my copyright report. It makes me very happy to know that you found them useful, and I sincerely hope you find future editions just as helpful.

Also, should you have any ideas or questions that will help you use music and sound more effectively, please drop me a line. I'm always looking for topics to explore. And if you have suggestions or the solution to a problem facing film, video, radio, and TV producers, I'd love to feature it.

I was happy to duplicate your radio commercial for you. And should something like this come up again (or any other audio or music needs) please do not hesitate to call. I'm looking forward to helping you on an upcoming project. Thanks again!

WHEN YOUR MUSIC IS DECLINED

I was sorry to hear yesterday that our proposal was declined. Thank you for taking a minute from your day to leave a message for me.

Please understand that I still hope we can do business together soon. I've had many successful relationships with other production companies in the past. I hope that soon we can work together as well.

Until then, I will keep you up to date with my activities by sending you my *FOR SCORE* newsletter and calling periodically to see how I might help you. And I would be grateful if you would keep me informed about all the activities and successes at your company.

SAMPLE PROJECT LISTING

- AMATORE PRODUCTIONS needed some dramatic, chase, and urban rhythms on their trailer for an independent feature titled *Bad Dreams*. Budget was tight, so we adapted some of my past work to fit the scenes.
- Peggy Berent and I added theme music as the open and close to her documentary highlighting MAERCKER SCHOOL DISTRICT #60. The music was light and positive to complement this production's message.
- I wrote some bouncy theme music for J MARC GROUP'S sales tape for ETI.
- Theme music, underscore, and general sound design for two *HRMS* computer presentations used for corporate image building.
- LAKESIDE HOSPITAL asked for a jingle proposal to kick off their *"We deliver more than babies"* campaign.
- J MARC GROUP again asked me for theme, dramatic, and general underscoring for their PBS project *Street Smarts: Straight Talk for Kids, Teens, and Parents*.

You should be on this list, too. Call me when you need original music to enhance *your* latest project.

Jeffrey P. Fisher Music specializes in scores, jingles, and sound design for business and commercial presentations. When your budget is small, he can help with a special option for productions not needing to buyout the music license.

TESTIMONIAL LETTER

Use this letter to solicit a testimonial recommendation from your satisfied clients. Send a thank you note to clients who give you both unsolicited and solicited testimonials. You may wish to send a small gift, too. I usually send a copy of one of my articles or booklets. It's up to you. Once you have several testimonials, print them together and include this sheet with your marketing materials. This third-party validation is evidence of your past success and shows prospective clients that you can and will do the same for them. (Check out the "About This Book" section of this book to see what I mean.)

It makes me very happy to know that the music I wrote and recorded for your *Above and Beyond* project worked so well. It was an exciting and challenging project. Can't wait to see the final master.

Since you were so pleased with my work, I hope you won't mind my asking you for your opinion of both my music and my company's services. You don't need to write a letter. You can just put your comments on the back of this one, sign below, and return it to me in the enclosed envelope. Please keep the second copy for your files. I hope you take a few minutes to tell me what you like and offer your suggestions about how I might improve my services in the future. Thanks! I'm looking forward to your reply.

May I have permission to quote your comments and use them in promotions when marketing my music and services?

[client signature, date].

SAMPLE MEDIA RELEASE ONE

Use this model media release when seeking publicity for your work. Another good example of a news release is the biographical sketch earlier in this section.

JEFFREY P. FISHER MUSIC recently completed the musical score for *The Capital Trip*. Produced by *XYZ* for *Tours Inc.*, the video promotes class trips to our nation's capital to area junior high school students. Composed, produced, and recorded at Jeffrey P. Fisher's suburban project studio, the score centers around two main themes.

"First there is a light and upbeat rock track," Fisher explains, "featuring bass, drums, and synthesizer. The other piece has a more serious tone with a heavy military, almost drum and bugle corps influence." He also confessed that this was his favorite kind of project. "I really enjoy doing scores like this. They're challenging and fun. And when you get to work with a straightforward director, it makes the experience even better."

SAMPLE MEDIA RELEASE TWO

If you work part-time, try this promotion.

I may be a marketing guy by day, but music is such a big part of my life that I couldn't ignore it. My day job at Software Solutions doesn't interfere with my moonlighting. Many corporate video producers don't mind meeting at night or on Saturdays. Plus, they really don't care when I write, just that I meet their needs. So, I compose at night and get them a demo during the day; they listen, and I make changes the next night. I meet my deadlines, and no client has complained so far.

SAMPLE MEDIA RELEASE THREE

This short bit appeared in an in-house newsletter at a cable company. It was not meant to go to the general public, but I use a reprint with my marketing materials.

Who says local cable television can't have original soundtracks? We've found a solution to one of the most difficult aspects of commercial and local origination productions: good music scores and jingles. Finding the right music has often been a frustrating experience complicated by the time wasted searching for the right sound for a particular production.

What's our solution? Jeffrey P. Fisher Music. A nearby composer who uses a variety of synthesizers and recording gear to produce custom music soundtracks for our commercials and other productions. To date he has produced our news theme and several tracks for some new local commercials. He doesn't work for free, but the savings in time and aggravation have more than made up for his music fees. And so far, our clients have loved the music Jeffrey has created. We know that as Jeffrey's skill gets better recognized by other producers, we'll have to stand in line. Meanwhile, let's keep this our little secret.

SAMPLE ARTICLE FORMAT

Here's one of my recent articles published in Screen.

FISHER MUSIC GOES DIGITAL . . .

. . . not. I'm hoping most of those busy creative types out there in *SCREEN*-land will stop reading at the headline. They will be content to know that just one more music house has the latest gear. That's fine by me. I had to write that headline to stay competitive. Or at least appear competitive. Because unless you have the latest and greatest digital kazoo, you will be left behind in the Great Technology War of the '90s.

You know what I mean. Every other week someone has a new toy in their studio to promote. So-and-so has a new AUDIOFAZZMATIC, while Da-other-guys just purchased the latest digital THINGAMAJIG. It brings new meaning to the phrase "keeping up with the Joneses." This Great Technology War is ludicrous. Innovation for innovation's sake. They have this, I gotta have this; they have that, so now I gotta have that, too. When is it going to end?

What ever happened to good, old-fashioned workmanship? You know, where someone practices his craft with pride, quality, commitment, consistency, and dependability. If you break the heel of your shoe, do you care if the local cobbler uses a hammer? Do you only patronize the shoe repair shop with the latest cordless hydraulic hammer like Norm Abrams uses on *This Old House*? Let's face it. You just want your damn shoe fixed, right? Who cares *how* it gets done, just *that* it gets done! So why is our industry preoccupied with technology? Machines don't make the music. People do!

I must confess that I too have been guilty of the

worst forms of technological lust (say it isn't so, Jeffrey!). My project studio is sufficiently digitalized with a smattering of what's-new. But I learned a lesson from a musician friend of mine. Each day J.S.A. grew progressively electronic. Then something inside him snapped. I think it was a rap version of "Ina Gadda Da Vida" (yo!) that finally burst his bubble. He proceeded to dump all his electronic gear and concentrate on solo guitar. Isn't that radical?

People ask me all the time: "What kind of setup do you have?" After years of rattling off my equipment list, I settled on simplifying my answer: "Quill pen and parchment." Hey, it was good enough for Mozart. It's good enough for me. The only person who gets my equipment list now is my insurance man. And the IRS. Of course.

Don't you wish everyone would just listen to the music? After that, they can ask how it was done. If they really want to know. It's not that I'm cantankerous. Rather, I'm very passionate about the art and craft of *music*. I know that using electronics is a necessary evil, but it is only a tool to help realize the end. Music existed long before recording technology reduced it to 0's and 1's. I think music will survive despite attempts to squeeze the life out of it.

Take my friend A.M. We've never met face-to-face. Yet, he asked me to compose his latest score. He didn't care about my studio. He didn't care what equipment I owned. He listened to my tape, liked what he heard (I'm guessing here), and hired me. Subsequently, we conducted all our business by phone, mail, and UPS. Hard as it is to believe, we didn't even use a fax machine. Technology (though we used quite a bit if it for this score) didn't matter. It was the music, after all, that he wanted. Nothing more. Nothing less.

Just as I finished writing the above, my mail brought news of another technological advance. Guess what, folks? All that stuff that is under a year old is already antiquated. With all this new gear coming out, my project studio is starting to look like a museum. It's time to put my older gear into a glass case with a brass plaque:

DX7 *(1983-1985) Dee Exus Sevenus—Famous synthesizer that ruled the Earth for one bright, shining moment.*

So, when I read about the latest purchases by my fellow creatives, I just laugh. I take a lesson from my friend and go back to playing my acoustic guitar. You know, that instrument where you pluck strings with your fingers and they vibrate over the hole in an oddly shaped wooden box. And then, through some highly scientific process, it moves the air around us in a way that our ears perceive as sound. Sound, that in the hands of a dedicated craftsman, becomes . . .

. . . beautiful music. That's what it is all about. Isn't it?

SAMPLE ARTICLE QUERY LETTER

Dear Editor,

As you well know, making it in today's highly competitive music world is hard. To reach their goals, your readers need to use many resources: time, talent, knowledge, money, and more. Unfortunately, some feel lost and overwhelmed. They need a coherent plan and a push in the right direction. Your magazine can help them succeed.

I propose to write a 2000-2500 word article titled "YOUR EIGHT STEP PLAN TO MUSICAL SUCCESS." This feature story details eight problems facing musicians today. It offers specific and practical advice to help your readers overcome these obstacles so they can build and sustain their career at the level of success they need, want, and deserve. The steps in the plan are:

- Prepare yourself mentally. You must make sure your mind is ready for both the demands and rewards of success.
- Master your technique. Make sure your skills, image, presence, demo tape, and other factors showcase your best work.
- Understand the real problem. Too many musicians concentrate on production and not marketing and selling.
- Create the necessary promotional material. You won't succeed without collateral material to promote your work.
- Do what is necessary for success. You must determine where it is you wish to head and must pledge that you will make the appropriate sacrifices to reach your goal.
- Plan how and what you are going to do. Scrutinize your competition, consider your promotional gambits, study the many options available to you, and set a plan of action in motion.
- Determine how to measure your success. What does making it mean to you? You need a one-year plan, a five-year plan, and a life plan.
- Review these steps regularly. You need to periodically review these steps and see what is working . . . so you can keep on doing it. And what is failing . . . so you can fix it FAST.

This outline is the basis for the article. As author of the music book, *How to Make Money Scoring Soundtracks and Jingles*, I will draw on personal experiences for the article content.

I'd like to write "YOUR EIGHT STEP PLAN TO MUSICAL SUCCESS" for your magazine. How does this sound? I've enclosed a SASE for your reply.

Should you have questions or need additional information, please call. Thank you for your consideration.

CASSETTE PRODUCTION SALES LETTER

Now you can easily record your most important information on inexpensive audio cassettes and deliver it to those people who need it most.

You need to deliver your message more effectively, don't you? Why not put it on tape? Low-cost audio cassettes tell *and* sell. They are electronic brochures that let you deliver vital information directly to customers, prospects, members, staff, and more. Plus, audio cassettes have a higher value than print. They are more likely to be kept, listened to, and remembered. And that means a better opportunity for success. *Your success.* Here's how it works:

• Get on-location recording of your meeting, seminar, speech, etc.
• Complete audio cassette production and duplication.
• Sale of cassettes before, during, and after your meeting.
• Fast turnover of all mail orders.
• Skilled audio technicians and top quality recording equipment.
• Highest quality cassettes guaranteed against defects.
• Free initial consultation and planning session to make sure all goes smoothly.

Take a minute right now to call and tell us about your next meeting. We'll take it from there and do all the necessary preparation. And when your meeting is held, we'll get it down on tape, duplicate it fast, and have them ready for your people to take home.

ON-HOLD SALES LETTER

Sell more products and services, improve your image, solve problems, and promote, educate, and motivate your clients.

Use your on-hold system to deliver your message to callers. This simple, easy, and inexpensive system lets you use your existing phone system as an effective marketing, advertising, publicity, and sales weapon. With on-hold messaging you get the tool you need to:

• Sell more products and services faster.
• Strengthen your marketing and advertising.
• Build your company's identity.
• Improve client relations.
• Lower caller anxiety by providing assistance to them while on hold.

With on-hold messaging you replace negative time (waiting in limbo) with your positive message. Here's what you get with your on-hold messaging program:

• Scriptwriting made-to-order using your specific information. We follow your guidelines when developing your on-hold messages.
• Complete production services including studio time, voice talent, and all music licensing fees so you get the professional result you need and deserve.
• Tape or digital playback systems. It's easy to add to your existing music on-hold system, and it's virtually maintenance free. Turn it on, press play, and your message starts helping your clients instantly.

This is one hot marketing idea. Recent studies show that using on-hold messaging increased revenues by 8-12%. Also, 16-20% of callers made purchases following an offer heard while on hold. One company even said that hang-ups were reduced a whopping 73% following an aggressive phone hold marketing program.

Couldn't you use these results? On-hold messaging is the solution. Don't put it off. Call today and start reaching your clients on-hold tomorrow.

FLYER TO PROMOTE YOUR MUSIC LIBRARY

Need original music?

Choosing the right music for your productions is often a frustrating and costly experience. That's why you need help. Whatever your project, big and small, let Jeffrey P. Fisher Music be your one-stop source for ALL your music needs. When you need instrumental soundtracks and jingles, you get these three options:

• Full service original music options. Let us score your project exactly to your specification and grant you full, buyout rights to the music. This option is ideal for jingles, commercial scores, and other big budget productions.
• Secondary original music options. We created this option for smaller budgets and productions that don't need to buyout the music license. You still get the music you want, but at a price that makes sense. We own the music and have the unrestricted right to sell the music outside your market area.
• Nonexclusive tracks. Still need effective music, but you have a tiny budget? This resource is just for you. You have access to our collection of music cues that you can use on a nonexclusive basis. This is the easiest way to get the music you need and deserve and save some cash at the same time.

Please note: An added benefit to our exclusive library is you get some control over the final mix. We can adjust tempo, instrumentation, mix, and more when we deliver your tracks. Ask for our latest demo, take a few minutes to listen, then select the tracks you need. Tell us what you need changed and we'll deliver completed tracks, remixed to your specifications, the very next day. All this for one low price.

Call now to discuss your project in detail. Then let us help you make the proper musical decision. Get exactly what you need to deliver your message effectively with original music.

$AVE MONEY WHEN YOU CHOOSE ORIGINAL MUSIC

sing modern musical and recording technology is the key to getting low cost original music. Many composers, like myself, have a project studio stocked with equipment. Such a creative arsenal produces finished compositions that rival the quality of many big budget recording studios. That translates to lower overhead with the savings passed on to you.

My sophisticated project studio handles all phases of music production: composing, arranging, recording, and mixing the master tape. I can deliver a finished score for just the price of my time. The result is that you pay for the creative work — *you only pay for the music* — and not high-priced studio time.

Today's synthesizers and samplers reproduce any sound, real or imagined. In the hands of an accomplished composer/arranger, it's hard to tell the difference. Not that having the real thing is bad, on the contrary, there's nothing better or more beautiful than a room full of the world's greatest musicians playing a full symphonic score.

But this is about economics. Plain and simple. If you can afford the orchestra, GET THE ORCHESTRA! You won't regret it. But when you need music that works, sounds great, and is also surprisingly affordable, the 'synthesizer orchestra' is the way to go.

AN EFFECTIVE HYBRID

However, your original score doesn't need to be all electronic. Often using a real solo instrument like sax or flute brings an added dimension to a mostly electronic score. This subtlety simply makes the music come alive. I call this technique an electro-acoustic hybrid. It's my particular specialty. Basically, this method combines synthetic textures with real instruments like guitars, bass, and percussion. It is these particular *feel* instruments that give you a more compelling and exciting score.

More importantly, the blend of electronic and traditional instruments saves you money while still delivering a powerful music soundtrack. This is not a compromise either. Using electronics is just different. It is your creative choice! Plus, if your score needs rock, jazz, new age, exotic, or 'out there', an electro-acoustic score is definitely the right way to go.

Make sure you only pay for the music, not high-priced studio time!

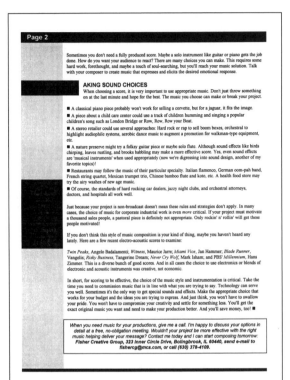

Sometimes you don't need a fully produced score. Maybe a solo instrument like guitar or piano gets the job done. How do you want your audience to react? There are many choices you can make. This requires some hard work, forethought, and maybe a touch of soul-searching, but you'll reach your music solution. Talk with your composer to create music that expresses and elicits the desired emotional response.

MAKING SOUND CHOICES

When choosing a score, it is very important to use appropriate music. Don't just throw something on at the last minute and hope for the best. The music you choose can make or break your project.

■ A classical piano piece probably won't work for selling a corvette, but for a jaguar, it fits the image.

■ A piece about a child care center could use a track of children humming and singing a popular children's song such as London Bridge or Row, Row, Row your Boat.

■ A stereo retailer could use several approaches: Hard rock or rap to sell boom boxes, orchestral to highlight audiophile systems, aerobic dance music to augment a promotion for walkman-type equipment, etc.

■ A nature preserve might try a folksy guitar piece or maybe solo flute. Although sound effects like birds chirping, leaves rustling, and brooks babbling may make a more effective score. Yes, even sound effects are 'musical instruments' when used appropriately (now we're digressing into sound design, another of my favorite topics)!

■ Restaurants may follow the music of their particular specialty. Italian flamenco, German oom-pah band, French string quartet, Mexican trumpet trio, Chinese bamboo flute and koto, etc. A health food store may try the airy washes of new age music.

■ Of course, the standards of hard rocking car dealers, jazzy night clubs, and orchestral attorneys, doctors, and hospitals all work well.

Just because your project is non-broadcast doesn't mean these rules and strategies don't apply. In many cases, the choice of music for corporate industrial work is even *more* critical. If your project must motivate a thousand sales people, a pastoral piece is definitely not appropriate. Only rockin' n' rollin' will get these people motivated!

If you don't think this style of music composition is your kind of thing, maybe you haven't heard any lately. Here are a few recent electro-acoustic scores to examine:

Twin Peaks, Angelo Badalamenti; *Witness*, Maurice Jarre; *Miami Vice*, Jan Hammer; *Blade Runner*, Vangelis; *Risky Business*, Tangerine Dream; *Never Cry Wolf*, Mark Isham; and PBS' *Millennium*, Hans Zimmer. This is a diverse bunch of good scores. And in all cases the choice to use electronics or blends of electronic and acoustic instruments was creative, not economic.

In short, for scoring to be effective, the choice of the music style and instrumentation is critical. Take the time you need to commission music that is in line with what you are trying to say. Technology can serve you well. Sometimes it's the only way to get special sounds and effects. Make the appropriate choice that works for your budget and the ideas you are trying to express. And just think, you won't have to swallow your pride. You won't have to compromise your creativity and settle for something less. You'll get the exact original music you want and need to make your production better. And you'll save money, too! ■

When you need music for your productions, give me a call. I'm happy to discuss your options in detail at a free, no-obligation meeting. Wouldn't your project be more effective with the right music helping deliver your message? Contact me today and I can start composing tomorrow: **Fisher Creative Group, 323 Inner Circle Drive, Bolingbrook, IL 60440, send e-mail to fishercg@mcs.com, or call (630) 378-4109.**

Final Word

The ultimate quest has no ending, and that
fact is what gives the quest its ultimate value.

—David Carradine

Now you have a workable studio, a great sounding demo, a huge list of possible prospects, a smaller list of qualified prospects, and a few paying clients. What's next? Run your business effectively and efficiently. That means keeping your demo up to date, promoting continuously, and staying in touch regularly with all your hot prospects and clients. You'll probably get 80% of your business from 20% of your client list. You'd better keep them happy. And keep looking for new markets and client sources, too.

The real secret to making it with your music is to start your own business and pursue a diverse range of music products and services. You must run your own company and ignore that nagging voice inside your head. Work hard to get some prospect leads, turn them into clients, and then springboard each success into bigger and better things.

There's no security anywhere, so prepare to make your own way and live your own life. Your best weapon is knowledge. When you know what to do, you can do anything and everything. And, as you realize your goals, you will get a steady income, benefits, some security, great rewards, boundless enthusiasm and confidence . . . and autonomy, self-esteem, love, and all the other things that make life special and worthwhile.

There is no end to your quest to succeed. You never stop marketing, you never stop developing your skills, and you never stop building and enhancing your personal studio. You just continue. As Taoist thought says: There is no beginning, middle, or end. And there is no status quo. There is only one constant and that is change. At any point in time you are in transition from one point in your life to another. Since there is no pinnacle, prepare yourself for all there is to do. There will always be something more requiring your attention. The universe unfolds around us, not under some preordained plan, but naturally—it cannot help but do so. Everything follows nature's way. And when you understand that you too are part of nature—not separate from it—you will begin to understand what that means.

So, get started *now.* Right away! Don't put it off. Take a small step today . . . another tomorrow . . . another after that . . . and so on and so forth. Soon you shall arrive. You don't have to jump in unprepared because you already have a basic understanding of what you must do to succeed. If you write good music, charge fairly for your music services, give more than anyone ever expects, and learn to exploit superior marketing skills and opportunities, you'll have nothing but success. Don't worry. While it won't be easy, it will be fun and, ultimately, worthwhile. What are you going to do first?

CONGRATULATIONS

An ounce of action is worth a ton of theory.
—FRIEDRICH ENGELS

- -

You made it! You now know exactly how you can make money composing in the commercial music industry. Your business can supplement your band or full-time job income or it can be your only source of income. It's a natural extension of your musical pursuits. How far to take it is completely up to you. It's your choice. You now have the tools you need to make big money scoring soundtracks and jingles. It won't be easy. This is hard work, but *you can do it!* You have a distinct advantage because you chose this valuable resource to help you along the way.

Now that you've finished this manual, you're ready to start applying all the details found in these pages. After a few days have passed, pick up *How to Make Money Scoring Soundtracks and Jingles* and read it again. You'll discover useful pieces you may have missed the first time. Let me also suggest you keep this resource around for future reference and let it help you along your road to success.

Usually when you buy a book, that's all there is. Not anymore. Just because you've finished *How to Make Money Scoring Soundtracks and Jingles,* that doesn't mean the relationship we started on page one need end. Let's keep the door open for further conversations. I'm available to help you—just as I have already helped you through my book. When you need additional help improving your promotional materials, demo tape, music, and commercial music business, I'm here for you. If you have any problems, need some sound advice, or maybe just a little encouragement, please contact me. I want you to keep in touch. Let me know about your successes, any problems you come across, all *your* tricks of the trade, and most of all, your milestones, so I can share your celebration. All you need to do is drop me a note: Fisher Creative Group. 323 Inner Circle Drive, Bolingbrook, IL 60490; send e-mail to fishercg@ mcs.com; or call (630) 378-4109. Let's talk. Remember, *you* need to take the initiative. I want to hear from you. If you don't keep in touch, I can't help you succeed. It's that simple.

MUCH SUCCESS!

Index

A Music Bookstore At Your Fingertips...
FREE!

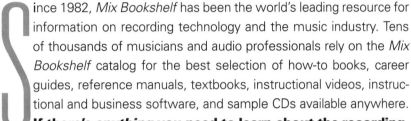